LEVERAGED MANAGEMENT BUYOUTS

LEVERAGED MANAGEMENT BUYOUTS

edited by YAKOV AMIHUD

BeardBooks
Washington, D.C.

Library of Congress Cataloging-in-Publication Data

    Leveraged management buyouts : causes and consequences /edited by Yakov Amihud.
        p. cm.
    Papers presented at a conference held at the Leonard N. Stern School of Business, New
York University, on May 20, 1988, and sponsored by the Salomon Brothers Center for the
Study of Financial Institutions.
    Originally published: Homewood, Ill. : Dow-Jones-Irwin, 1989.
    ISBN 1-58798-138-6
    1. Management buyouts--Congresses. 2. Leveraged buyouts--Congresses. I. Amihud,
Yakov, 1947-. II. Salomon Brothers Center for the Study of Financial Institutions.

HD2746.5 .L53 2002
338.7--dc21

                                         2002066568

Printed in the United States of America

CONTENTS

PREFACE

As this book goes to print, leveraged management buyouts are expanding to unprecedented levels, both in number and in size of transaction. Recent large buyout offers—like the one for RJR Nabisco for $24.88 billion—have intensified the public debate on the merit of MBOs. MBOs are distinct from ordinary acquisitions in that management itself is the acquirer and thus its interests may well conflict with those of shareholders, toward whom it has a fiduciary duty. This inspires the question of fairness and the question of whether this form of restructuring has real *economic* benefits.

This book is intended to expand the understanding of the causes and consequences of leveraged management buyouts and to contribute to the debate on the appropriate public policy to be applied. Its contents originated as papers presented by academics, legislators, and practitioners at a conference at the Leonard N. Stern School of Business, New York University, on May 20, 1988, organized by the Salomon Brothers Center for the Study of Financial Institutions under the direction of Dr. Arnold Sametz. The book includes a comprehensive review of the evidence of the effects of MBOs on firms' performance; it reviews the tax considerations unique to MBOs as well as the legal issues raised in these transactions, focusing on those that emanate from the potential conflict of interests between management and shareholders; and it presents a debate on whether and how MBOs should be regulated.

The book includes three sections:

The first section presents research findings on the characteristics and consequences of leveraged management buyouts. The first chapter by **Y. Amihud** surveys the empirical evidence on the effects of MBO announcements on stock prices as well as on bond prices, discusses the relationship between these price changes and the characteristics of the transactions, and surveys the evidence on the premiums offered and the determinants of their magnitude. It also considers the arguments for and against the proposal to mandate auctioning of the target firm in an MBO and analyzes the arguments and the evidence on the conflict of interests between management and shareholders. Finally, it critically evaluates some of the motivations for MBOs, such as tax benefits and improved managerial incentives. The next chapter by **R. L. Kieschnick** identifies the characteristics of public corporations subject to MBOs that distinguish them from other firms. The findings are useful in assessing the likelihood of a firm's becoming an MBO target and sheds light on the motives for MBOs. The next two chapters, by **I. O. Bull** and by **S. N. Kaplan** compare the performance of the target firms in the post-MBO period to that in the pre-MBO period. These studies are unique and especially commendable given the difficulty in obtaining data on privately held firms. Kaplan considers public firms that became private, whereas Bull also considers divisional and private firm LBOs, and both reach a similar conclusion: the buyouts were followed by significant improvements in firms' performance. Bull includes interviews with CEOs that provide insights into the expectations and motives for LBOs and their effects on managerial behavior afterwards. Kaplan considers the division of the value created in the MBO between the target shareholders and the buyout investors—an often-debated issue. In the concluding chapter in the first section, **A. C. Eckert** surveys the evolution of LBOs in recent years as seen by a practitioner engaged in this activity; he also discusses the developments in the financial markets (such as junk bonds) that facilitated LBOs.

The second section focuses on the legal and tax aspects of MBOs. The first two chapters are by **L. Lederman** and **B. A. Bryer** and by **R. N. Macris**, academics as well as practicing lawyers involved in MBOs. Lederman and Bryer focus on the role of management in MBOs, the potential conflict with shareholders' interests, and the issue of fairness. They survey related court decisions, analyze the proposed remedies to the problem, and evaluate the legal consequences of various business practices applied in MBOs. Macris analyzes the tax considerations that play a prominent role in the economics of MBOs. He critically discusses the sources of tax benefits and evaluates the tax-related consequences of commonly applied methods of financing and acquisition mechanics, with a particular focus on ESOPs. This section's concluding chapter, by **R. Romano**, discusses the issues raised in Lederman's and Bryer's and Macris's chapters in the context of recent research and questions the reasons for MBOs given that their tax and organizational advantages can be replicated to a great extent by other means.

The third section is on policy and legislative proposals concerning MBOs. **E.J. Markey,** a prominent Congressman, examines the fairness of LBOs to target shareholders and bondholders and the concerns over the increase in corporate debt level; he also discusses legislative proposals intended to resolve these concerns. **R. J. Gilson** reviews the debate on the motives for MBOs and the potential conflict between them and management's duty of loyalty to shareholders. He then presents the American Law Institute's proposal on MBOs, which is intended to promote competitive bidding by outside investors for the target firm after the MBO proposal has been made, and discusses its merits in resolving the conflict. **J. A. Grundfest**, an SEC Commissioner, considers the principles that should guide public policy regarding MBOs. He presents the economic benefits that MBOs generate, both at the firm and the macroeconomic level, and critically evaluates the arguments that call for constraining this activity. Finally, **M. C. Jensen** challenges the claims that MBOs are unfair to target shareholders and that they have disruptive economic effects. He suggests that MBOs enable entrepreneurs to avoid the inhibiting characteristic of the current regulatory environment and rejects the view that MBOs should be constrained.

This book is intended for academics, practitioners, and policymakers. It contains practical analyses of MBOs by people who are themselves involved with these transactions, the most recent academic research analyses of MBOs, and critical evaluation of the related regulatory proposals. It is hoped that this book will enrich the public's knowledge of the issues associated with MBOs, ultimately contributing to a better understanding of this important business reorganization activity.

Yakov Amihud

Contributors

Yakov Amihud
Leonard N. Stern School of Business, New York University and
Faculty of Management, Tel Aviv University

Barry A. Bryer
Wachtell, Lipton, Rosen & Katz, New York

Ivan Bull
University of Illinois at Urbana-Champaign

Alfred C. Eckert III
Goldman, Sachs & Co., New York

Ronald J. Gilson
School of Law, Stanford University

Joseph A. Grundfest
Securities and Exchange Commission

Michael C. Jensen
Harvard Business School

Steven N. Kaplan
Graduate School of Business, University of Chicago

Robert L. Kieschnick, Jr.
School of Business, University of Manitoba

Lawrence Lederman
Wachtell, Lipton, Rosen & Katz, New York and School of Law,
New York University

Robert N. Macris
Wachtell, Lipton, Rosen & Katz, New York and School of Law,
New York University

Edward J. Markey
Chairman, Telecommunications and Finance Subcommittee,
United States House of Representatives

Roberta Romano
Yale Law School

PART 1

THE CHARACTERISTICS AND EFFECTS OF MANAGEMENT BUYOUTS

CHAPTER 1

LEVERAGED MANAGEMENT BUYOUTS AND SHAREHOLDERS' WEALTH

Yakov Amihud *

1. INTRODUCTION

Management buyouts (MBOs) are assuming an increasingly important role in the restructuring of corporate America. Although the subject of corporate takeovers and mergers has been studied extensively,[1] MBOs have only recently become the subject of research in finance. On the face of it, MBOs are not different from ordinary corporate acquisitions: normally, a group of investors forms a shell holding corporation, whose equity is privately held, to acquire the target company. In other cases, the investors buy into the target firm directly. The distinctive features of these acquisitions are that

1. the group of investors in an MBO includes members of the management of the target company (it is this feature that gives these transactions their name);
2. subsequent to the acquisition, the newly formed company goes private; and
3. the acquisition is financed mainly by borrowing such that the new company has a very high level of debt compared to the norm among publicly traded companies. This feature gives these transactions

*I thank Bernard Black, Jean-Francois Dreyfus, Deborah Goldstein, Avner Kalay, Robert Kieschnick, Robert Macris and Nickolaos Travlos for helpful comments, and Vernon Budinger for assistance in data processing.

3

the name "leveraged buyouts" (LBOs). We sometimes observe LBOs without feature (1), that is, the acquiring investors' group does not include managers from the acquired firm.

These features of MBOs are not unique. Whenever a company is acquired by another and merges into it, its shares (which are then held by the new owner) are subsequently eliminated from the market. Acquisitions are often financed by heavy borrowing, and it is often the case that the incumbent management stays after the acquisition. What distinguishes MBO transactions is that the incumbent management acquires a substantially greater proportion of the firms' equity than it previously had and the public firm is merged into a privately owned firm that usually continues to operate the acquired firm as an independent company (although it often sells assets and even whole divisions and subsidiaries to other firms).

This chapter reviews the evidence on the effects of management buyouts of public companies on shareholders' wealth. It focuses on the effect on the wealth of the "old" shareholders, complementing the other discussions in this book, which analyze the firms' performance and value increases *after* the MBO.

Section 2 presents findings on the increase in stock prices of companies where buyouts were announced, on the premiums offered by the bidders over the pre-announcement stock prices, and on the factors and firms' characteristics affecting these price increases and these premiums.

Section 3 focuses on 15 buyouts that were the largest ever up to 1987. The average value of the deals in these buyouts was $2.4 billion, the average premium offered was about 30%, and the average price increase at the buyout announcement was 22% (higher if we bring into account the effect of earlier rumors).

Section 4 discusses the effect of buyout announcements on the wealth of bondholders who, together with stockholders, share the value of the firm. The evidence, though inconclusive, suggests that LBOs are detrimental to bondholders.

Section 5 analyzes the relationship between competition in the bidding process and shareholders' wealth. First, evidence is presented showing that competitive bidding is associated with higher premiums paid to shareholders. Then, there is a discussion of whether this implies that shareholders' wealth is increased under mandated auctioning.

Section 6 examines whether shareholders are exploited by management in MBOs, and presents evidence which is inconclusive. It is often observed that part of the firms' insiders do not participate in the buyouts, indicating that the offers are not underpriced; there is no evidence that management manipulates accounting reports in order to mislead shareholders prior to the MBO into underestimating the firm; and there is evidence that managements apply measures to signal high value about the firm prior to the MBO. On the other hand, the performance of firms before MBOs is below that of firms in buyouts led by outsiders. More research is needed on this issue.

Section 7 discusses the effect of MBO-related tax issues on shareholders' wealth and on total tax collection and considers the significance of tax gains in explaining MBOs.

Section 8 presents a summary and concluding remarks and raises questions about some of the explanations of the MBO phenomenon.

2. THE EFFECT OF MBOs ON STOCK PRICES

This section presents the evidence on the effect of the MBO announcement on stock prices, on the magnitude of the offered premiums and on the determinants and implications of these price increases and premiums.

All studies on the subject document large increases in the stock prices (net of market) of the target firms upon the MBO announcement. [2] Table 1-1 summarizes these findings.

Comparing the increases in stock prices at the buyout announcement to those found in studies on ordinary mergers and acquisitions, we observe that they are rather on the low side: in buyouts, stock prices increase by about 20%. The average increase in target firms' stock prices at the announcements of tender offers was 30%, and the average increase at merger announcements was 20%, all net of market.[3] The average price increase at the buyout announcements is thus closer to the low end of this range. Noticing that acquisitions for cash and debt securities are known to generate greater price increases than acquisitions financed by stock exchange offers, and given that MBOs are for cash and debt securities, their announcement-induced price increases are probably lower than the price increases of cash-financed ordinary acquisitions of firms.

The price increases at the buyout announcements were considerably lower than the average premium offered to shareholders,[4] reflecting investors' assessments that the offers could fail. The stock price at the announcement date reflects the expected value assessed by shareholders, considering the outcomes in each state—a successful completion or a failure—weighted by the probability of each such event occurring. That is,

Table 1–1
Excess (net-of-market) stock returns at the announcements of leveraged buyouts

Study[a]	Period of Study	Event Period[b]	Number of Cases	Cumulative Excess Return
DeAngelo, DeAngelo & Rice (1984b)	1973-80	-1,0 days -10,+10 days	72 72	22.27% 28.05%
Grammatikos & Swary (1986)	1975-84	-1,0 days -10,0 days	131 131	14.04% 19.52%
Lehn & Poulsen (1987)	1980-84	-1,0 days -10,+10 days	93 93	13.93% 20.76%
Marais, Schipper & Smith (1987)	1974-85	-1,0 days	79	13.00%
Torabzadeh & Bertin (1987)	1982-85	0 month	48	18.64%
Travlos & Millon (1987b)	1975-83	-1,0 days -10,+10 days	56 56	16.20% 19.24%
This study[c]	1983-86	-20,0 days	15	19.60%

[a]The results of these studies are not independent due to partial overlapping of samples.
[b]Date 0 is when the announcement about the offer appeared in *The Wall Street Journal*. The sign on the days is relative to day 0.
[c]Sample of 15 largest LBOs described in section 3.

$$\text{price} = (\text{expected final offer price}) \times (\text{probability of success}) +$$
$$(\text{price of firm going on as is}) \times (\text{probability of failure})$$

The evidence thus indicates that the public usually perceives the MBO price offer to exceed the value of the shares if the firm goes on as is, without the MBO. This valuation is made *after* the private information about the potential value increases under the MBO has been released by the offer and reflects the fact that the final offer price may be higher than the initial offer price, as is often the case. Thus, it seems that on average the public attributes the potential value increase in the MBO to the specific team of investors that initiated it. This could also suggest that the target shareholders in MBOs are not exploited by the initiators of these transactions, in the sense that they are offered more than their firm's value without the MBO (although the offer may still be less than the value of the firm after the MBO; see section 6).

The hypothesis that the company's value to the initiators of an MBO is higher than shareholders can otherwise attain is corroborated by the evidence that when the offer is withdrawn, the average return (net of market) is negative, between -8.88% and -10.86% at the two-days' withdrawal announcement period and -15% in the period between the MBO announcement date and the withdrawal of the offer.[5] Again, since by then the MBO initiators have already revealed their private information about the prospective value of the firm, if shareholders expected others to acquire the firm and offer at least as high a value for it, there would be no decrease in stock price. Thus, the MBO offer is perceived as not being fully substitutable by others and the value increase as being (in part) uniquely attributable to the team that has made the offer.

Examining factors accounting for differences in stock price reaction to the buyout announcements, Travlos and Millon (1987b) found that the price increase was higher (1) the lower the price/earnings (P/E) ratio of the firm relative to the P/E ratio of its industry and (2) in cases of management buyouts compared to third-party buyouts. The first finding indicates that the market assessed a greater potential gain in firms whose price performance relative to earnings was below their industry's. The second finding is consistent with that of Grammatikos and Swary (1986), who found that the increase in stock prices at the announcement of the buyout proposals was significantly higher when the proposals were made by managers than when the proposals were made by nonmanagement groups (the difference was 3.24%, net of market, measured over days -2 to 0, with date 0 being the day on which the announcement about the offer appeared in *The Wall Street Journal*. The fact that the market reacts more favorably to management buyouts than to buyouts by outsiders can reflect higher offered premiums in management-led buyouts;[6] or higher potential gains, implying that firms under MBOs are more undervalued than firms in nonmanagement LBOs (see section 6); or higher probability of a successful completion of the MBO when the incumbent managers are leading the buyout.

Examining the relationship between the control exercised by the management of the target firm and the stock price reaction to the buyout announcement, DeAngelo, DeAngelo and Rice (1984b) found that the average increase in stock price in firms where management owned over

50% of the stock was 20% higher than in firms where management owned less than 50% of the stocks. However, Grammatikos and Swary (1986) found this pattern only when the buyout proposals were made by nonmanagement groups. Then, the average increase in stock price at the announcement was significantly higher the greater the managers' ownership proportion in the firm (the difference was 3.15% over days -2 to 0). In buyout proposals made by management, the increase in stock price was significantly higher (by 4.69%), the *lower* the managers' ownership proportion in the firm. These findings suggest that in buyouts where difficulties might arise—when outsiders make the buyout proposal and the incumbent management holds substantial interest in the firm or when the proposal is made by management that holds small interest in the firm—a higher expected premium is necessary for the offer to succeed, taking into account the fact that in these cases even if the offered premiums are higher, the probability of success is lower. Another interpretation of these results is that the potential value increases were higher in the cases where higher price increases were recorded, but again this explanation is incomplete, and more research is needed on this issue.

Stock prices exhibited greater increases at the buyout announcements of firms whose risk (measured by the standard deviation of returns) was lower. This difference was particularly pronounced in cases of nonmanagement bids, where the average price increase (net of market) for low-risk firms during days -2 to 0 was 4.69% greater than that in firms with high risk (see Grammatikos & Swary, 1986). This finding may indicate a greater potential for leveraging and the associated tax shield in low-risk firms, or that in high-risk firms there were greater inefficiencies prior to the buyout. Finally, Travlos and Millon (1987a) found that the price increase at the buyout announcements were unrelated (1) to the size of the transaction and (2) the extent of the increase in debt following the transaction. More research is needed on this issue, as well as a joint estimation of all the target firms' characteristics on the price reaction to the buyout announcements. The premiums offered to public shareholders over the firms' stock prices before the offers are given in Table 1-2.

Examining what accounts for differences in premiums, DeAngelo et al. (1984b) found that the average premium was not much different between firms where management owned at least 50% of the stock and those where management ownership was below 50%, suggesting that the power exercised by insiders-managers had little effect on the premiums offered to outside

Table 1–2
Average premiums offered in LBOs[a]

Study	Premium	Compared to Period before Offer	Number of Firms
DeAngelo, DeAngelo & Rice (1984b)	56.3%	40 days	72
Lowenstein (1985)	56.0%	30 days	28
Lehn & Poulsen (1987)	40.0%	20 days	89
Easterwood, Hsieh & Singer (1988)	48.6%	40 days	110
Kaplan (1988)	45.9%	2 months	75
This study[b]			
First offer	31.1%	20 days	15
Last offer	42.9%		

[a]Compared to stock price on a specified period before the offer
[b]See section 3.

shareholders. These findings on the offered premiums should be noted, for, as pointed out above, these authors found that the increase in the stock price (net of market) at the announcement was higher for the group of firms where management owned at least 50%, perhaps reflecting the higher probability of success of the MBO offer.

However, Easterwood, Hsieh, and Singer (1988) found significant evidence that lower premiums were offered in firms with higher ownership concentration (measured by the proportion of the firm owned by the board of directors and other top managers). This finding was interpreted as evidence that one motive for buyouts is a reduction in the costs associated with the conflict of interests between management and owners-shareholders. Because this cost is lower in firms with high ownership concentration, the improvement due to the buyout is lower, and hence the offered premium is lower. They also found that the offered premiums were not significantly different in firms where the buyouts were carried out by management, compared to third-party buyouts.

The findings on the relationship between the ownership structure in the firm, the offered premiums, and price increases at the announcements seem inconsistent across the various studies. The relationship between the offered premiums and the ownership concentration found by Easterwood et al. (1988) is consistent with the pattern of price increases at the announcements found by Grammatikos and Swary (1986) for buyouts proposed by management, but not with the pattern of price increases found by DeAngelo et al. (1984b). As pointed out above, the price increases reflect not only the offered premiums but also the probability of success.[7]

Higher premiums were offered for firms with higher undistributed cash flows and higher effective tax liabilities relative to equity values (Lehn & Poulsen, 1987).[8] The higher cash flows indicate a potential for increasing efficiency under a reorganization that will bring about a reduction in free cash flows and put management under more pressure, consistent with Jensen's (1986) "free cash flows" hypothesis. The high tax ratio represents greater potential for tax savings under an MBO. Finally, Easterwood et al. (1988) found that the offered premiums were significantly lower in firms that subsequently obtained competing offers, compared to premiums offered in firms with a single bid. This issue is discussed in section 5.

How do stock prices react at the announcement of the outcome of the buyout attempts? Grammatikos and Swary (1986) found that at the final announcement of approval of going private by shareholders, there was a positive but insignificant stock price reaction in the cases where the bids were made by management (1.41% over days -2 to 0), whereas the price increases in the cases of bids made by nonmanagement groups were about three times higher (4.50%) and highly significant. This implies that the surprise at the approval of a nonmanagement proposal was greater. At the announcements of the failure of buyout attempts, there was an average price change of -11.5% (over days -2 to 0), regardless of which party made the proposal. DeAngelo et al. (1984b) found a price change of -8.88% at the withdrawal announcement dates (-1 to 0), yet the total price change over the period beginning 40 days before the initial proposal and ending at withdrawal was positive, 21.89%, and this was maintained through 40 days after the withdrawal. This may reflect the information released during the buyout attempt on potential increases in the values of the target firms.

3. FINDINGS ON RECENT LARGE LBOs

The above-mentioned studies included firms of all sizes, large and small alike. In order to study the nature of very large MBOs, I examined those that appeared in the "25 Largest Leveraged Buyouts of All Time" list in the

November–December 1987 issue of *Mergers & Acquisitions*. Ten out of the 25 were of subsidiaries, and thus the analysis was confined to a sample of 15 firms, where the value of the transactions ranged between $977 and $6,250 million, with a mean of $2,443 million and a median of $1,690 million (the distribution was positively skewed). In six of these 15 firms, management made the initial buyout offer, and in seven cases (those six plus another), the final buyout was led by management. In the other cases, the buyout was initiated or led by outsiders, although there was sometimes management involvement.

The average premium offered by the initial bidder was 31.1% over the stock price of those firms 20 trading days before the offer announcement date, and it climbed up to 42.9% at the final offer that constituted the acquisition price. The average initial premium was lower than the average premiums documented in previous studies, suggesting the finding that the premiums in large firms are lower. The stock price increase from 20 days before the initial offer through the day of the offer was 19.6% on average, about the same as found in other studies, and similarly lower than the offered premium. The premiums were smaller after controlling for marketwide price changes: the mean net-of-market premium in the initial offer was 29.0% and 26.0% in the final offer.[9]

In some firms there were acquisition-related rumors in *The Wall Street Journal* sometimes before the first buyout announcement, and thus part of the value increases have occurred earlier. The two-day price increases at these rumors dates add 4.0% to the 19.6% reported above, giving a total value increase of 23.6% that could be attributed to the buyout.[10]

4. THE EFFECTS OF LBOs ON BONDHOLDERS' WEALTH

Not all the firm's claimholders benefit from the increased leverage associated with the buyouts. While shareholders' wealth increased in these transactions, and while holders of claims convertible into stocks gained too, there is evidence that bondholders might have incurred losses. This could suggest that part of the increase in shareholders' wealth, albeit a small part, constitutes a wealth transfer from bondholders.

The available studies on bondholders' returns at the announcement of going-private transactions are less comprehensive than those on stockholders' returns, and the results are less reliable, for data on bond prices are not readily available. Altogether, the evidence is inconclusive, although there are indications that bondholders suffer losses at the buyout announcements. Lehn and Poulsen (1987) examined the change in bond prices from 10 days before to 10 days after the LBO announcement. Data were available for nine firms' nonconvertible bonds, and the average return was -1.16%, significantly negative.[11] Travlos and Millon (1987b) examined the bond returns on 10 firms' nonconvertible bonds and found that the average cumulative return from 5 days before to 5 days after the announcements (net of the average returns on these bonds before the buyout) was -3.51% and significant. However, Marais, Schipper and Smith (1987) found that in a sample of 26 nonconvertible bonds, the announcement of going private produced negative but insignificant effect on nonconvertible bond prices (controlling for market effects and the average pre-announcement bond returns).[12]

In my own sample of 15 large LBOs, I checked for announcements of downgrading of the debt of the companies by either Moody's or Standard and Poor's right after the announcements of the going-private transactions. In 8 of the 15 companies in the sample, there were definite downgradings, and the other 7 were announced to be put on credit watch or considered for possible downgrading. This is consistent with the findings by Marais et al. (1987) of pervasive downgradings of Moody's ratings of debt following successful MBO proposals. For a subsample of nonconvertible securities whose ratings were downgraded or where leverage increased substantially, they found negative abnormal bond returns.

In sum, buyout announcements usually meant bad news for bondholders because of the reduction in the quality of the debt.

In these cases, shareholders may have taken advantage of incomplete protection of bondholders' interests in the bond covenants. It could also be that shareholders realized that they have been providing bondholders with greater protection than had been contracted in the bond indenture and acted to reverse the situation.[13] It should be emphasized, however, that the increase in the total firm value was overwhelmingly greater than the decline in the value of nonconvertible securities. When one looks at the firm as a whole, the value of the sum of its claims increased at the MBO announcement. In fact, Travlos and Millon (1987a) found no relationship between the change in capital structure at the buyout and the increase in stock prices at the buyout announcement.

5. THE EFFECT OF AUCTIONING ON SHAREHOLDERS' WEALTH

There are suggestions that shareholders are not adequately compensated in MBOs. Thus, Brudney and Chirelstein (1978) proposed to limit MBOs, and Longstreth (1983) and Lowenstein (1985) proposed to mandate auctioning for the target firms. The ensuing competitive open bidding will drive up the premiums obtained by shareholders, thus increasing their share in the MBO-generated benefits. This section examines the effect that auctioning might have on shareholders' wealth, considering both its effect on the offered premiums and on the probability of offers. A related issue also considered here is payoffs to the investors in MBOs and the ability of target shareholders to adopt measures that amount to "homemade" substitutes to mandated auctioning.

Lowenstein (1985) examined large MBOs, each worth at least $100 million to their shareholders at the winning bid price. His sample included 28 such cases, which took place between 1979 and 1984. The median company size in his sample was $401 million and the mean size was $498 million. His findings are presented in Table 1–3, panel A. The table shows that the premiums offered above the pre-MBO stock prices were substantially higher when there were three or more competing bids. Lowenstein (1985) concluded that "presumably, shareholders benefit from a climate of competitive bidding even if the bidding is not intense, but the benefits increase dramatically with the number of bidders" (p. 738). Consequently, he proposed to mandate a public auctioning of the target firm after the initial MBO offer has been made to encourage competition from other bidders, which will lead to a higher compensation to the target shareholders. The conclusion that competition among bidders results in higher premiums is, however, not supported by the findings of Easterwood et al. (1988). After adjusting for other factors they found no significant effect of the numbers of bidders on the buyout premiums.

Naturally, the initial bidder may err in assessing the target's worth. If the bidder overvalues the target, the bid will go unchallenged and the bidder will eventually lose. This is the "winner's curse."[14] If the bidder underestimates the target, other bidders may compete and lead to the elimination of the initial bidder's possible gain. Competition among bidders in takeovers is known to lead to increases in the compensation to target firms' shareholders. Examining shareholders' returns in tender offers with

Table 1–3
Premiums paid in LBOs and their relationship to competition[a] among bidders

Panel A: Lowenstein (1985, p. 738), 28 firms.

	Premium of Winning Bid over Market Price 30 Days before First Significant Announcement			Disclosed Number of Actual or Potential Bidders	Premium of Successful Third-party Bids over Management Bids
	All Bids	Less than 3 Bids	3 or More Bids		
Median	58%	48%	76%	2.0	8%
Mean	56%	50%	69%	2.5	14%

Panel B: Amihud (current study), 15 large firms, of which 9 had competing bids. Premiums over market price 20 days before first announcement.

Panel B.1: Premium of initial bid price.

	Unadjusted			Net of Market[b]		
	All Bids	Without Competition	With Competition	All Bids	Without Competition	With Competition
Median	30.2%	23.7%	30.9%	28.3%	23.8%	27.5%
Mean	31.1%	29.3%	33.4%	29.0%	27.4%	30.6%

Panel B.2: Premium of final bid price.

	Unadjusted			Net of Market[b]		
	All Bids	Without Competition	With Competition	All Bids	Without Competition	With Competition
Median	43.2%	28.8%	50.8%	24.7%	9.4%	39.3%
Mean	42.9%	30.7%[c]	52.2%[c]	26.0%	11.9%[c]	35.8%[c]

[a]Competition in panel A is when there were more than three bidders. In panel B, it is when there was at least one bidder in addition to the initial one. Information was obtained through reports in *The Wall Street Journal.*

[b]Net-of-market premium = unadjusted premium − (a + b [market return]). See description in note 9.

[c]The difference in the mean premiums between the two groups is statistically significant.

single bidders relative to those in tender offers with multiple bidders, Bradley, Desai, and Kim (1983) found that under multiple bidding the returns to target shareholders were over 10% higher and the returns to bidders were 2% to 3% lower, compared to single-bidder bases. Some academics and legislators have long proposed to enact an auctioneering rule in all types of takeovers that would mandate a delay period after the initial tender offer has been made in order to enable potential bidders to enter the bidding process and compete for the target company.[15]   It has been suggested that such a rule would not only increase the reward to the target shareholders but would also facilitate the allocation of the target's resources to their most efficient user, that is, the highest bidder. The question is whether the finding that competition among bidders drives up the price of the target firm's shares implies that auctioning the target firm increases shareholders' wealth.

Although successful MBOs generate large returns earned by the initiators of the deals, we do not observe the investment of resources, including the investment of specialized human capital, in searching for a buyout target and arranging the transaction, and we also have to consider the fact that there is no certainty that the bid succeeds. If the expected gain to bidders from this process is reduced by auctioning, the investment in it will be as well, simply shifting the market to a new equilibrium where investors still earn "normal" returns, as they may well be earning today. In the new equilibrium, some buyouts will not be initiated and their potential economic gains will be lost.

It is thus erroneous to infer from the higher premium obtained under competition among bidders that target shareholders will surely benefit under a law mandating auctioning of the MBO firms. Indeed, *conditional* on the event that an initial offer has been made, competition among bidders helps increase shareholders' wealth, but mandated auctioning can reduce the probability of the initial offer being made. When a potential bidder knows that the likelihood of a successful completion of the acquisition is reduced because of possible competition, and that the expected profit will be reduced because of the need to outbid competitors, the propensity to start the process (search for an appropriate target and initiation of a buyout transaction) is reduced.[16] When the expected value of mandated auctioning is considered—that is, when the additional premium under auctioning is balanced against the lower probability of an offer's being made—it is unclear whether it increases shareholders' wealth. In fact, mandated auctioning could be detrimental to shareholders. Proponents of auctioning observe the higher premium but not the buyouts that were not initiated because of the threat of auctioning.

While mandated auctioning involves some tradeoffs from the target shareholders' viewpoint, it can cause an overall economic loss, for it discourages the search and bidding for undervalued firms and thus the potential value increases will not be realized. Even without a mandated auction, the Williams Act which mandates a delay period following a tender offer,[17] causes this kind of an economic loss, for the information produced about the target firm becomes publicly available and can be utilized freely by any potential competing bidder. Thus, even under the current regime there may well be too few MBOs (and takeovers in general), and the potential value increases are lost.[18]

This issue can be viewed as a "public good" problem associated with the production of information: the MBO specialist invests resources in searching for a target and in the bidding process but cannot enforce property rights on the information he or she has produced.[19] This information can be freely used by any other bidder who has not invested resources in producing the information. Since the reward to the initial bidder is not commensurate with the cost (because someone else shares the reward but not the cost), there will be a less-than-optimal level of search. That is, the expected economic marginal benefit from search for buyout targets will exceed the marginal cost, yet there will be no incentive to search. In addition, acquisitions where potential benefits are relatively low or where competition is expected to be intense will be ignored, and the potential increases in value (regardless of how they are split between the MBO initiators and the target shareholders) will be forgone—a net economic loss.

Proponents of auctioning propose that without it, target shareholders are insufficiently compensated, implying that the MBO initiators earn above-normal returns from their activity.[20] It is unclear, however, who has property rights on the value gain generated in a MBO and what is the proper benchmark to determine how this gain should be divided between the buyers and the selling shareholders. There is no uniformly agreed-upon standard of fair division when a deal between two parties generates a gain, and under some models any division of these gains is equally "fair."[21] In an ordinary corporate acquisition, it has been observed that most (perhaps all) of the gains accrued to the sellers rather than to the acquiring firm. This led Roll (1986) to propose that bidding firms infected by "hubris" pay too much for their target. In MBOs, the bidding firms are private; hence, it is impossible to obtain a direct market assessment of the effect of the acquisition on the bidder.[22]

It may be possible to make some inferences about the returns to buyout investors from the fact that there are no barriers to entry into the "MBO industry." There are no constraints on acquiring firms in general and on MBOs in particular, and they can be undertaken by any group of investors with sufficient resources. While we observe large funds established by MBO specialists, investment banks, and other financial institutions, the size of these funds is limited and the intensity of the buyout activity is not boundless. At some point, the market attains an equilibrium where the marginal gains from MBOs to their initiators are commensurate with the marginal cost of initiating these deals. In other words, at equilibrium investors should be earning only "normal" returns, regardless of whether or not auctioning is mandated. Auctioning will not change the equilibrium return to MBO investors, but it will change the intensity of this activity.

Even without auctioning, if shareholders consider the buyout offer price to be too low, they can refrain from tendering their shares. While not having the information about the firm that insiders do, outside shareholders with rational expectations about the firm's value will tender at a price that is an unbiased estimate of what they consider a "fair" price, given the private information disclosed by the MBO offer. However, the bidders can structure the offer to exert a pressure on target shareholders to tender by squeezing out the minority at inferior terms. Such pressure may be necessary, for without it the acquisition may never take place[23] and the resulting increase in value may be forgone. Shareholders, however, can remove the pressure to tender if they so wish by adopting defensive measures that also can effectively delay the takeover process.

The availability of takeover-impeding measures can be viewed as a "homemade" substitute to a mandatory auctioning. The empirical evidence suggests that the adoption of defensive measures was not considered valuable by shareholders.[24] Still, the initial bidders, especially if they are (or are associated with) the firm's management have the advantage in the bidding process, both in respect to time and information. The proposal of the American Law Institute, discussed by Gilson in Chapter 10, is designed to bring about a division of the MBO-induced gains in a way that approximates the division under an arm's-length transaction.

Finally, a company considering a buyout and wishing to enjoy the benefits of auctioning while providing an incentive to a buyout specialist can have both by providing that the latter will be paid a cancellation fee if the buyout is carried out with a competing investor.[25] Under such an arrangement, the auctioning is compatible with shareholders' wealth maximization.

6. ARE SHAREHOLDERS EXPLOITED BY MANAGEMENT IN MBOs?

MBOs are found to generate large economic gains to the parties involved, as well as to the economy as a whole.[26] But why do managers buy out the firm in order to attain these improvements? Being in charge, they can improve their firm's performance while leaving unchanged the organizational and ownership structure of the firm. This section will examine the hypothesis that MBOs are motivated by management's ability to exploit the company's shareholders and take advantage of them by buying the firm for a price that is "too low."

It has been suggested that management can apply "techniques [that] are intended directly or indirectly to depress the price of the company's shares, so that the public can be offered the bait of a 'premium' price" (Lowenstein 1985, p. 740).[27] The company's shareholders, being unorganized, suffer from the "free rider" problem: none of the small shareholders has the incentive to spend resources on monitoring the management, for he or she alone will bear the cost, whereas the benefit will accrue to all shareholders. Thus, each (small) shareholder refrains from monitoring the management, enabling these managers to exploit the firm's resources to serve their interests[28] and, in the case here, to buy the firm at a "low" price.

The argument that MBOs are made feasible by the inability of the company's dispersed shareholders to monitor management cannot explain the often-observed MBOs of subsidiaries or divisions of corporations. Out of the 25 largest LBOs through 1987, 10 were subsidiaries or divisions of corporations, and 5 of those were acquired by management. In the largest buyout, that of Beatrice Corporation, five divisions of the company with an estimated total value of $3.2 billion were sold by the buyout group, headed by Kravis, Kohlberg, Roberts & Co. (KKR), to investors' groups that included the divisions' management.[29] Similarly, Kraft Inc. has recently announced the $1.8 billion sale of its Duracell battery business to a buyout group that includes Duracell's top management and is led by KKR. In an MBO of a subsidiary, the free-rider argument that monitoring of managers by shareholders is impeded does not hold. Although monitoring is still costly, the management of the parent company can certainly expend resources to monitor the managers of the subsidiary, for then the benefits accrue to the firm as a whole. If the parent company considers the subsidiary to be more valuable as an independent entity, it can auction it or spin it off as an independent, publicly traded firm. Then, the value increases can be attained under *any* management, not necessarily under the incumbent one. If the parent company chooses to sell the subsidiary to a group of investors that includes the subsidiary's managers, there must be unique benefits in MBOs that cannot be duplicated by another type of organizational restructuring.

Examining the gains of the parent companies' shareholders in divisional MBOs, Hite and Vetsuypens (1988) found that the two-day stock price increase at the announcement of divisional MBOs was 0.55% and weakly significant. In a subsample of firms where the sale constituted more than 30% of the parent firm's pre-buyout equity, the two-day announcement price increase was 2.72% and highly significant. Against these gains, the 14% to 22% two-day increase in stock prices of target firms in MBO announcements of entire firms compares favorably (adjusting linearly for size), and suggests that target shareholders in MBOs may not be receiving unusually low offers, as is often claimed. Also, the gains of the parent firms' shareholders at the MBO announcements were not affected by whether the parent company's management participated in the buyout, indicating that the apparent conflict of interest when management acts as both buyer and seller did not harm shareholders. Finally, Abbott and Johnson (1988) found that the average increase of parent firms' share prices in divisional MBOs was higher (but insignificantly so) than those in the sell-off of divisions to outside buyers. In sum, the evidence from divisional MBOs suggests that this form of organizational restructuring increases value and may well be attributed to the human capital of the managers and to the form of ownership.

The evidence on the premiums offered in MBOs does not support the hypothesis that management exploits the shareholders. Easterwood et al. (1988) and Kieschnick (1988) found no difference in the premiums offered in MBOs compared to those offered in third-party buyouts, and my findings for the 15 large buyouts are similar, both for the initial offer and the final offer.[30]

In addition, the evidence presented in section 2 shows that the increases of stock prices at the buyout announcements are significantly higher when they are initiated by management,[31] and in my sample there was no significant difference between the two groups. While these findings suggest that the premiums in MBOs are not unusually low, they cannot refute the hypothesis that managements exploit the shareholders in MBOs, since the pre-offer stock prices could have been deliberately depressed by management.

There is some evidence that stock prices of firms that undergo MBOs show inferior performance in the period before the offer announcement, compared to other public firms. Kieschnick (Chapter 2) found that in the year up to the quarter before the buyout, the stock return of firms that went private was lower than that of a control sample of public firms.[32] Maupin, Bidwell, and Ortegren (1984) found that the stock price/book value ratios were lower before the transaction in firms that underwent MBOs compared to firms remaining public.[33]

However, in my sample of 15 large LBOs, the stocks of firms that went private outperformed the market in the five-year period preceding the announcement, by an average of 0.41% per month.[34] When splitting the sample according to whether the buyout was led by management (7 firms) or by outsiders (8 firms), I found that the pre-buyout overperformance was, on average, 0.21% per month (median = 0.29%) for the first group and 0.57% (median = 0.57%) for the second group. While this could suggest that the performance of the stocks of firms subject to MBOs was lower than that of firms subject to buyouts by outsiders, the difference between the means was not statistically significant.[35]

Significant evidence that the performance of firms subject to MBOs was worse than that of firms subject to buyout by nonmanagement groups was found by Grammatikos and Swary (1986). Over the period between 90 days and 11 days prior to the buyout announcement, firms of the first group earned between 11% and 14% less than firms of the second group, after controlling for differences in risk (measured by standard deviation of returns or by the beta coefficient). Kieschnick (1988) found that the lower the prebuyout performance of the firm, the more likely the buyout would be led by management than by a third party. These findings have two possible interpretations. They could support the hypothesis that in MBOs managers exploit shareholders by depressing the firm's performance before they offer to buy it. Alternatively, they could reflect what the majority of surveyed financial officers of firms that went private said: "The primary reason for the buyout transaction was that the stock had been selling so far below its real value that the best way to enable shareholders to realize the maximum amount on their investment was through a management buyout" (Maupin, et al. 1984, pp. 441-442). This interpretation suggests that management maximizes shareholders' wealth, and the buyout proposal is motivated by the observation that the firm has been doing poorly in the market. Unable to convey the favorable inside information about the firm in a credible and less costly way, management offers to buy the firm at its "fair" value. One can then ask why a less drastic method, such as a partial share repurchase, has not been applied before resorting to a buyout.

It is of interest to note that most of the firms in my sample (12 out of 15) announced increases in dividends in the year prior to the MBO announcement.[36] An increase in dividends is a well-known means for insiders to convey favorable information about the firm to outsiders, and it is generally followed by large price increases. Managers who wish to depress the price of their firm's stock prior to a MBO will hardly choose to raise dividends.[37]

Management can reduce the compensation it would have to offer in a buyout by misleading outside shareholders about the true value of the firm. DeAngelo (1986) tested whether management understates reported earnings in the period just preceding the buyout, but found no evidence supporting that hypothesis. It should be noted that the buyout offer price is often carefully scrutinized by the target firm shareholders, who can challenge it in court if considered inadequate (see Lederman & Bryer, Chapter 6). This serves to monitor the management and prevent underpricing.

Still, given the nature of MBOs, the problem is, who represents the interests of the shareholders when management itself is on the opposite side of the deal? Shareholders have recourse to the courts, and they can litigate against the management for breaching its fiduciary duty, as discussed in Chapter 6. MBOs are very often litigated, but the process is costly.

In Chapter 4, Kaplan presents a number of observations suggesting that the MBO offers are not underpriced by the better-informed investors: there are often informed insiders who do not participate in the buyout and prefer to sell their shares at the offer price. In fact, the equity share of nonparticipating insiders is larger, on average, than that of the participating ones. In addition, Kaplan asserts that the projections provided by the buyout management in the proxy statements exceed the actual performance of these firms after the buyout.[38]

It seems that more research is needed on whether management deliberately exploits the target shareholders and whether the latter obtain a fair price.

7. THE TAX-INDUCED BENEFITS OF MBOs

Tax considerations play a major role in MBOs, and have induced a public debate on their merit. As Robert Macris discusses in detail in Chapter 7, MBOs give rise to the following three types of tax benefits: increased depreciation deductions with respect to the acquired assets (due to an increase in the depreciable basis); the deductibility of interest payments on debt, and the tax advantage of stock acquisition through employee stock ownership plans (ESOPs).[39] Naturally, these tax benefits may be reflected in the MBO offer price and thus contribute to shareholders' wealth. Some argue[40] that these tax benefits constitute an unintended subsidization of MBOs by the public and cause a loss in tax revenues to the government. More important is the claim that the MBO-induced tax benefits encourage wasteful use of resources in order to generate them, thus leading to social loss, a view that is certainly not new.

These arguments regarding the tax benefits associated with MBOs can be disputed. The tax benefits that accrue to shareholders and investors in MBOs do not constitute a net loss in tax revenues to the government, and in fact, the net effect on government tax revenues is not always clear. Shareholders who realize gains on the sale of their stock in the MBO tender offer are subject to income tax on these gains currently. It may be argued that this tax would have been paid some time in the future in any event, but this is not always the case. Shareholders may plan to realize the gains on the sale of their stocks in periods when their marginal tax is lower, thus paying lower tax than that incurred upon a tender of shares in a MBO. Some shareholders eliminate taxation of appreciation in stock by holding their shares until death, at which time their beneficiaries receive a fair market value tax basis (and thus the appreciation is not subject to income tax), whereas upon selling their shares to the bidder in an MBO, these shareholders immediately pay ordinary income tax on the appreciation. Finally, even if the taxpayer's bracket does not change, advancing the tax payment on gains implies higher present value of tax collection.

In addition, the individual tax paid by tendering shareholders could exceed the tax benefits generated by the MBO. If these benefits constitute a fraction of the MBO offer premium and if the tendering shareholder's gain is that premium (i.e., if the individual shareholder's tax basis is the pre-MBO market stock price), the aggregate individual tax that the shareholders pay may exceed the MBO-generated tax benefits. If the shareholder's gain is greater than the premium (i.e., if the shareholder's tax basis is below the pre-buyout price),[41] the individual tax paid may exceed the tax gain due to the MBO.

In sum, it is not necessarily the case that MBOs result in a "subsidization" or loss in tax revenues. And it may well be that at the margin, the tax advantage to the MBO investors is offset by the tax paid by the tendering shareholders.[42]

Another counterargument to the tax subsidization argument is that some of these tax benefits can be realized without MBOs, and others have been eliminated. A major source of tax shield in MBOs is attributed to the increase in leverage, although it is well known that this benefit might have been offset, at least until the recent change in the tax code, by the higher individual tax on interest income (Miller, 1977).[43] However, these tax benefits were available without undergoing an MBO. Publicly traded firms often undergo restructuring, issuing debt and using the proceeds to purchase their own stock. These transactions are known to generate large gains to shareholders.[44] Clearly, the tax benefits due to interest deductibility are available there too and can be enjoyed without undergoing an MBO. What might limit the corporate borrowing is the agency costs of debt that arise from the conflict of interests between bondholders and stockholders.[45] The increase in borrowing associated with MBO may reflect the lowering of these debt-related costs under the new organizational structure. In MBOs, the line between equity holders and lenders is less firmly drawn than in publicly traded firms,[46] and the contracts between borrowers and lenders are designed to lower agency costs. But these contracts are available to public corporations as well. Finally, given that the informed public knows the unutilized debt capacity of the firm, it may be argued that unless new information is revealed by the increased debt, the value of the available tax shield should be incorporated, at least in part, in the stock price.

The tax benefits generated by the use of ESOPs in MBOs are, again, not uniquely associated with MBOs and can be obtained by a public corporation that decides to encourage an ESOP. Just as with leverage, one may wonder why we do not observe more firms taking advantage of this potential tax benefit.

The tax advantages from stepping up the depreciable basis of "inside" assets that were available prior to the Tax Reform Act of 1986 are almost totally eliminated now (see Chapter 7). This legislation generally imposes a tax cost at the sale upon the election to step up the basis of the assets for federal income tax purposes. Therefore, since the present value of the future tax benefits is almost always exceeded by the tax cost imposed upon the election, there is no economic advantage in this transaction. If MBOs were propelled mainly by these tax benefits, we should observe now a reduction in MBO activity or a reduction in the premiums offered.[47] Some of these tax benefits were attainable before this Act without a "qualified" stock purchase,[48] which essentially changes the control in the firm. However, any qualified stock purchase, whether or not in the form of an MBO, could generate similar tax benefits, and thus if there were a potential tax benefit, the economic cost of such a transaction would have been incurred even without an MBO.

Given that some of the tax advantages associated with a MBO can be attained without it and that other advantages that could be obtained mostly under a change-of-control transaction were eliminated under the 1986 Tax Recovery Act, the argument that MBOs are motivated only by tax benefits needs more support than is currently available.

8. CONCLUDING REMARKS

The available evidence suggests that the effect of MBOs on shareholders' wealth is favorable: a buyout announcement generates significant increases of about 20% in stock prices. These price increases were larger in management-led buyouts and in firms whose P/E ratios were low relative to their industry. The offered premiums were about 50% of the pre-offer prices, and were higher in firms with relatively high cash flows and high effective tax liabilities. [49] The average stock price after an offer has been made was lower than the average offered buyout price, reflecting the likelihood that the offer could fail and then the firm would continue to operate without the buyout-generated benefits. The evidence does not seem to support the hypothesis that the buyout investors gain at the expense of the shareholders, nor that managements deliberately exploit or mislead the outside shareholders in order to make the acquisition less costly. There is some evidence, however, that the pre-buyout performance of firms in MBOs was below that of firms when the buyout was led by outsiders.

Although the evidence suggests that buyouts generate real economic gains (see Chapters 3, 4, 11, and 12), the question is why they are needed to attain these gains. Couldn't the same gains be produced without changing the organizational structure of the firm?

A buyout is costly, for going private substantially reduces the liquidity or marketability of the firm's claims (in particular, of the equity claims), which leads to a reduction in value. Amihud and Mendelson (1986a, 1986b) showed that the lower the liquidity of a financial asset, the higher its expected return after controlling for risk. This implies that given two firms that generate the same cash flows, the one with the less liquid claims will have a lower value. Amihud and Mendelson (1988) thus argue that "going public" can be considered a value-increasing investment in improving liquidity. The value of liquidity can be inferred from the fact that in firms where part of the stock is publicly traded and the other part restricted (or "letter") stock, the price of the illiquid restricted stock is about 25% to 30% below the price of the publicly traded stock.[50] Thus, it might be that the high returns required by buyout investors are, in part, a compensation for the cost of illiquidity of their claims and do not constitute abnormally high returns. In sum, the great reduction in the liquidity of the firm's claims when going private constitutes a substantial cost. It is thus questionable what the unique benefits in going private are that could offset this cost.

The cost savings in going private, associated with public ownership (savings in the cost of listing, registration with the SEC, reporting and servicing the shareholders) was often cited as a motivation for MBOs. However, these costs are relatively small for large corporations and cannot explain the large value increases in MBOs.

The benefit from linking the managers' compensation more closely to the firm's stock value, as is the case in MBOs where managers become major shareholders, can also be achieved in public corporations by properly designing the managerial compensation contracts.[51] If the corporate managerial compensation does not provide sufficient incentives to managers, a raider can take over the firm and change it, without the need to go private. If the value of MBOs lies in the concentration of ownership and the unchallenged power of management or if the separation between ownership and control is a source of inefficiency in public corporations, these issues can be resolved by having insiders hold a substantial control (e.g., more than 50% of the voting power). That is, the management and the buyout specialist could buy a controlling interest in the firm without taking it private. Such large shareholders will also have the incentive to monitor management better than do dispersed public shareholders. If such an organizational structure is valuable, we should observe public firms with highly concentrated ownership. What we observe instead is that in most firms ownership concentration is very low.

The tax benefits associated with MBOs can be obtained by a change-of-control acquisition without going private or can be obtained under the existing corporate organizational structure and control. The tax advantages associated with stepping up the basis of depreciable assets have been almost entirely eliminated under the Tax Reform Act of 1986. Regarding leverage, it is not entirely clear why a public corporation cannot leverage itself in the same way that a private corporation does, especially when ownership is concentrated.[52] Contracts between lenders and shareholders of the type used in MBOs, designed to reduce the conflict of interests between the two parties and thus reduce the agency cost of borrowing, are also available to public corporations, and it is unclear why they are necessarily associated with privatization.

The benefits to a private corporation that cannot be duplicated in a public one are fewer regulatory constraints[53] and, perhaps more importantly, retaining property rights on information. Privately owned firms avoid the need to release private information that can be useful to competitors and/or may hamper the carrying out of some policies. Perhaps it is the cost to the public corporation of being under public scrutiny that motivates MBOs.

NOTES

1. See Jensen and Ruback (1983) for a comprehensive review of the literature and Jarrell, Brickley, and Netter (1988) for more recent evidence.
2. Prices are adjusted for dividends; thus, a price change implies total return.
3. See Jensen and Ruback (1983).
4. DeAngelo, DeAngelo, and Rice (1984b) report that the offer price exceeded the stock price, measured five days after the proposal, by 13.86%. There were cases where the price increase at the announcement exceeded the offered premium, reflecting investors' assessment that the offer price would rise or that

the value of the firm, conditional on the buyout information, was higher than the offer price. The analysis of the implication of this evidence follows the discussion in DeAngelo et al. (1984b), p. 390. Note, however, that in cases of partial acquisitions with minority squeezeouts, it is natural for the stock price to be below the (partial) offer price.

5. See DeAngelo et al. (1984a), Grammatikos and Swary (1986), and Marais, Schipper, and Smith (1987), respectively. Since the studies also cover hostile LBOs, the decline in stock price at the withdrawal announcement also reflects the public's recognition that management is entrenched and refuses value-increasing changes.

6. However, Easterwood et al. (1988) found no difference in premiums offered in MBOs compared to third-party buyouts.

7. More research is needed on this issue. The *joint* effect of the management's control in the firm and of whether the offer is made by insiders or outsiders is a worthwhile topic for further study.

8. Undistributed cash flows equal operating income minus taxes, interest, and dividends; tax liability equals income tax minus charges for deferred taxes.

9. These premiums are significantly greater than zero. The exact calculation was done as follows. For each firm i we estimated the market model

$$R_{it} = a_i + b_i R_{mt} + e_{it},$$

where R is the firm's monthly return, R_m is the market value-weighted monthly return, a and b are parameters, and e is the residual. The data source is the University of Chicago CRSP data base, and the estimations are over 60 months up to at least 2 full months before the initial buyout announcement date, which is the day the information appeared in *The Wall Street Journal*. The expected return on the firm's stock between 20 days before the first announcement and the announcement date, or the final date when the transaction was consummated, equals ($a_i + b_i$[change in the market index over the respective period]). The net-of-market premium is the premium minus the expected stock price change over the respective period (for three firms that concluded the deal in 1987, the S&P 500 index was used then). The net-of-market price increase is the firm's return over the 20-day period minus the expected return over this period.

10. In some cases, information was unfolding gradually between the first rumor and the formal announcement, and thus the cumulative price increase may be even higher.

11. Lehn and Poulsen's (1987) sample included 13 bonds, but four of them were convertible.

12. The ratio between the number of observations on bonds and the number of observations on stocks in these three studies was 9:93, 10:56, and 26:79, respectively.

13. Kalay (1982) has documented the fact that firms often hold a "reservoir" of funds above the level required in the bond covenants. In my sample of 15 large LBOs, 9 firms decreased their debt/equity ratio in the year prior to the LBO compared to the year beforehand.

14. See Black (1988) on bidders' overpayments in takeovers.

15. See Bebchuk (1982) and Senator William Proxmire in a floor speech on March 20, 1985. This idea might have been behind the Williams Act, which mandated a delay period of 20 business days following the tender offer, and the more recently enacted state laws that mandate substantial disclosure requirements, effectively delaying the takeover and enabling competitors to enter the bidding process. For arguments against auctioneering and in favor of a management passivity rule in tender offers, see Easterbrook and Fischel (1982). Gilson (1982) presented a comprehensive discussion of the issue.

16 Indeed, Lederman and Bryer point out in Chapter 6 that a buyout group often requests the company to refrain from soliciting or encouraging others to make competing bids, citing the expense borne in putting together the buyout proposal.

17. Robert Kieschnick (Chapter 2) has found that the period between the initial offer and the final stockholders' vote on the buyout proposal averaged 158 days with a median of 145 days.

18. See Amihud and Burnovski (1987) for a comprehensive analysis. It should be pointed out, however, that the cost to the incumbent management of initiating a buyout may be far lower than the cost to outsiders, for management has the information. Thus, the negative effect of auctioning on the initiation of MBOs may be lower than in cases of LBOs initiated by outsiders.

19. The current legal regime protects the property rights of the producers of goods. There are laws that protect patents and designs, there are copyright laws, but the information produced about a firm that is a potential acquisition candidate is not only unprotected but by law is also made freely available to all.

20. This view is often supported by the well-publicized returns earned by some buyout specialists, such as in the case of Beatrice: "Buying and breaking up the consumer products giant proved more profitable than anyone's wildest dream" (Sterngold, 1987).

21. See a discussion in Amihud and Burnovski (1987) on the property rights on the value generated in corporate acquisitions and the division of this value.

22. See, however, Chapter 4 for Kaplan's findings on this issue.

23. See Grossman and Hart (1980). The reason is that shareholders know that the acquisition entails cost to the offerer and that the offer price must be less than the postacquisition value in order for the acquirer to make a profit, and therefore they will not tender. However, in MBOs insiders usually hold large blocks of stocks, so the profit they make on their stocks could be sufficient to cover the

offer cost, and hence a dilution of the minority interest may be unnecessary for the success of the offer (Shleifer & Vishny, 1986).

24. See a discussion and a review of the evidence in Amihud and Burnovski (1987). These measures may be hard to institute if the management opposes them.

25. See Chapter 6, where Lederman and Bryer cite the agreement between Beatrice and the buyout specialist Kohlberg, Kravis, Roberts & Co. This arrangement can raise the issue of "moral hazard" when the incumbent management is involved.

26. Bull and Kaplan (in Chapter 3 and 4, respectively) analyze the real economic improvements during the period after the MBO. Grundfest discusses the economic benefits of MBOs in Chapter 11.

27. See also Longstreth (1983). Markey (see Chapter 9) suggests regulation of MBOs to protect the interests of the target shareholders, and this is also the concern of the American Law Institute, as Gilson notes in Chapter 10. But Grundfest argues that "MBOs...are already among the most regulated transactions in our economic system" and details the extensive protection of the target's shareholders interests, (see Chapter 11).

28. See also Easterbrook and Fischel (1983). This problem can be viewed in the context of the conflict of interests between shareholders and management, a classical "agency problem" (Jensen & Meckling, 1976). Self-serving managerial actions, at the expense of shareholders, include consumption of perquisites, preferring sales growth over profit maximization, and having a higher propensity to engage in risk-reducing, size-increasing conglomerate mergers. See Amihud and Kamin (1979), Amihud and Lev (1981), Amihud, Dodd, and Weinstein (1986), and the references therein. However, the principal-agent relations between shareholders and managers are regulated by "homemade" means (i.e., by contracts between the parties), and it is thus questionable why we do not observe employment contracts barring managers from buying out the company they manage.

29. See Sterngold (1987).

30. The initial net offer premium (= offer price minus the stock price 20 days earlier, net of market) was, on average, 30.1% for management-led buyouts compared to 28.6% in buyouts led by others. The final net offer premiums were, respectively, 25.8% and 26.6%, on average. The differences were insignificant. In one case, Fruehauf Corporation, the initial buyout offer was made by outsiders led by Asher Edelman, but the buyout was finally led by the management.

31. As pointed out in section 2, the greater price increases in MBOs than in LBOs by outsiders may reflect the higher probability of successful completion of the transaction rather than indicating anything about the relative value of the transactions.

32. This evidence was weakly significant. The return was measured relative to the S&P 500 Index during the respective period.
33. The stock prices of firms that went private were also lower than their book value.
34. This result was obtained from the monthly market model (see footnote 9). Here, the returns on both the firms and the market were in terms of premiums over each month's 90-day Treasury bills rate (source: *Citibank Economic Database*). The average β for the sample was 1.046 with standard error of .072 (average β is not significantly different from 1.0) and the average α was 0.41% with standard error of 0.16 (t-value is 2.56), significantly greater than zero. The median α was 0.41, indicating that the result is not affected by extreme values.
35. The β coefficients of the two groups were nearly the same, 1.075 and 1.021 for buyouts led by management and by others, respectively, with no significant difference.
36. Often there was a sequence of announcements of dividend increases. In one case, Northwest Industries, there were three dividend increases followed by a dividend decrease. There, the LBO was not initiated by management.
37. Maupin, Bidwell and Ortegren (1984) found that firms that went through MBOs were distinguished in their above-industry dividend yields and that these cash dividends dropped to zero after the MBO transaction, reducing tax payments by equityholders.
38. This is consistent with Roll's (1986) 'hubris' hypothesis discussed in section 5 above.
39. There are additional tax benefits associated with the management stock transaction; see Chapter 7. For a comprehensive discussion of tax motivation for corporate acquisitions, see Gilson, Scholes, and Wolfson (1988).
40. See Lowenstein (1985) and the references therein.
41. As reported above, firms that underwent MBO enjoyed good performance prior to the offer, relative to the market.
42. Because of the different tax base of individual investors, each will have a different reservation price, giving rise to a supply function of stocks that is increasing in price; see Dreyfus (1987).
43. Under the Internal Revenue code of 1986, as amended, capital gains and ordinary income are taxed at the same rate, but individuals can still reduce the effective capital gains tax by deferring the realization of the gains or by realizing them in times when their marginal tax rate is low.
44. Masulis (1980) found that the average excess returns to shareholders at the announcement of exchanging equity for new debt was 9.79%.
45. See Jensen and Smith (1985). Bankruptcy costs can play a role too, although they could be eliminated; see Haugen and Senbet (1978).
46. See the discussion in Lowenstein (1985, p. 758). He points out (Note 105) that "if the lenders are also equity investors—and the large amount of debt in some

MBOs effectively makes them such, regardless of the form of the security—it is more likely that the terms will be renegotiated when interest payments cannot be met rather than that the company will be forced into bankruptcy reorganization."

47. Controlling, of course, for other factors. This will make an interesting study that will shed light on the importance of some tax considerations in MBOs.

48. Usually, this requires an acquisition in a taxable sale transaction of at least 80% of the stock (in vote and in value) of the target company.

49. Absent is a study that examines jointly the factors affecting the offered premiums and the stock price reaction. Such a study should consider additional factors, e.g., ownership concentration and prior takeover offers and other pre-buyout characteristics, see Chapter 2.

50. The illiquidity problem of the claims of firms in buyouts is recognized by the investment community, and there are recent attempts to mitigate it; see Donnelly (1988).

51. If a managerial compensation contract that is linked to the firm's equity value is beneficial to both managers and shareholders, there will be no conflict of interests between the two parties in establishing it, and the associated agency cost will be low. Arguing that shareholders will oppose value-maximizing compensation to managers for being "too generous" is tantamount to assuming shareholders' irrationality.

52. There is evidence that in public firms, high leverage is associated with high ownership concentration by insiders; see Kim and Sorensen (1986) and Amihud, Lev, and Travlos (1988).

53. Jensen describes in Chapter 12 here how the legislature restricted major shareholders from taking active part in managing their firms when they are publicly held.

REFERENCES

Abbott, A. & Johnson, D. J. (1988). Management buyouts: Boon or bane? [Working paper].

Amihud, Y. & Burnovski, M. (1987, September). A priority rule in tender offers [Working paper].

Amihud, Y., Dodd, P. & Weinstein, M. (1986). Conglomerate mergers, managerial motives and stockholders' wealth. *Journal of Banking and Finance*, 401-410.

Amihud, Y. & Kamin, J. (1979, January). Revenue vs. profit maximization: Differences in behavior by the type of control and by market power. *Southern Economic Journal*, 838-846.

Amihud, Y., Lev, B. & Travlos, N. (1988). Corporate control and the choice of investment financing [Working paper].

Amihud, Y. & Lev, B. (1981).   Risk reduction as a managerial motive for conglomerate mergers. *Bell Journal of Economics, 12*, 605-617.

Amihud, Y. & Mendelson, H. (1986a; May-June).   Liquidity and stock returns. *Financial Analysts Journal*, 43-48.

Amihud, Y. & Mendelson, H. (1986b, December).   Asset pricing and the bid-ask spread. *Journal of Financial Economics*, 223-246.

Amihud, Y., & Mendelson, H. (1988, spring). Liquidity and asset prices: Financial management implications. *Financial Management*, 5-15.

Bebchuk, L. A. (1982). The case for facilitating competing tender offers. *Harvard Law Review, 95*, 1028-1056.

Black, B. (1988, forthcoming).   Bidder overpayment in takeovers. *Stanford Law Review*.

Bradley, M., Desai, A. & Kim, E. H. (1983). Specialized resources and competition in the market for corporate control. University of Michigan [Working paper].

Brudney, V. & Chirelstein, M.A. (1978).   A restatement of corporate freezeouts. *Yale Law Journal, 87*, 1354-1376.

DeAngelo, H., DeAngelo, L. & Rice, E. (1984a, summer). Going private: The effect of a change in corporate ownership structure. *Midland Corporate Finance Journal, 2*, 35-43.

DeAngelo, H., DeAngelo, L. & Rice, E. (1984b).   Going private: Minority freezeouts and stockholder wealth. *Journal of Law and Economics, 27*, 367-401.

DeAngelo, L. (1986, July). Accounting numbers as market valuation substitutes: A study of management buyouts of public stockholders. *Accounting Review, 56*, 400-420.

Donnelly, B. (1988, May 5). Firms offering buy-out funds with new twist. *The Wall Street Journal*, p. 35.

Dreyfus, J.-F. (1987). Personal taxes and the optimal design of takeover bids. New York University [Working paper].

Easterbrook, F. H. & Fischel, D. R. (1982). Auctions and sunk costs in tender offers. *Stanford Law Review, 35*, 1-21.

Easterbrook, F. H. & Fischel, D. R. (1983). Voting in corporate law. *Journal of Law and Economics, 26*, 395-427.

Easterwood, J. C., Hsieh, V. & Singer, R. F. (1988, June). The motivation for going private. [Working paper].

Gilson, R. J. (1982). Seeking competitive bids versus pure passivity in tender offer defense. *Stanford Law Review, 35*, 51-67.

Gilson, R. J., Scholes, M. & Wolfson, M. (1988). Taxation and the dynamics of corporate control: The uncertain case for tax motivated acquisitions. In J. Coffee, L. Lowenstein, & S. Rose-Ackerman (Eds.), *Knights, raiders and targets: The Impact of hostile takeover* (Chapter 18). New York: Oxford University Press.

Grammatikos, T. & Swary, I. (1986, April). Incentives for public firms to go private: Superior information or organizational efficiency. [Working paper].

Grossman, S. & Hart, O. D. (1980). Takeover bids, the free-rider problem, and the theory of the corporation. *Bell Journal, 11*, 42-64.

Haugen, R. & Senbet, L. (1978). The insignificance of bankruptcy costs to the theory of optimal capital structure. *Journal of Finance*, 383-393.

Hite, G. L. & Vetsuypens, M. R. (1988). Management buyouts of divisions and shareholder wealth. [Working paper].

Jarrell, G. A., Brickley, J. A. & Netter, J. M. (1988, winter). The market for corporate control: The empirical evidence since 1980. *Economic Perspective, 2*, 49-68.

Jensen, M. C. (1986). Agency costs of free cash flow, corporate finance and takeovers. *American Economic Review, 76*, 323-329.

Jensen, M. C. & Smith, C. W. (1985). Stockholders, manager, and creditor interests: Application of agency theory. In E. I. Altman & M. G. Subrahmanyam (Eds.), *Recent development in corporate finance* (pp. 93-131). Homewood, IL: Richard D. Irwin.

Jensen, M. C. & Meckling, W. H. (1976). Theory of the firm's managerial behavior, agency costs, and ownership structure. *Journal of Financial Economics, 3*, 305-360.

Jensen, M. C. & Ruback, R. S. (1983). The market for corporate control: The scientific evidence. *Journal of Financial Economics, 11*, 5-50.

Kalay, A. (1982, June). Stockholder-bondholder conflict and dividend constraints. *Journal of Financial Economics, 10*, 211-233.

Kieschnick, R. (1988). A comparison of management led versus third party led going-private transactions. [Working paper].

Kim, W. S. & Sorensen, E. H. (1986). Evidence on the impact of the agency costs of debt on corporate debt policy. *Journal of Financial and Quantitative Analysis, 21*, 131-144.

Lehn, K. & Poulsen, A. B. (1987, February). Sources of value in leveraged buyouts. [Working paper].

Linn, S. C. & Rozeff, M. S. (1984, summer). The corporate sell-off. *Midland Corporate Finance Journal, 2*, 17-26.

Longstreth, B. (1983, October 3). Management buyouts: Are public shareholders getting a fair deal? Remarks to the International Bar Association, Toronto, Canada.

Lowenstein, L. (1985). Management buyouts. *Columbia Law Review, 85*, 730-784.

Marais, L., Schipper, K. & Smith, A. (1987, September). Management buyout proposals and corporate claimholders: Explicit recontracting and differential wealth effects. [Working paper].

Masulis, R. W. (1980). The effect of capital Structure change on security prices: A study of exchange offers. *Journal of Financial Economics, 8,* 139-177.

Maupin, R. J., Bidwell, C. M. & Ortegren, A. K. (1984). An empirical investigation of the characteristics of publicly quoted corporations which change to closely held ownership through management buyouts. *Journal of Business & Accounting, 11,* 435-450.

Miller, M. (1977, May). Debt and taxes. *Journal of Finance,* 261-275.

Roll, R. (1986). The hubris hypothesis of corporate takeover. *Journal of Business, 59,* 197-216.

Shleifer, A. & Vishny, R. W. (1986). Large shareholders and corporate control. *Journal of Political Economy,* 461-488.

Sterngold, J. (1987, September 6). Shaking billions from Beatrice. *The New York Times,* Section 3, p. 1.

Torabzadeh, K. M. & Bertin, W. J. (1987). Leveraged buyouts and shareholder return. *Journal of Financial Research, 10,* 313-319.

Travlos, N. G. & Millon, M. H. (1987a). An examination of the motivation for leveraged buyout proposals. *Spoudai, 37,* 177-202.

Travlos, N. G. & Millon, M. H. (1987b, April). Going private: Buyouts and determinants of stockholders returns. [Working paper].

ABOUT THE AUTHOR

Yakov Amihud is currently Visiting Professor at New York University Leonard N. Stern School of Business from the Faculty of Management, Tel Aviv University. Teaching and research interests include corporate finance and securities market microstructure. Editor of *Market Making and the Changing Structure of the Securities Industry* (with T. Ho and R. Schwartz); he has published numerous articles on topics including the effect of ownership structure and control in firms on corporate policies, the effect of asset liquidity on expected returns, the effect of securities markets' trading mechanisms on price behavior, and market-making and dealership in securities markets.

He received the BA degree from the Hebrew University and the MSc and PhD degrees from New York University.

CHAPTER 2

MANAGEMENT BUYOUTS OF PUBLIC CORPORATIONS: AN ANALYSIS OF PRIOR CHARACTERISTICS

*Robert L. Kieschnick, Jr.**

1. INTRODUCTION

Although LBOs come in a variety of forms, they can be distinguished by the characteristics of the entity acquired. On this basis, two categories are clear: (1) leveraged buyouts of a firm and (2) leveraged buyouts of a division or subsidiary of a firm. Further, one may distinguish within the first category between firms that are public corporations and those that are private companies. Of the different types of leveraged buyouts, buyouts of public corporations have evoked the most public concern. And of these transactions, the majority have been management buyouts (MBOs). For the purposes of this discussion, an MBO is the purchase of a public corporation by a group involving some members of management, which may include members of the board of directors as well as operating officers.

It is the purpose of this study to examine the prior characteristics of public corporations which go private through an MBO. By examining their prior characteristics, evidence concerning the validity of selected arguments

*As some of the research reported herein comes from his dissertation, the author would like to especially thank his chairman, Dr. Seha Tinic, for his guidance, criticism, and support. Also, the author wishes to thank Dr. Yakov Amihud, Dr. Laura Starks, Dr. John Kensinger, Dr. Conrad Doenges, and Dr. Robert Thompson for their help, comments, and suggestions.

about the nature and purpose of these transactions can be established. In addition, the results should provide information about the characteristics of firms likely to engage in these transactions.

This chapter is organized into seven sections. Section 2 provides a brief discussion of various theoretical perspectives on LBOs in general and MBOs in particular to provide a survey of current thinking about these transactions. Following this, a review of selected previous empirical research is presented to discern which hypotheses warrant further examination.

Section 4 begins the examination of the prior characteristics of MBOs by setting forth the research design of this study. A logistic model of the probability of going private through an MBO provides the statistical framework for testing the signs and significance of selected characteristics. The selected characteristics are determined by the hypotheses identified earlier for further examination. The sources of data used in this study are set out in Section 5, along with an analysis of a number of relevant aspects of these transactions. Statistical results for the estimation of the logistic model are set out and discussed in Section 6. And finally, the paper concludes with a summary of the important results and tentative conclusions about MBOs of public corporations.

2. SURVEY OF THEORETICAL PERSPECTIVES

Within the collective literature on MBOs, LBOs, and going-private transactions, there are a number of arguments made about the nature and intent of these transactions. The following discussion will attempt to set out distinct themes in these arguments so as to define separate testable hypotheses about MBOs.

With this guiding principle in mind, I will discuss nine distinct hypotheses in the literature on these transactions: (1) the transactions cost hypothesis, (2) the tax hypothesis, (3) the takeover defense hypothesis, (4) the free cash flow hypothesis, (5) the control hypothesis, (6) the defective managerial compensation hypothesis, (7) the bondholder expropriation hypothesis, (8) the inadequate leverage hypothesis, and (9) the risky arbitrage hypothesis.

Transactions Cost Hypothesis

This explanation was first proposed in a study by DeAngelo, DeAngelo, and Rice (1984a) of "going private" transactions.[1] While the authors acknowledge that public corporations entail certain agency costs, they point to the regulatory costs of being a public concern that are avoided by becoming a private concern as a motivation for these transactions. For example, the firm is no longer required to file 10K and insider trading reports, or to bear certain accounting costs. The essential point of this argument is that the costs of continuing as a public concern outweigh the benefits of access to public capital markets. I call this a transactions cost hypothesis because the identified costs of continuing as a public concern are essentially the transactions costs associated with this organizational form.

Tax Hypothesis

Another explanation of MBOs is a tax argument presented in Lowenstein (1985,1986).[2] From Lowenstein's perspective, a primary motivation of managers in an MBO is to exploit the firm's unused tax shields. These shields are also the source of funds to pay for the buyout.

Two basic types of tax shields are increased by MBOs. The first type is any nondebt-related tax shields that result from a step-up in the tax basis of the assets of the target firm (e.g. increased depreciation deductions). The second type is any debt-related tax shields created by the buyout, for these transactions are primarily debt financed (e.g. increased interest deductions). As a result of these combined tax shields, the purchasers of the firm can use the associated sheltered cash flows to pay the debt claims used to finance the buyout.

Prior to the transaction, under this hypothesis, one should observe candidates for an MBO with higher relative tax payments, lower relative interest payments, and greater opportunities for asset write-ups than firms that remain public concerns. From this perspective, the firm's expected revenues and operating expenses (excluding interest expense) should not change. Rather, any premiums paid to stockholders should be funded from the cash flows created by increased tax shields.

Takeover Defense Hypothesis

A third argument made about the motivation for an MBO is set out by Michel and Shaked (1986). Their basic notion is that MBOs are a defensive strategy against hostile takeovers by outside parties. By buying the company, existing managers protect their jobs from the vicissitudes of a hostile takeover. In this case, one would expect firms that are likely MBO candidates to have hostile control bids made prior to the buyout.

Why a firm that engages in an MBO is a takeover target to begin with is not directly addressed by Michel and Shaked, though they do mention the possibility of poor performance immediately prior to a takeover attempt. In addition, they do not really have a theory that explains why or when a takeover candidate would use an MBO defense rather than some other type of defense. In terms of the premiums paid in buyouts, they mention reduced regulatory costs, increased tax shields, and improved managerial efficiency as sources of cash flows that pay for these transactions.

The Free Cash Flow Hypothesis

As proposed by Jensen (1986a), the primary targets for takeovers are firms that have cash flows in excess of their positive net present value (npv) investment projects. Because management's compensation is often based upon the growth in firm size, managers will tend to use these excess cash flows to fund zero or negative npv projects rather than paying off stockholders.

This explanation implicitly entails a notion that there is a defect in managerial compensation contracts that creates conditions conducive to buyouts. The defect concerns management's incentives relative to "free cash flows." Further, it indicates that potential MBO candidates are also viable candidates for takeover. In a sense, Jensen's explanation is very similar to Michel and Shaked's argument in that potential MBOs are also potential takeover targets. However, Jensen does not specify a takeover defense rationale for MBOs.

Rather, he suggests that leveraged (management) buyouts are a new organizational form in which (1) managers divert free cash flows to stockholders in the form of buyout premiums, (2) managers perform more efficiently due to the control function played by debt, and (3) debtholders have an incentive to mitigate bankruptcy costs and equity/bondholder conflicts because of an equity interest they obtain arising from the use of strip financing in these transactions.

This line of thought implies that likely MBO candidates should have more free cash flows and fewer growth prospects than firms that do not engage in MBOs. Further, the premiums paid in these transactions should be directly related to these free cash flows.

Control Hypothesis

This argument focuses upon the monitoring costs associated with the principal-agent relationship and was called the control hypothesis in Hsieh, Easterwood, and Singer (1987). The notion behind this hypothesis is that there is a free-rider problem faced by large shareholders in public corporations in determining how much to monitor managerial actions. Because investments made in monitoring managerial actions benefit all shareholders and are therefore not fully compensated, any individual shareholder has an incentive to underinvest in monitoring activities. However, if the firm goes private, then the equity will be held by fewer and larger shareholders. Consequently, shareholders will be more willing to invest in monitoring activities and improve firm performance. Under this argument, the primary source of buyout premiums is clearly the increased net cash flows that accrue to the firm as a result of lower agency costs.

Defective Managerial Compensation Hypothesis

The first presentation of this line of thought was in the DeAngelo et al. (1984a, 1984b) studies of going-private transactions. As a secondary theme to their transactions cost notion, they propose that managers in public corporations are not always able to receive a proportional share of any gains produced by the investment decisions they make. As a result, by taking the firm private, management can design compensation contracts that more closely tie their compensation to the firm's performance. This argument was recently repeated in a paper by Jensen and Murphy (1987) in which they argue that managers in public corporations do not receive proper compensation for their efforts. This proposal implies (1) a defect in the way some managers are compensated in public corporations and (2) a defect in the managerial labor market for public corporations.

However, this argument fails to account for the "reverse LBO" phenomenon observed for a number of firms that have undergone buyouts. For why would the firm's managers wish to return to public capital markets if being a public corporation makes it difficult for the firm to compensate them properly for their efforts?

Bondholder Expropriation Hypothesis

This argument posits that buyouts represent a transfer of wealth from bondholders to equityholders as they are paid premiums, a portion of which represents a diminution of bondholder wealth.[3] This explanation has some of the elements of an agency cost argument, for it involves a conflict of interest between the different financial claims on the firm. Clearly, under this hypothesis, one should observe bondholders suffering significant losses of wealth when buyouts are announced.

Inadequate Leverage Hypothesis

This hypothesis is based on the idea that likely candidates for buyouts are firms that have underutilized their debt-carrying capacity. Consequently, the firm's value can be improved by increasing the firm's leverage. This increased value will be both the source of premiums paid and the motivation for parties to the buyout.

However, why shareholders have allowed such conditions to arise is not clear. Some type of agency cost might be implied. Further, this hypothesis is related to the tax hypothesis, for a primary source of value in leveraging will come from increased debt tax shields.

Risky Arbitrage Hypothesis

The basic argument presented in Kieschnick (1987) is that the firm can be viewed as a collection of assets/projects that may have higher-valued alternative uses. If this is true, then the firm's break-up values may exceed its "going concern" value. This condition implies that there is an opportunity for a "risky arbitrage" that entails purchasing the equity of the firm and restructuring its asset/project composition. In executing this arbitrage, there is an advantage to using debt financing, for the primary goal of this action is to acquire the capital gains that accrue from the restructuring of the firm's asset/project composition. This creates a type of call option on the firm's real assets.

Additionally, the argument posits that an existing management team has an advantage in executing this arbitrage for several reasons. First, they possess potentially better information about the market values of the firm's existing real assets or projects. Second, they have the operational experience necessary to execute the type of levered acquisition required. In other words, they are in a good position to operate the firm so as to meet debt payments and convince potential lenders of that possibility, a particularly important factor due to the degree to which specific human capital is required to control the costs of operating the firm in order to meet the debt repayment schedule. Third, they possess an existing share of the firm, which lowers the total acquisition costs of the firm. The more they possess, the smaller the difference between the firm's stock market value and breakup value has to be for them to effectively "arbitrage" the difference using debt financing. Fourth, because of their existing position, they are in a good position to use the resources of the firm to effect its purchase and fight off alternative bids.

Despite these advantages, it is important to note that any party willing and able to develop private information about these divergences will find advantage in playing this type of arbitrage. Consequently, it is not surprising that we should observe specialists in the use of LBO techniques seeking out and organizing buyout groups. By including management in these groups, some of the advantages described above still hold for such groups.

The critical components of this explanation are (1) that there is a divergence between the firm's "going concern" and breakup values, which occurs when there are potential gains to be had from restructuring the firm's asset/project composition and (2) the greater the share of management in the firm's pre-buyout equity, the greater the likelihood of their executing or participating in a buyout of the firm under these conditions.

With the above survey in mind, we now turn to an examination of some previous empirical research on these transactions.

3. SURVEY OF PREVIOUS EMPIRICAL RESEARCH

Of the various empirical studies of MBOs, LBOs, and going-private transactions, I discuss only those that provide evidence about the prior characteristics of MBOs. A review of empirical studies on the stock and bond price reactions associated with these transactions is presented elsewhere.[4] Suffice it to say that this evidence does not provide much support for the bondholder expropriation argument.

In a study of the prior characteristics of MBOs, Maupin, Bidwell, and Ortegren (1984) analyze the pre-buyout characteristics of 63 MBOs over the period January 1972 to August 1983. They use discriminant analysis to compare a matched sample of firms that subsequently go private through an MBO with those that remain public corporations. The comparison firms are chosen to be similar in terms of size and industrial classification.

The purpose of their research is to determine whether it is possible to distinguish firms that subsequently engaged in an MBO from those that do not on the basis of accounting and stock market data prior to the transaction date. This is established by testing whether the group means between the two sets of firms are equal for 25 chosen variables. The variables employed were identified by an examination of the literature on going private transactions and conversations with financial officers of buyout firms in their sample.

They reject the null hypothesis of no difference in the multivariate means between the two groups for measurements on these variables for both one and two years prior to the event period. Further, employing three different variable reduction techniques, they develop a five-variable discriminant function that compares well with their larger model in terms of classification errors. The variables in this reduced model are (1) concentration of ownership (COWN), (2) cash flow to net worth ratio (CFNW), (3) cash flow to total assets ratio (CFTA), (4) price of common stock to book value ratio (PBVR), and (5) dividend yield (HDYR). In all cases except for PBVR, where the opposite result holds, the means of the buyout group exceed those of the comparison group for these variables.

The implications of these results should be drawn cautiously for several reasons. First, the distributional assumptions underlying the use of discriminant analysis do not hold. The joint distribution of the independent variables does not form a multivariate normal distribution. Second, their sampling scheme introduces sample choice bias, which is not accounted for in their estimation procedure. This sampling bias is a result of their specifically selecting firms that subsequently engaged in an MBO to be included in their sample. Third, the variables included in the analysis were not intended to test any hypotheses about the nature and motivation of MBOs. They were included to determine whether it is possible to employ financial data prior to a buyout to distinguish between those firms that are likely to engage in an MBO from those that are not.

With these caveats in mind, I suggest that these results are not inconsistent with the transactions costs hypothesis, but do raise some doubt about either the free cash flow hypothesis or the defective compensation hypothesis. First, the positive significance of the dividend yield variable is inconsistent with the free cash flow argument, for it indicates that whatever free cash flows are generated by the firm are distributed to stockholders. Second, the positive significance of the ownership concentration variable is not consistent with either the free cash flow or defective managerial contract argument. The data of Maupin et al.(1984) indicate that the mean equity ownership of management in MBOs is roughly 56%, whereas in the comparison sample the mean equity ownership of management is 37%. At such high levels of management equity in the firm, it is not clear why managers can not effect the design of what they feel to be appropriate compensation contracts.

As a side point, an interesting study by DeAngelo (1986) concerning MBOs of public corporations provides some comfort in the use of pre-buyout data. DeAngelo studied whether there is evidence of management manipulation of earnings information prior to an MBO proposal in a sample of 64 firms, whose managers made a buyout proposal during the period 1973 to 1982. In summary, she finds no evidence of any significant systematic reductions in accruals prior to a buyout offer. As a result, she concludes that the evidence does not support a manipulation hypothesis. This result indicates that pre-buyout accounting data are not subject to systematic distortion by management.

As mentioned earlier, we will not consider the bondholder expropriation hypothesis further in this study. As to the takeover defense hypothesis, although it has not been tested directly, there are several reasons to question it as an explanation of MBOs. First, the reasons why the firm is subject to a takeover attempt are not well specified in those studies that cited this explanation for MBOs. Second, why managers choose an MBO rather than some other defense is left unanswered. A number of alternative defensive strategies are available to management that would appear to be less costly (e.g., poison pills). So the question remains: why an MBO? Consequently, this hypothesis about MBOs is not a sufficiently rich explanation to warrant further testing.

Of the hypotheses discussed earlier, I will directly test (1) the transactions cost hypothesis, (2) tax hypothesis, (3) the free cash flow hypothesis, (4) the inadequate leverage hypothesis, and (5) the risky arbitrage hypothesis.

4. RESEARCH DESIGN OF THE PRESENT STUDY

In order to test for the significant prior characteristics of firms that subsequently engaged in an MBO, it is necessary to choose an appropriate statistical framework. Three statistical methodologies are often employed when the dependent variable is a categorical variable: (1) discriminant analysis, (2) logit analysis, and (3) probit analysis. Of these three, the first two are most often employed, for the third tends to be cumbersome to manipulate and computationally expensive relative to the other two. Concerning the choice between discriminant and logit analysis, much has been said for the purposes of prediction. However, we are concerned with hypothesis testing in this application and will be employing data that cannot be expected to follow a multivariate normal distribution.[5] In this context, the discriminant analysis estimators are not consistent and would appear to be not as robust as maximum-likelihood logit estimators.[6] Consequently, the logit framework is used for modeling the odds of a firm engaging in an MBO.[7]

The next question to confront concerns sampling design. Because of the relatively infrequent incidence of MBOs within the population of all public corporations in the United States, a simple random sample may not be the most effective design in terms of cost, size, or information content about the population of interest. Therefore, it may be appropriate to specifically identify firms taken private through MBOs included in a sample. This is a choice-based sampling scheme, and it is employed in this study.

Fortunately, there has been some attention in the literature to this type of sampling scheme and the appropriate choice of sample design, particularly with regards to the multinomial logit model. As a primary source of guidance in these issues, I use the analytical and simulation results of Cosslett (1981). The basic conclusion from his work is that the efficiency of an equal shares sample design is close to the optimal design (in a relative asymptotic variance sense). And further, if the underlying population proportions are known, then the choice-based design is always more efficient than the random sample. Based on these results, an equal-shares, choice-based sample design is used.

However, it should be clear that this sampling design will require some modification in the estimation procedure in order to account for the obvious bias introduced by this design. Therefore, I have used a conditional maximum likelihood estimator developed in Manski and Lerman (1977) because (1) external information about the underlying population is used in the estimation procedure, (2) for the simple binary logit model estimated, this estimator will be a consistent estimator, and (3) it is the easiest estimator to implement.[8]

To set out the above more formally, I start with the assumption:

$$P(j = 1 \mid x_i, b) = F(x'_i\, b) \quad i = 1, \cdots n \tag{1}$$

where
$$F(z) = \left[\frac{e^z}{1 + e^z} \right]$$

$j = 1$ if the firm goes private through an MBO; 0 otherwise

$x_i = $ a vector of k known constants

$\beta = $ a vector of k unknown parameters

$z = x'\beta$

This is a standard qualitative response model with the additional assumption that $F(z)$ is a logistic distribution. Based on this specification of the probability of a firm going private through an MBO, we can derive an expression for the likelihood of such an occurrence conditioned on the firm's characteristics and likelihood of observation.[9] From this likelihood expression, Manski and Lerman (1977) propose an estimator, β^*, that maximizes

$$S_n = \sum_{i=1}^{n} W(j_i)\, \log[P(j_i \mid x_i, \beta)] \tag{2}$$

where
$$W(j_i) = \left[\frac{Q_0(j)}{H(j)} \right] \quad \text{and}$$

$Q_0(j) = $ the probability that a firm in the population goes private

$P(j_i \mid x_i, \beta) =$ the probability that the *i*th firm goes private (when j=1), given x_i, β

$H(j) =$ the probability that a researcher draws j in the sample

It is perhaps useful to note two additional points about the assumed model of the probability of a firm subsequently engaging in an MBO. The first point is that one can express the log of the odds of a firm engaging in an MBO as a linear combination of the independent variates. More formally, this statement means that

$$\log \left[\frac{P(j=1)}{P(j=0)} \right] = \log \Omega = x' \beta \tag{3}$$

This fact will be used latter to set out the model estimated in this study.

The second point of relevance is that the partial derivative of the probability of a firm engaging in an MBO with respect to a change in the *k*th variable, x_k, is

$$\frac{\partial F(x'\beta)}{\partial x_k} = \frac{e^{x'\beta}}{(1+e^{x'\beta})^2} \beta_k \tag{4}$$

This last result indicates that a unit change in x_k does not imply a β_k change in the probability of a firm engaging in an MBO. Rather, one should interpret β_k as the increment in the log of the odds of an MBO for a unit change in x_k. This is pointed out to aid the reader in interpreting the statistical results reported in Table 2–8.

5. DESCRIPTION OF THE DATA

The sample of firms for study was created in the following manner. First, a list of rumored MBOs was drawn up by (1) examination of the journal *Mergers & Acquisitions*, from 1981 through 1986, (2) examination of W.T. Grimm's *Mergerstat Review* for 1981 to 1985, and (3) references in the literature on MBOs.[10] These procedures led to the identification of 224 rumored MBOs during the period January 1, 1981, to January 1, 1986. By examining *The Wall Street Journal Index* and company 10K reports, this list was culled to 135 completed transactions. From this list, 102 firms possessed sufficient information on critical variables for inclusion in the

Table 2–1
Going-private transactions, 1981 to 1985

		1981	1982	1983	1984	1985
1.	Number of Going-Private Transactions[a]	17	31	36	57	76
2.	Total Public Takeovers[b]	168	180	190	211	336
3.	Percent of Total Public Takeovers	10.1%	17.2%	19.0%	27.0%	22.6%
4.	Number of Common Stocks Listed on Exchanges[c]	2,687	2,639	2,535	2,452	2,423
5.	Number of Foreign Common Stocks Listed on Exchanges[d]	98	96	101	106	106
6.	Number of Quoted Securities - NASDAQ[e]	3,687	3,664	4,467	4,723	4,783

[a]The source for these data is *MergerStat Review, 1985,* (Chicago: W.T. Grimms & Company, 1985), p.117.
[b]The source for these data is *MergerStat Review, 1985,* p.117.
[c]The source for these data is *S.E.C. Monthly Statistical Review,* Table A-130, various issues.
[d]The source for these data is, again, Table A-130, from the *S.E.C. Monthly Statistical Review.* These figures are included in this table because they are subtracted from the figures in line 4 to arrive at total number of domestic corporations with listed common stocks. This study is concerned only with MBOs in the United States.
[e]The source for this data is *Securities Industry Yearbook, 1986-1987,* (New York: Securities Industry Association, 1986), p. 661.

final sample.[11] Table 2–1 places this sample in its population context. During the period 1981 to 1985, there were 217 going-private transactions. This represents about 20% of the total public corporation takeovers occurring during this same period. And it implies that about 6% of the public corporations engaged in a going-private transaction during this period, whereas 94% did not.

The sample of comparison firms was identified by randomly sampling from the Security Exchange Commission's (SEC) lists of firms filing 10K reports for the appropriate period until a match between an MBO firm and its comparison firm in terms of fiscal year was achieved.[12] Firms were not matched in terms of market value or industrial classification as with the study by Maupin et al. (1984). There were two reasons for this. First, there were no a priori reasons to suppose that controlling for these influences was relevant to testing hypotheses about MBOs. Second, this would bias the statistical results by further conditioning the sampling distribution.

The data sources for information about the prior characteristics of firms that subsequently engaged in MBOs were 10K reports and proxy statements filed with the SEC. The data sources for comparison firms were their 10K reports and associated proxy statements.

The definitions of all variables examined in this study are presented in Appendix 2–1. Appendices 2–2 and 2–3 present information about the distributional characteristics of a number of these variables for the two sets of firms in our sample. Notice that a number of these variables do not appear to be normally distributed. And further note, though not reported in Appendix 2–2, that for all but one of the MBO transactions included in the sample, the percentage of debt financing exceeded 50%. This confirms the earlier point that the typical MBO is also a LBO.

Several other observations can be made about the sample of firms, and so before discussing the statistical results it is appropriate to consider the following tables. First, Table 2–2 presents data on the industrial distribution of MBOs. While the distribution of the sample is rather wide, it also appears that there is some clustering in certain industries. The top four industries in this distribution are (1) apparel products, (2) food products, (3) textile products, and (4) transport equipment. Interestingly, these are primarily manufacturing sectors that have been recently subject to keen foreign competition.

The next tables of interest concern the frequency distribution of prior hostile control bids for various segments of the sample. The first analysis, presented in Table 2–3, concerns the frequency of prior hostile control bids for MBOs and comparison firms.[13] The chi-square statistics for this table indicate that the sample is not homogeneous; therefore MBOs and the comparison firms are not alike in facing hostile alternative control bids. Further, the size of Cramer's V (0.38) indicates that there is a strong association between a firm going private through an MBO offer and the firm having faced a prior hostile control bid. However, as also shown in Table 2–3, 71% of the MBOs did not face a prior hostile control bid.

Table 2–2
Industrial distribution of management buyouts in the sample

SIC	Frequency	Percent	SIC Description
15	3	2.9	Building construction
16	1	1.0	Construction (other)
20	9	8.8	Food products
22	7	6.9	Textile products
23	11	10.8	Apparel products
26	1	1.0	Paper & allied products
27	4	3.9	Printing industries
28	2	2.0	Chemicals
30	3	2.9	Rubber & plastics
31	2	2.0	Leather products
32	1	1.0	Stone, clay, glass
33	2	2.0	Primary metals
34	4	3.9	Fabricated metals
35	3	2.9	Nonelectric machinery
36	2	2.0	Electric machinery
37	6	5.9	Transport equipment
38	3	2.9	Measuring, photo equipment (and the like)
42	1	1.0	Motor freight
48	2	2.0	Communication
49	1	1.0	Electric, gas, sanitation services
50	4	3.9	Wholesale trade: durables
51	3	2.9	Wholesale trade: nondurables
53	4	3.9	General merchandise stores
54	2	2.0	Food stores
56	3	2.9	Apparel and accessory stores
57	1	1.0	Furniture stores (and the like)
58	3	2.9	Eating and drinking places
59	3	2.9	Miscellaneous manufacture
61	1	1.0	Credit, other than banks
62	1	1.0	Insurance
65	1	1.0	Real estate
67	1	1.0	Holding & other investment firms
70	1	1.0	Hotels
73	3	2.9	Business services
78	1	1.0	Motion pictures
79	1	1.0	Amusement
80	1	1.0	Health services

102

Table 2–3
Frequency distribution of prior hostile control bids by type

	Non-MBO	MBO	Total	
No prior hostile control bid	101 (49.51)	73 (35.78)	174 (85.29)	Frequency (Total percent)
Prior hostile control bid	1 (0.49)	29 (14.22)	30 (14.71)	
Total	102 (50.00)	102 (50.00)	204 (100.00)	

Statistic	DF	Value	Prob
Likelihood ratio Chi-Square	1	37.346	0.000
Cramer's V		0.388	
Sample size		204	

An extension of these results is presented in Table 2-4, where the frequency distribution of prior hostile control bids by MBO type is displayed. Categories 1 and 2 in this table correspond roughly to third-party buyouts and MBOs as defined in DeAngelo et al. (1984) or Travlos and Millon (1987). Category 3 represents ESOP-financed buyouts. This category was created because these transactions are sometimes discussed separately in the literature. The likelihood ratio chi-square is significant (at the .002 level) for this table, indicating that the distribution is not homogeneous. This would tend to imply that these categories face different prior-takeover patterns. Visually, one can not help noticing that the ESOP financed buyouts are predominantly faced by a prior hostile control bid. This would tend to support the contention of some that the primary use of this buyout financing technique is in defensive buyouts.[14]

The last set of tables concern the distribution of prior beneficial ownership of equity by management in the various sample segments. Table 2-5 presents the frequency distribution of firms in the combined sample across various categories of prior management ownership shares. Based on the significant likelihood ratio chi-square statistic, one can infer that there is a significant difference between MBOs and comparison firms in terms of

Table 2–4
Frequency distribution of prior hostile control bids by buyout type

	Management Buyout Type[a]				
	1	*2*	*3*	*Total*	
No prior hostile	32	39	2	73	Frequency
control bid	(31.37)	(32.23)	(1.96)	(71.57)	(Total percent)
Prior hostile	14	8	7	29	
control bid	(13.73)	(7.84)	(6.86)	(28.43)	
Total	46	47	9	102	
	(45.10)	(46.08)	(8.82)	(100.00)	

Statistic	*DF*	*Value*	*Prob*
Likelihood ratio Chi-Square	2	12.830	0.002
Cramer's V		0.369	
Sample size		102	

[a]The Management Buyout Type definitions, intended to be consistent with Travlos and Millon (1987), are as follows:
  1: "Third party buyout," MBO with management equity participation less than 50%
  2: "Management buyout," MBO with management equity participation more than 50%
  3: MBO financed through ESOP

pre-buyout management equity. In fact, notice that while over 50% of the non-MBOs show a managerial equity share of less than 20%, the contrary is true for MBOs. For this group, a little over 50% of the firms show a prior managerial beneficial share of over 20%. According to accounting conventions, such an ownership pattern, if held by another firm, would indicate "significant influence." And such a degree of influence would also suggest that management has some control over the design of its compensation scheme.[15] Consequently, these results do not support the defective managerial compensation hypothesis discussed earlier.

Within the sample of MBOs, the distribution of ownership for the three categories of buyouts is displayed in Table 2-6. Again, the likelihood ratio chi-square statistic indicates that this sample is not homogeneous. Rather, it indicates that there are differences between "third-party" buyouts, "management" buyouts, and ESOP-financed buyouts. Of particular note is the Cramer's V statistic of 0.417. These results show that ESOP financed

Table 2–5
Frequency distribution of firms by pre-buyout managerial beneficial equity share

Management Stock Ownership	Non-MBO	MBO	Total	
0 - 10%	45	27	72	Frequency
	(22.06)	(23.24)	(35.29)	(Total percent)
10% - 20%	22	15	37	
	(10.78)	(7.35)	(18.14)	
20% - 50%	28	40	68	
	(13.73)	(19.61)	(33.33)	
> 50%	7	20	27	
	(3.43)	(9.80)	(13.24)	
Total	102	102	204	
Mean	17.71	29.1		
Std deviation	19.4	22.0		
Median	11.1	26.6		

Statistic	DF	Value	Prob
Likelihood ratio Chi-Square	3	14.536	0.002
Cramer's V		0.264	
Sample size		204	

buyouts are associated with low pre-buyout managerial equity interest. This point is particularly interesting given their higher incidence of pre-buyout hostile control bids. In fact, by observing the patterns for the three groups in Tables 2–4 and 2–6, one might infer a negative relationship between pre-buyout managerial beneficial ownership and pre-buyout hostile control bids. This is a reasonable result, as an increasing managerial beneficial ownership share should increase the cost of an alternative hostile control bid.

With these observations about the sample employed in this study, it is now appropriate to turn attention to directly testing specified hypotheses by examining the significance of selected prior characteristics.

Table 2–6
Frequency distribution of pre-buyout managerial beneficial ownership of equity by MBO type

	Management Buyout Type[a]			Total	
	1	2	3		
0 - 10%	18	3	6	27	Frequency
	(17.65)	(2.94)	(5.88)	(26.47)	(Total percent)
10% - 20%	10	4	1	15	
	(9.80)	(3.92)	(0.98)	(14.71)	
20% - 50%	16	22	2	40	
	(15.69)	(21.57)	(1.96)	(39.22)	
> 50%	2	18	0	20	
	(1.96)	(17.65)	(0.00)	(19.61)	
Total	46	47	9	102	
	(45.10)	(46.08)	(8.82)	(100.00)	

Statistic	DF	Value	Prob
Likelihood ratio Chi-Square	6	39.255	0.000
Cramer's V		0.417	
Sample size		102	

[a]The Management Buyout Type definitions, intended to be consistent with Travlos and Millon (1987), are as follows:
1: "Third party buyout," MBO with management equity participation less than 50%
2: "Management buyout," MBO with management equity participation more than 50%
3: MBO financed through ESOP

6. STATISTICAL RESULTS

As set out earlier, a binomial logit framework is employed for testing the different hypotheses about MBOs. Within this framework, the log of the odds of a firm engaging in an MBO can be viewed as a linear function of selected variables (see Equation 3). From this viewpoint, we estimate the following model:

$$\log \Omega = b_1 + b_2 NCC + b_3 RIE + b_4 FCF + b_5 RDEP + \\ b_6 MKTBKV + b_7 PCBD + b_8 SOD + b_9 RPM + b_{10} DERATIOM \qquad (5)$$

where

NCC, represents a change in financing measure

RIE, represents a measure of relative interest expense

RDEP, represents a measure of depreciation expense

MKTBKV, represents a measure of the firm's growth expectations

FCF, represents a measure of the firm's "free cash flows"

PCBD, is a prior control bid dummy

SOD, is the beneficial stock ownership of management

RPM, is a measure of the firm's stock market performance

DERATIOM, is a measure of the firm's debt to equity ratio

In Table 2–7, the expectations concerning the signs and significance of the coefficients of each variable under each of the selected hypotheses are displayed. The reasons for these expectations are as follows.

Under the transactions cost hypothesis, one would expect the firm to do little new financing prior to the buyout. The logic of this argument is that the costs of being a public concern exceed the benefits, so a potential MBO candidate firm should do little new financing prior to a buyout. This aspect is captured in the variable NCC, which represents the relative change in long-term debt and equity financing. The sign of this variable should be negative, for increases in new financing should lead to decreased odds of engaging in an MBO. As a corollary, the lower the growth expectations for the firm, the greater incentive for an MBO. This is captured in the MKTBKV variable, for a primary determinant of the market value of equity relative to its book value will be market expectations about its future growth

Table 2–7
Summary of expectations regarding signs and significance of selected variables under the different hypotheses[a]

	Transaction Cost Hypothesis	Tax Hypothesis	Free Cash Flow Hypothesis	Arbitrage Hypothesis	Inadequate Leverage Hypothesis
NCC	-	0	-	0	0
RIE	0,-	-	0,-	0	0
RDEP	0	+	0,+	0	0
MKTBK	-	+	-	0,-	0
FCF	+	0,+	+	0	+
SOD	0,+	0	0	+	0
PCBD	0	0	+	+	0
RPM	0	0	-,0	-	0
DERATIOM	0	-	-	0	

[a]   + represents significantly positive sign expected
- represents significantly negative sign expected
0 represents sign not specified or insignificant

For exact definitions, see Appendix 2-1, however,
NCC represents a change in financing measure
RIE represents a measure of relative interest expense
RDEP represents a measure of depreciation expense
FCF represents a measure of the firm's "free cash flows"
MKTBKV represents a measure of growth expectations
PCBD is a prior control bid dummy
SOD is the beneficial stock ownership of management
RPM is a measure of the firm's stock market performance
DERATIOM is a measure of the firm's debt to equity ratio

possibilities. Consequently, the sign on this variable, under this hypothesis, should be negative. In contrast, an increase in free cash flows (FCF) should increase the odds of a firm engaging in a buyout under this hypothesis. For the remaining variables, our expectations under this hypothesis are not well specified and are therefore neutral.

Under the tax hypothesis, MBOs should be paying less in interest expense and should have more fully depreciated assets than do firms that do not subsequently engage in such buyouts. Consequently, one would expect a significant negative sign on the relative interest expense variable RIE and a significant positive sign on the relative depreciation variable RDEP. If the potential MBO pays lower interest expenses than firms remaining public concerns, then an increase in the variable DERATIOM should be associated with a lowered likelihood of a firm engaging in an MBO. The contribution of the remaining variables should be weak at best under this hypothesis, with signs as set out in Table 2-7 if they are significant. Of these, MKTBKV is perhaps the most important, for unless growth expectations are positive, why attempt to shelter income?

The appropriate characterization of a potential buyout firm under the free cash flow hypothesis is of a firm with limited growth prospects and excess cash flows. While the measurement of free cash flows is somewhat problematic, we can be reasonably assured that it will bear some direct relationship to working capital from operations. In addition, because cash dividends are a cash flow that goes to shareholders and reduces free cash flows, they should be deducted. Consequently we employ the FCF variable, as defined in Appendix 2-1, to capture the firm's free cash flows.[16] The limited growth prospects, and hence limited investment opportunities, are captured by the variable MKTBKV, which should have a significantly negative coefficient under this hypothesis. Similarly, this hypothesis should imply a negative sign on both the RPM and DERATIOM variables. And finally, as firms that have free cash flows will be potential takeover candidates under Jensen's line of argument, the PCBD variable should have a positive coefficient.

Likewise, under the risky arbitrage hypothesis, potential MBO candidates should also be potential takeover candidates. Hence, we also expect a positive coefficient on the PCBD variable under this hypothesis. In addition, we would expect that an increased share of the equity on the part of management, measured by the SOD, will be associated with an increased odds of a firm engaging in a buyout. Consequently, we would expect a positive coefficient on this variable. And finally, we would expect a negative sign on the RPM variable, for this would potentially imply that there are grounds for the arbitrage implied under this hypothesis.

Under the inadequate leverage hypothesis, we would primarily have expected a negative sign on the variable DERATIOM, for this would imply that likely MBO candidates have lower levered capital structures than firms that remain public concerns. In addition, we might expect a positive sign on the FCF variable, for higher free cash flows might be expected to be associated with lower debt in the capital structure of an MBO candidate.

The results of estimating the model implied by Equation 5 are displayed in Table 2-8. At the bottom of Table 2-8, the derivatives of the distribution with respect to each of the independent variables gives the reader a feel for the effect of a unit increase in each variable on the probability of a firm engaging or not engaging in an MBO.

The results reported are not consistent with the transactions cost hypothesis. Although both the MKTBKV and NCC variables have negative signs, as anticipated, neither are significant. As a result, the data are not consistent with the transactions cost hypothesis.

For the tax hypothesis, the results are neither supportive nor consistent. The coefficients on the RIE, RDEP, and DERATIOM variables are insignificant. Consequently the data do not support the tax hypothesis.

Turning to the free cash flow hypothesis, the results are again neither supportive nor consistent. While the signs of the MKTBKV and RPM variables are consistent with this hypothesis, the insignificance of the MKTBKV and DERATIOM variables are not supportive. But more important, the sign and insignificance of the FCF variable is totally inconsistent with this hypothesis. As a result of these findings, one can infer that the data are not consistent with the free cash flow hypothesis.

For the risky arbitrage argument, the data are most supportive. The signs and significance of the RPM, SOD, and the PCBD variables in this equation accord well with this hypothesis.[17]

And finally, the insignificance of both the DERATIOM and FCF variables, along with the sign of the FCF variable, implies that the data do not support the inadequate leverage hypothesis.

7. SUMMARY AND CONCLUSIONS

In light of the evidence presented in the previous sections, a transactions cost type argument for MBOs appears unsupported. This conclusion is especially reinforced when one considers the transactions cost of concluding these buyouts.

DeAngelo et al. (1984) estimate the potential savings from going private to be about $100,000 annually. They suggest that if one treats this amount as a perpertuity, then at a 10% interest rate this represents a present

Table 2–8
Statistical analysis of MBO determinants[a]

Parameter		Estimate [b]	Standard Error	T-Statistic
1	CONSTANT	4.76771	5.16205	.92361
2	NCC	-0.388654E-02	.176454	-0.22026E-01
3	RIE	3.10044	3.13148	.99009
4	RDEP	2.73657	3.13473	.87298
5	FCF	-1.11198	.972473	-1.1435
6	MKTBKV	-0.55329E-02	0.905314E-02	-.61117
7	PCBD	4.51310	1.08516	4.1589
8	SOD	0.357751E-01	0.153122E-01	2.3364
9	RPM	-9.34735	5.07615	-1.8414
10	DERATIOM	-1.38689	.963446	-1.4395

−2 times LOG likelihood ratio (Chi Squared): 33.5540
    with 9 degrees of freedom

Independent Variable Derivatives (evaluated at group means)

Variable [c]		MBO	Non-MBO
1	CONSTANT	.1147	-.1147
2	NCC	-.9354E-04	0.9354E-04
3	RIE	0.7462E-01	-.7462E-01
4	RDEP	0.6586E-01	-.6586E-01
5	FCF	-.2676E-01	0.2676E-01
6	MKTBKV	-.1332E03	0.1332E-03
7	PCBD	.1086	-.1086
8	SOD	0.8610E-03	-.8610E-03
9	RPM	-.2250	.2250
10	DERATIOM	-.3338E-01	0.3338E-01

[a]This equation is estimated using the Manski-Lerman estimator utilizing population proportion estimates based upon the W.T Grimm & Co. data set out in Table 2-1. This gives (a) [Q0(1)/H(1)] = .1209 and (b) [Q0(0)/H(0)] = 1.879.

[b]There were 204 observations used for this estimation.

[c]For exact definitions, see Appendix 2-1, however,

NCC represents a change in financing measure
RIE represents a measure of relative interest expense
RDEP represents a measure of depreciation expense
MKTBKV represents a measure of growth expectations
FCF represents a measure of the firm's "free cash flows"
PCBD is a prior control bid dummy
SOD is the beneficial stock ownership of management
RPM is a measure of the firm's stock market performance
DERATIOM is a measure of the firm's debt to equity ratio

value of $1 million. For our sample of 102 buyouts the mean transactions cost of a buyout was around $9.7 million.[18] Clearly, the mean transaction cost in a going-private transaction in this study's sample is more than the potential direct savings from going private.

As to the tax argument, while it might play a role in financing leveraged buyouts, it does not seem to play a significant role in explaining the likelihood of a firm engaging in an MBO. In addition, the evidence examined was generally inconsistent with the kind of story the tax hypothesis tells. Probably the greatest logical flaw in this argument is that the tax incentives at issue are available to any third party purchaser of the firm, not just a buyout group involving management. Consequently, this line of thought is inadequate to explain MBOs of public corporations as distinct from any other type of buyout of a public corporation.

For the free cash flow argument, the data are inconsistent and unsupportive. While the Maupin et al. study (1984) finds that a number of liquidity variables are significantly different between their samples, they also find likely MBO candidates to pay higher dividends than firms that remain public concerns. Further, we find the sign and insignificance of our free cash flow variable to be inconsistent with this hypothesis. Consequently, the data from this sample did not support the free cash flow hypothesis.

While not testing the defective managerial compensation contract argument directly, some evidence on the prior characteristics of MBOs would seem not supportive. This is a tricky hypothesis to test, for it can quite easily become a tautology. For instance, if one is to conclude that managerial compensation contracts are defective whenever managers pursue their self-interest, then one has really set up a tautology. For why else but for gain would managers engage in any economic activity—particularly a buyout of their company? Consequently, one must be circumspect in interpreting this line of reasoning.

The most often-stated theme under this line of reasoning is that managers in public corporations are not rewarded properly for their corporate *investment* decisions. Under this notion, the evidence from this study's sample raises some questions. Management's pre-buyout share of equity would indicate that they are likely to have some influence on the design of their compensation contracts. Consequently, one must be skeptical about the presumptions of this line of argument. This skepticism is further reinforced by the reverse LBO phenomenon. However, further testing of this hypothesis requires an analysis of the post-buyout behavior of MBO firms.[19]

Of the different hypotheses about MBOs of public corporations, the risky arbitrage hypothesis is most consistent with the data in this study. The essential point of this argument is that anytime a firm has assets or projects with higher valued alternative uses, there is a basis for an arbitrage involving a restructuring of the firm's asset/project composition. This will occur whenever sufficient information about its existence is available to parties who can execute it. That this information will typically be private information does not mean that third parties will not participate; rather, it suggests that there are advantages to involving the firm's management in the buyout group.

This is not to suggest that in an MBO the management of the firm will not operate the post-buyout firm more effectively—in the cash flow sense. As suggested earlier, one of the advantages to involving management in a buyout group that is organized by a third party is management's specific human capital or operating experience. This is because an emphasis on cash flow generation should be expected when the buyout is a levered transaction. Another advantage of management participation in the buyout group is its existing share of the firm's equity.

Finally, as the opportunity for arbitrage increases so will the interest on the part of other parties. Hence, an MBO will sometimes occur in the context of a hostile takeover attempt. In these cases, there may be much to the argument that an MBO operates as a takeover defense. And yet, one must not lose sight of why the firm is in such a position.

APPENDIX 2-1

Variable definitions employed in study

TA Total assets (book value).

TE Total equity (total assets minus liabilities, book value).

MKTVAL Stock price on balance sheet date times number of shares issued and outstanding.

CURRAT Ratio of current assets to current liabilities.

DERATIOM Ratio of long term debt (book) to stockholder's equity (market value).

NCC New financing variable defined as the change in total capitalization relative to prior year's capitalization; where total capitalization is defined as long-term debt plus common stock plus additional paid in capital minus treasury stock (all using book values).

ROH Overhead expenses (measured by selling and administrative expense) relative to net revenue.

RTE Total income tax expense relative to total revenue.

RIE Net interest expense relative to total revenue.

FCF A free cash flow proxy defined as funds provided by operations, minus dividends, plus the change in funds, all relative to total revenues.

SALGROW Average continuously compounded rate of growth over prior two-year period.

RDEP Accumulated depreciation provision relative to total plant and equipment.

SOD Percentage share of beneficial ownership of the common stock of the firm held by officers and directors.

RPM The ratio of the geometric average of the quarterly yields on the firm's stock price (including dividends), lagged one quarter prior to the announcement date, and the geometric average of the quarterly yields on the Standard & Poor's 500 over the same period (4 quarters).

TC The transactions costs associated with the buyout (fees, etc).

DAYS The number of calendar days between the management buyout announcement and the stockholders approval date.

NPREMPS1 The difference between the stock price of the firm one week before the first MBO announcement and the final traded price of the stock.

NPREM1 The above difference in stock prices, NPREMPS1, times the number of shares issued and outstanding (on balance sheet date).

HCB A dummy variable for hostile control bids within one year prior to the announcement date determined from listings in either *The Wall Street Journal Index* or the company's 10K report (same date used for chosen comparison firm).

PCBD   A dummy variable for prior control bids, hostile or otherwise, within one year prior to the announcement date determined from listings in either *The Wall Street Journal Index* or company's 10K report.

MBO   Dummy variable that takes on the value 1 if the firm subsequently engages in an MBO (during the sample period) and 0 if the firm does not.

APPENDIX 2–2

Simple Descriptive Statistics for the Sample of Management Buyout Firms

Variable	Mean	Median	Standard Deviation
TA	373,175,174	131,284,992	1,083,457,969
TE	140,689,068	59,927,664	279,114,435
MKTVAL	194,668,263	60,439,128	397,688,964
MKTBKR	1.39747	1.09102	1.18984
CURRAT	2.79092	2.19748	3.59832
DERATIOM	0.568269	0.298025	0.883327
NCC	0.127656	-0.0309166	2.40789
ROH	0.193233	0.181529	0.115699
RTE	0.0383372	0.029954	0.0462983
RIE	0.0187742	0.00905244	0.039213
FCF	0.089488	0.0636826	0.243655
SALGROW	0.0882498	0.0951197	0.136418
RPM	0.983525	0.977628	0.101268
RDEP	0.407695	0.409376	0.137692
SOD	29.1452	26.62	22.0979
TC[a]	9,698,497	3,000,000	23,195,561
DAYS[a]	157.176	145.5	75.8142
NPREMPS1[a]	6.19118	4.9375	5.01775
NPREM1[a]	63,288,780	160,386,365	21,210,456

[a]Measures unique to this sample.

APPENDIX 2–3

Simple Descriptive Statistics for Comparison Sample Firms

Variable	Mean	Median	Standard Deviation
TA	843,222,816	245,434,000	1,540,787,504
TE	368,427,930	87,621,992	742,133,334
MKTVAL	544,643,664	133,286,960	1,021,642,624
MKTBKR	15.5303	1.31869	138.944
CURRAT	2.27452	1.98797	1.28562
DERATIOM	1.20809	0.344643	5.76485
NCC	0.538685	0.030883	4.00616
ROH	0.230743	0.1945227	0.169011
RTE	0.0306272	0.0212204	0.0522402
RIE	0.029148	0.0135699	0.101285
FCF	0.146804	0.0848375	0.405308
SALGROW	0.111767	0.0879809	0.177632
RPM	1.03831	1.0291	0.0921163
RDEP	0.39897	0.406314	0.13006
SOD	17.7474	11.1	19.4447

NOTES

1. In their sample of 72 going-private transactions over the period 1973 to 1980, 28 of these transactions were classified as LBOs.
2. See Lowenstein (1985) for the most complete presentation of this argument. In the 1986 paper, he simply reiterates most of his earlier arguments and calls for a formal public auction when management makes a buyout proposal.
3. One source for this argument is Forsyth (1986).
4. See Chapter 1.
5. The reader is referred to Amemiya and Powell (1983) for a good discussion of these issues and empirical support for concern about the use of discriminant analysis estimators in hypothesis testing situations.
6. There are other reasons to choose the logit framework, but for our purposes the robustness of this framework is sufficient justification.

7. For other options, the reader is referred to Manski and MacFadden (1981) or Hensher and Johnson (1981).
8. A more formal development of the statistical framework used in this study is given in Kieschnick (1987).
9. There are a number of LBOs identified in DeAngelo (1986), Dubendorf and Storey (1985), Lehn and Poulsen (1986), and Wallner & Greve (1984).
10. This does pose a potential problem with sample selection bias, but the estimation procedures should be robust with respect to this potential problem because I condition the probability of inclusion. Further, there was no evidence of a systematic pattern in exclusions, for large and small buyouts were excluded.
11. The lists employed were from the SEC's regular publication "Directory of Companies Required to File Annual Reports with the Securities and Exchange Commission under the SEC Act of 1934."
12. See Appendix 2-1 for how prior hostile control bids were determined.
13. See Michel and Shaked (1986).
14. Even though management compensation is often set by a compensation committee of the board of directors, the level of management stock ownership indicated in the statistics for MBOs would imply that management will have some influence on the composition of the compensation committee.
15. Their TYPED variable was a dummy variable for whether the buyout was a "management buyout" or a "third-party buyout." Their HOLDI variable was a measure of management's beneficial stock holdings.
16. Actually, our free cash flow variable definition is a modification of a definition employed in Mason (1984). The primary difference concerns the accounting of R&D expenses and net plant expenditures.
17. As an aside, note that the significantly positive sign on the SOD variable raises questions about the defective managerial compensation contract hypothesis.
18. See Appendix 2-2, the variable TC.
19. See Kieschnick (1988) for an analysis of some data on the post-buyout actions of firms that went private through an MBO. These data further support skepticism over the defective managerial compensation contract hypothesis.

REFERENCES AND ADDITIONAL READING

Amemiya, T. & Powell, J. L. (1983). A Comparison of the logit model and normal discriminant analysis when the independent variables are binary. In S. Karlin, T. Amemiya & L.A. Goodman (Eds.) *Studies in econometrics, time series, and multivariate statistics*. New York: Academic Press.

Amemiya, T. (1985). *Advanced econometrics*. Boston: Harvard University Press.

Barnes, P (1987). The analysis and use of financial ratios: A review article. *Journal of Business Finance and Accounting, 14*, 449-461.

Baron, D. P. (1982). Efficient estimation of discrete choice models. In C. F. Manski & D. MacFadden (Eds.), *Structural analysis of discrete data with econometrics applications*. Cambridge, MA: The MIT Press.

Cowan, A. L. (1987, July 16). White knights: The dark side. *New York Times*, p. 26.

Crawford, E. K. (1987). *A management guide to leveraged buyouts*. New York: John Wiley & Sons.

Dann, L. & DeAngelo, H. (1983). Standstill agreements privately negotiated stock repurchases and the market for corporate control. *Journal of Financial Economics, 11*, 275-300.

DeAngelo, L. (1986). Accounting numbers as market valuation substitutes: A study of management buyouts of public stockholders. *The Accounting Review, 61*, 400-420.

DeAngelo, H., DeAngelo, L. & Rice, E. M. (1984a). Going private: Minority freezeouts and stockholder wealth. *Journal of Law & Economics, 27*, 367-401.

DeAngelo, H., DeAngelo, L. & Rice, E. M. (1984b). Going private: The effects of a change in corporate ownership structure. *Midland Corporate Finance Journal, 2*, 35-43.

Demsetz, H. (1983). The structure of ownership and the theory of the firm. *Journal of Law & Economics, 26*, 375-390.

Diamond, S. C. (ed.) . (1985). *Leveraged buyouts*. Homewood, IL: Dow Jones-Irwin.

Dubendorf, D. R. & Storey, M. J. (1985). *The insider buyout*. Pownal, VT: Storey Communications, Inc.

Fama, E. F. (1980). Agency problems and the theory of the firm. *Journal of Political Economy, 88*, 288-307.

Fama, E. F. & Jensen, M. C. (1983a). Separation of ownership and control. *Journal of Law & Economics, 26*, 301-325.

Fama, E. F. & Jensen, M. C. (1983b). Agency problems and residual claims. *Journal of Law & Economics, 26*, 327-349.

Feder, B. J. (1987, May 28). $2.7 billion Forstmann war chest. *New York Times*.

Forsyth, R. W. (1986, February 24). Bad grades: Takeovers teach a costly lesson to bond holders. *Barron's*, pp. 24-26.

Gargiulo, A. F. & Levine, S. J. (1982). The leveraged buyout. AMA Management Briefing. New York: American Management Association.

Heckman, J. J. (1979). Sample selection bias as a specification error. *Econometrica, 47*, 153-161.

Hensher, D. A. & Johnson, L. W. (1981). *Applied discrete-choice modelling.* New York: John Wiley & Sons.

Hector, F. (1987). Are shareholders cheated by LBOs. *Fortune, 115* (2), pp. 98-104.

Hsieh, V., Easterwood, J. & Singer, R. (1987, October). The role of large shareholders in the control of corporations: Evidence from going-private transactions. Paper presented at the Financial Management Association meetings, New York.

Hite, G. L. & Owers, J. E. (1984). The restructuring of corporate America: An overview. *Midland Corporate Finance Journal, 2*, 6-16.

Jensen, M. C. & Meckling, W. (1976). Theory of the firm: Managerial behavior, agency costs, and ownership structures. *Journal of Financial Economics, 3*, 305-360.

Jensen, M. C. & Ruback, R. S. (1983). The market for corporate control: The scientific evidence. *Journal of Financial Economics, 11*, 5-50.

Jensen, M. C. (1986a). Agency costs of free cash flow, corporate finance and takeovers. *American Economic Review, 76*, 323-329.

Jensen, M. C. (1986b). The takeover controversy: Analysis and evidence. *Midland Corporate Finance Journal, 4*, 6-32.

Jensen, M. C. & Murphy, K. J. (1987). Are executive compensation contracts structured properly? (MERC-86-14). Rochester, NY: University of Rochester, Managerial Research Center.

Kieschnick, R. L. (1987). Management buyouts of public corporations: An empirical study. (Doctoral dissertation, University of Texas, Austin).

Kieschnick, R. L. (1988). Management buyouts of public corporations: A selective examination. Faculty of Management working paper, University of Manitoba, Winnipeg, Canada.

Klein, B. (1983). Contracting costs and residual claims: The separation of ownership and control. *Journal of Law & Economics, 26*, 367-374.

Klein, R. (1987, January-February). The private lives of textile industry LBOs. *Mergers & Acquisitions*, 61-65.

Lehn, K. & Poulsen, A. (1986). Leveraged buyouts: Wealth created or wealth redistributed? Unpublished SEC working paper.

Lowenstein, L. (1985). Management buyouts. *Columbia Law Review, 85*, 730-784.

Lowenstein, L. (1986, January-February). No more cozy management buyouts. *Harvard Business Review*, 147-156.

Maddala, G. S. (1983). *Limited dependent and qualitative variables in econometrics.* Cambridge, England: Cambridge University Press.

Manski, C. F. & Lerman, S. R. (1977). The estimation of choice probabilities from choice-based samples. *Econometrica, 45*, 1977-1988.

Manski, C. F. & MacFadden, D. (1981). Alternative estimators and sample designs for discrete choice analysis. In D. F. Manski & D. MacFadden (Eds.) *Structural analysis of discrete data with econometric applications.* Cambridge, MA: The MIT Press.

Marais, L., Schipper, K. & Smith, A. (1986). Management buyout proposals and corporate claimholders: Explicit recontracting and differential wealth effects. Graduate School of Business working paper, University of Chicago.

Mason, L. R. (1984). *Structuring and financing management buyouts: A case history digest.* San Diego, CA: Buyout Publications, Inc.

Maupin, R., Bidwell, C. & Ortegren, A. (1984). An empirical investigation of the characteristics of publicly-held corporations that change to private ownership via management buyouts. *Journal of Business Finance & Accounting, 11*, 435-450.

Michel, A. & Shaked, I. (1986). *Takeover madness: Corporate America fights back.* New York: John Wiley & Sons.

Ross, S. A. (1987). The interrelations of finance and economics: Theoretical perspectives. *Papers and Proceeding of the 99th Annual Meeting of the American Economic Association, 77*, 29-34.

Salamon, G. L. & Smith, E. D. (1979). Corporate control and managerial misrepresentation of firms' performance. *Bell Journal of Economics, 10*, 319-328.

Travlos, N. G. & Millon, M. H. (1987). Going private buyouts and determinants of shareholder returns. Unpublished working paper.

Wallner, N. & Greve, J. T. (1984). *How to do a leveraged buyout or acquisition.* (2nd cd.). San Diego, CA: Buyout Publications, Inc.

Wayne, L. (1987, April 23). Reverse LBOs bring riches. *New York Times*, p. 29.

Williamson, O. E. (1983). Organization form, residual claimants, and corporate control. *Journal of Law & Economics, 26*, 351-366.

Wright, M. & Coyne, J. (1985). *Management buyout-outs.* London: Croom Helm Ltd.

Vetsuypens, M. R. (1985). Two essays on voluntary corporate divestiture. (Doctoral dissertation, working paper No. PHD-13, University of Rochester, Rochester, New York).

ABOUT THE AUTHOR

Robert L. Kieschnick, Jr., is an Assistant Professor of Finance at the University of Manitoba, Winnipeg, Canada. His current research interests concern corporate acquisition and divestitures, corporate debt decisions, and corporate investment analysis using contingent claims analysis.

Prior to completing his PhD in Finance at the University of Texas at Austin, he had an extensive career in both the public and private sectors, primarily involving natural resources extraction and distribution.

CHAPTER 3

MANAGEMENT PERFORMANCE IN LEVERAGED BUYOUTS: AN EMPIRICAL ANALYSIS

Ivan Bull *

1. INTRODUCTION

The purpose of this chapter is to compare the performance of a business unit before and after an LBO. A number of theoretical arguments suggest that performance can be expected to improve after an LBO. Some controversy exists, however, about whether wealth creation arises from improvement in "real" performance or whether wealth creation occurs because of a transfer of tax burden to other taxpayers.

One argument which supports improvement in real performance is the introduction of the entrepreneurial dimension. In LBOs, the new group of owners is small in number, and it includes top-level managers. Most owners tend to be personally involved in the business. They can be expected to observe and exploit opportunities for personal gain. Kirzner (1973, 1980) observes that all human beings tend to notice that which is in their interest to notice. He describes a pure entrepreneur as one whose role arises out of alertness to hitherto unnoticed opportunities. Selden (1980) describes Kirzner's statements as a pure theory of entrepreneurship, that the source of entrepreneurship is alertness to opportunity and imagination and vision to

*The assistance and advice of Charles M. Linke, Peter A. Silhan, Thomas J. Frecka, Norman Barnett, Joseph Lakonishok, and Yakov Amihud are gratefully acknowledged.

exploit or capitalize on it. Jensen (1984) alleges it is the change in management's interest, compensation, incentives, and performance that creates value in LBOs. Seely (1984) sees a small group of highly motivated stockholders and quasi-stockholders who will probably create more total wealth, in ways that he likens to Adam Smith's invisible hand. Halpern (1984) claims "one of the great benefits of the leveraged buyout is the impact of entrepreneurial management on a company" (p. 26).

Agency theory tends to predict similar results, but from a different perspective. Whereas entrepreneurial theory posits the introduction of entrepreneurial benefits, agency theory predicts the reduction of agency costs[1] after a buyout. The differences in utility functions between capital providers and resource managers are reduced when managers assume substantial equity positions. An agency relationship still exists, but the primary objective of debt repayment tends to be adopted by both principals and agents. Jensen (1984) suggests that the wealth creation potential of leveraged buyouts is partly based on organizational inefficiencies in a large firm. *Business Week* ("Behind the Scenes," July 20, 1987) suggests "a liberation from bureaucratic tyranny and, with that freedom, a return to common-sense management" (p. 120).

In his recently published free cash flow theory, Jensen (1986) holds that a major cause of takeovers is the high agency costs associated with conflicts between managers and shareholders over the disposition of corporate free cash flow. Free cash flow is defined as cash flow in excess of that required to fund all projects that have positive net values when discounted at the relevant cost of capital. Free cash flow should be paid out to shareholders to maximize shareholder value, but managers prefer to retain control. They may invest free cash flow in corporate assets that do not produce a return above the cost of capital, or waste it through organizational inefficiencies. The substitution of debt for equity reduces agency costs of free cash flow by reducing the free cash flow available for discretionary spending by managers. Therefore, the free cash flow theory would predict improvement in performance following an LBO because of the control function that debt exercises over agency costs.

Political costs are expected to be reduced for one segment of LBOs, namely, publicly held corporations that go private. Private firms do not incur significant out-of-pocket costs related to servicing public stockholders, meeting regulatory reporting requirements, maintaining relationships with analysts, and performing similar functions. Owners no longer need to be concerned about the political acceptability of such items as compensation arrangements. Rather, they can concentrate on achieving their private objectives without being subjected to public scrutiny.

Another source of improved operating results for LBOs is a reduction in income taxes. Under varying tax laws, depreciation may increase, inventory bases may increase, interest deductions will increase and other benefits may be obtained. Sloan, (1984) calls leveraged buyouts "a direct line into the federal treasury" (p. 41). Lowenstein (1985) states that "the large financial gains (to stockholders) should not be confused with real gains. To a large extent, they have been tax generated" (p. 784). Gleckman and Weiss (1986) predict that the Tax Reform Act of 1986 will curtail "billions of dollars worth of these [tax] benefits." However, Schipper and Smith (1986) find that considerable variability in premiums and proceeds paid to shareholders in LBOs is unexplained by tax savings. Gilson, Scholes, and Wolfson (1986) conclude that the source of acquisition premiums is something other than the attempt to secure a tax gain that is uniquely available because of an acquisition. From the viewpoint of society as a whole, a reduction in income taxes for LBOs can be categorized as a transfer of a burden to other taxpayers, arguably not a "real" improvement.

A continuing public policy debate, mostly about hostile takeovers but also including other forms of restructuring, has ensued in recent years. Congress considered over 20 bills in 1985 that proposed new restrictions on takeovers. The states of New York, New Jersey, Maryland, Pennsylvania, Connecticut, Illinois, Kentucky and Michigan have passed anti-takeover laws in the last several years.[2] In *Business Week* ("Do Mergers," 1985) it is alleged that "in an era of ever-increasing and ever-bigger mergers, a remarkable number—somewhere between a half and two-thirds—simply do not work" (p. 88). Drucker (1986) states that "altogether, the record is poor for all companies that have been merged, especially into a conglomerate or into a business with which they had little in common—for example, the typical financial conglomerate. Only three out of every ten such acquiring companies do as well two years later as they did before the merger. But the record of companies that have been acquired in a hostile takeover is uniformly dismal" (p. 14).

Empirical studies of results of different kinds of restructurings provide helpful evidence to judge the merits of each kind. For example, Meeks (1977) studied 233 acquisitions made by British firms between 1964 and 1972. A mild decline in profitability typified those acquisitions. Mueller

(1980) concluded that mergers had but modest effects on the profitability of the merging firms in the three to five years following merger. This LBO study provides empirical evidence about performance following certain kinds of LBOs. It documents performance improvement in the two years after a LBO as compared to the two years before the LBO.

Section 2 presents the research design including the tests employed to measure performance change, a description of the sample, a discussion of performance measurements, and the variables used to compare performance. Section 3 summarizes interviews with institutional investors, LBO specialists, and CEOs of companies that have undergone LBOs. Section 4 describes and interprets the principal findings, for example, comparisons of performance of the after-buyout years to performance in the pre-buyout years. Section 5 offers overall conclusions and speculates about implications of the findings.

2. RESEARCH DESIGN

Tests

This study compares the average performance of a business unit for the two years before an LBO to the average performance for the two years after the buyout.   Comparison periods are limited to two years because LBO managers are not status-quo managers. They acquire new businesses and sell old ones.   Adding a third comparison year would either materially decrease the sample size or create the necessity to attempt to adjust for major restructurings by the LBO. The year[3] of the buyout is excluded from comparisons because it frequently includes recognition of a number of atypical events that distort comparisons. Management must have acquired an equity interest as part of the buyout for the entity to be included in the study.

One set of tests computes the significance of changes in the average two-year post-buyout (T+) performance variables compared to the average two-year pre-buyout (T-) performance variables, after adjusting T- accounting bases and amortization policies to be consistent with T+ accounting bases and amortization policies. In another set of tests, performance measures of the sample buyout companies, similarly adjusted in the pre-buyout years, are converted to ratios of the same variables for a composite group of companies in the same primary industry. The post-buyout ratios of company performance statistics divided by the industry performance statistics are compared to the pre-buyout ratios. The first set of tests ignores changes in the environment. The second set controls for environmental changes to the extent that environmental changes similarly affect all companies in the same industry. The industry comparison data were compiled from *Financial Dynamics* (1985), published by Standard & Poor's Compustat Services.[4]

The LBO Data Base

Financial information needed for a study of LBO performance is not publicly available. The required financial data were obtained from six institutional investors with the understanding that the subject companies would not be identifiable from published descriptions or findings.[5]

The six institutions offered a potential population of more than 50 LBOs. However, over half are not included in the sample for one or more of the following reasons:

1. Some constraint was not met: for example, the company was sold within the pre-buyout two-year period or the post-buyout two-year period or management did not acquire equity as part of the buyout;
2. Restructuring in the pre-buyout period made it impracticable to determine the base performance against which post-buyout performance was comparable.
3. Restructuring in the post-buyout period made it impracticable to determine performance comparable to the base period; that is, a major business segment was divested.
4. Critical data were unavailable for either the pre- or post-buyout period.

The study sample consists of 25 different companies that emerged from LBOs that occurred between 1971 and 1983.

Table 3-1 shows that the aggregate transfer price of the 25 companies exceeded $3 billion. The lowest price was less than $5 million, the highest in excess of $500 million. The average price was approximately $125 million. Nineteen sold at a premium over book value, six at a discount and three at approximate book value. The average net premium was approximately $31 million, about 25 percent of the average transfer price.

Table 3–1
Year of purchase, type, and purchase price of the entities included
in the Sample of 25 Leveraged Buyouts

| Year of Purchase | Type of Leveraged Buyout | | | |
	Going Private	Subsidiary/ Division	Private Company	Price (Millions)
1971			1	$ 11,000
1977	2		1	104,000
1979		1	1	51,000
1980	1		1	514,000
1981	1	3	2	965,000
1982	2	3		666,000
1983	2	4		820,000
Totals	8	11	6	$3,131,000

Table 3-2 shows that the industries represented tend to be mature and not involved in high technology. Such industries would seem to include businesses with low growth prospects and high potential for generating cash flows, situations where Jensen (1986) would expect high agency costs because of free cash flows.

Eighteen industries are identified in Table 3-2 as the principal lines of business. Four of the sample companies are primarily involved in the metal fabrication industry. No other industry is represented by more than two companies.

Annual sales at the time of the buyout range from less than $10 million to more than $1 billion, with an average of about $277 million (median of $118 million). The number of employees varies from fewer than 200 to more than 10,000, with an average of approximately 3,000 and a median of 2,200 employees. Most of the sample companies are engaged in more than a single line of business. Management ownership after the buyout averages 27 percent of the common stock, ranging from 1.5 to 100 percent.

Table 3-2
Industries represented by the sample of 25 leveraged buyouts and
industries against which their performance is compared

Industry	Number of LBOs
Metal Fabricated Products	4
Machinery-Specialty	2
Electronics-Instruments	2
Conglomerates	2
Auto-Original Equipment Manufacturing	2
Food-Confectionery	1
Metals-Steel Products	1
Home Furnishings	1
Shoes	1
Containers-Paper	1
Chemicals-Miscellaneous	1
Retail Food	1
Paper	1
Textile Apparel Manufacturing	1
Textile Products	1
Abrasive Products	1
Office Equipment and Business Forms	1
Miscellaneous	1
Total	25

Performance Measures

The objective of the study I described in this chapter was to measure the extent of changes in management performance, yet no set of measurements has been generally accepted for that purpose. Return on investment (ROI) type of measures are frequently used when accounting variables are utilized to determine performance bonuses for managers.

Kaplan (1983, 1984) argues that clever managers have learned a variety of ways to meet ROI goals in the short term. He urges development of nonfinancial measures for manufacturing performance. He believes that measures that emphasize financial performance can be improved temporarily by reducing capital investment in intangibles such as research, product development, human resources development, advertising and promotion, maintenance, quality control, and customer service. Kaplan (1983) considers the practice of relying on a single measure to motivate and evaluate the performance of managers in complex settings to be naive: "Any single measurement will have myopic properties that will enable managers to increase their score on this measure without necessarily contributing to the long-run profits of the firm" (p. 699).

Unfortunately, measurement concepts that conform to Kaplan's criteria have not been well developed. This study therefore relies on traditional financial measurements. To some extent, the following seven performance variables that are used in this study are surrogates for efficiency, profitability, and market share:

Income from Continuing Operations (Earnings)/Beginning Equity

Earnings Before Interest and Income Taxes (EBIT)/Beginning Assets

Sales/Beginning Assets

Sales

Operating Income/Sales

Cash Flow/Sales

Income Tax Expense/Sales

Adjustments to the accounting data used to calculate the performance variables are required for comparison purposes because new values are assigned to inventory, fixed assets, and intangible assets when the transfer price is allocated among the transferred assets.[6] Comparability is reasonably achieved by adjusting pre-buyout balances and amortization policies to conform to those used in the post-buyout periods.[7] See Appendix 3-1 for details.

3. INTERVIEWS

The LBO environment is unlike that of traditional businesses. Interviews were conducted to gain insight into that environment and to develop expectations against which empirical results could be compared. Seven institutional investor executives, three LBO specialists, and five CEOs of companies that experienced LBOs were interviewed. The interviews were conducted concurrently with the data accumulation phase of the study. They provide insight, understanding and reinforcement to statistical findings.

Institutional Investor Executives

This group of investors tends to view LBO managers as (1) managing for cash flow, not for quarterly reportable profits, (2) managing assets better than other managers, and (3) possibly being more effective with their employees. These executives tend to believe that equity values increase when managers acquire equity in the company they manage. They tend to believe that LBO boards of directors oversee managers better than boards of publicly held corporations.

LBO Principals

This group strongly believes that executives manage more effectively after an LBO, although they have discovered that some managers cannot escape from their former highly structured corporate culture. The principals generally believe that managers of large companies tend towards procrastination in recognizing and solving problems, that they dissipate time and energy playing internal politics, and that large corporations require excessive documentation. In contrast, they perceive that LBO managers recognize losses early, pay attention to winning businesses, manage for cash flow, and spend their energy constructively in managing the business. One of the principals described the typical CEO of an LBO company as "not the salary-bonus-pillar of the community" type but the "got to pay the mortgage and make a million" type.

These principals tend to describe their own oversight philosophy as hands on, but without interfering in daily operations. They believe they pay what it takes to hire the best people, give the CEO the authority to manage effectively, and do not require formal documentation for capital expenditures. They ask pertinent questions and "shake the tree" when needed. Each one has replaced the CEO of a buyout company. They see the LBO business as a "people" business. They believe that the typical corporation prefers to invest in plant and equipment, whereas they prefer to invest in good managers.

Leveraged Buyout CEOs

With but one exception, the managers tended to state that they managed the same after the buyout as before. Then they proceeded to describe several changes. Changes involve employees, structure, compensation plans, product pricing, the internal climate, and support professionals outside the company. One CEO described the present environment as opposite of that when he managed the entity as a division of a larger firm. Following the LBO, each manager does what needs to be done, whereas before the LBO no one took a risk and each person prepared lots of "paper protection." Each CEO pays close attention to projecting and monitoring cash flow. Four of the five talked about minimizing the investment in inventory.

Three CEOs described the present board of directors as more committed, more involved, and more helpful than the previous board. Both the LBO specialist members and institutional investor members seem to be regarded favorably, less bound by constraints than prior board members. They are more willing, for example, to pay what it takes to hire the right person for a job.

The other two CEOs regard their former superiors as tougher. One misses phone calls with nasty questions, as well as the corporate pressure. He consults frequently with board members who are principals in a buyout firm but does not regard them as especially helpful. The second CEO owns the majority of the voting stock and seems to regard his board as typical for most corporations.

Interview Impressions

Persons interviewed shared a surprisingly uniform perception about management of an LBO company. Principals of LBO houses are active participants in management but stay relatively free of day-to-day operations. CEOs manage effectively or they are replaced. CEOs do not see themselves making broad strategy changes but responding promptly and decisively to changes in the environment. All persons interviewed tend to believe that LBO managers performed well, and the study results support that belief.

Table 3-3
Mean and *median* of major accounting variables for the Sample of 25 Leveraged Buyouts for the two years before and the two years after the buyout ($ millions) [a]

		Year		
	T-2	*T-1*	*T+1*	*T+2*
Sales	$276,502	$266,396	$282,329	$301,201
	104,270	*112,901*	*129,038*	*131,929*
Earnings before	20,622	19,297	20,112	21,460
interest and taxes	*9,671*	*8,316*	*10,568*	*13,061*
Operating profit	19,181	18,673	18,169	19,724
	9,671	*7,789*	*10,141*	*11,453*
Income tax	9,359	8,414	2,527	3,877
	4,500	*3,396*	*1,453*	*1,620*
Income continuing	10,791	9,473	2,826	5,471
operations	*5,171*	*4,284*	*3,311*	*2,720*
Depreciation and	8,592	9,088	9,402	10,221
amortization	*2,604*	*2,527*	*2,332*	*2,512*
Capital expenditures	11,013	8,240	5,211	7,246
	2,026	*2,446*	*1,583*	*1,909*
Cash available for	3,233	9,820	12,716	12,795
debt repayment	*2,199*	*3,555*	*3,053*	*2,954*
Interest	2,112	3,012	14,610	11,964
	596	*708*	*4,436*	*4,168*
Cash available to	5,345	12,832	27,326	24,759
debt and interest	*2,486*	*4,778*	*6,975*	*13,006*
Beginning assets	170,496	181,566	169,513	164,663
	70,557	*62,464*	*50,435*	*47,155*
Beginning equity	109,907	121,606	18,573	21,234
	46,798	*48,395*	*14,612*	*18,812*

[a]See Appendix 3-1 for adjustments included in the above totals for T- years.

Table 3–4
Plots of Mean and Median of major accounting variables for the 25 LBOs for the two years before and after the buyouts

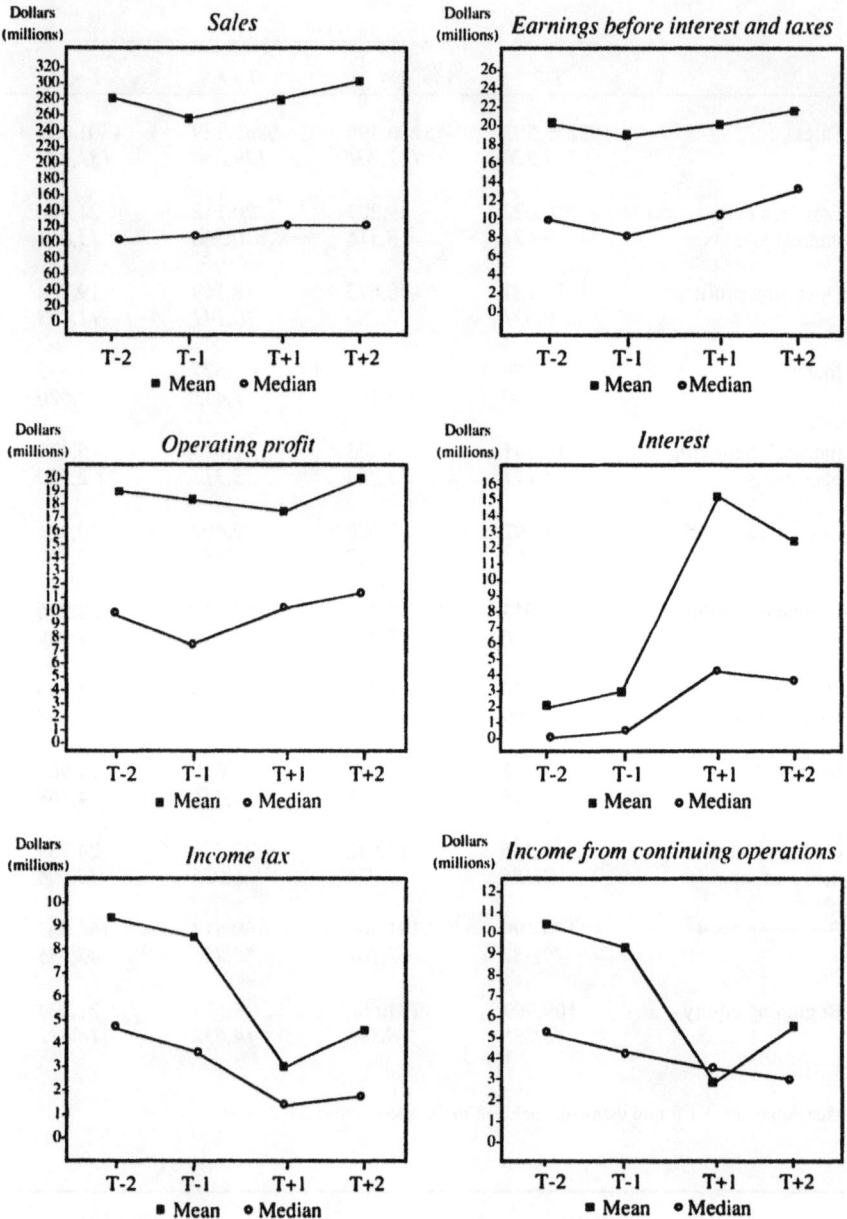

Dollars (millions)

Sales

320
300
280
260
240
220
200
180
160
140
120
100
80
60
40
20
0

T-2   T-1   T+1   T+2

■ Mean   ● Median

Dollars (millions)

Earnings before interest and taxes

26
24
22
20
18
16
14
12
10
8
6
4
2
0

T-2   T-1   T+1   T+2

■ Mean   ● Median

Dollars (millions)

Operating profit

20
19
18
17
16
15
14
13
12
11
10
9
8
7
6
5
4
3
2
1
0

T-2   T-1   T+1   T+2

■ Mean   ● Median

Dollars (millions)

Interest

16
15
14
13
12
11
10
9
8
7
6
5
4
3
2
1
0

T-2   T-1   T+1   T+2

■ Mean   ● Median

Dollars (millions)

Income tax

10
9
8
7
6
5
4
3
2
1
0

T-2   T-1   T+1   T+2

■ Mean   ● Median

Dollars (millions)

Income from continuing operations

12
11
10
9
8
7
6
5
4
3
2
1
0

T-2   T-1   T+1   T+2

■ Mean   ● Median

Table 3–4—Continued

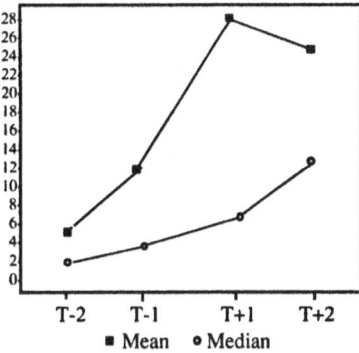

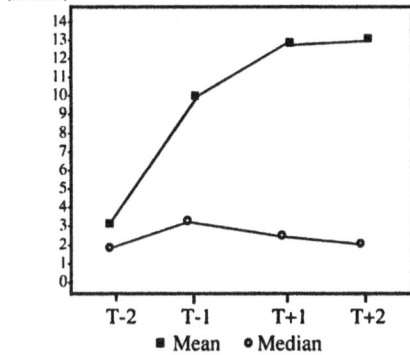

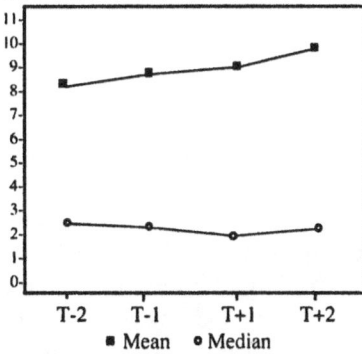

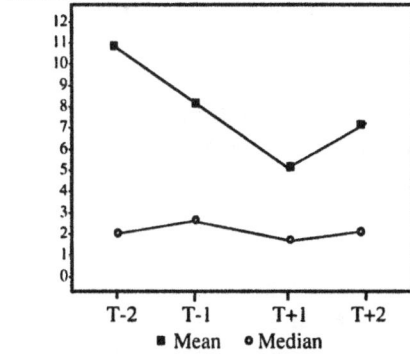

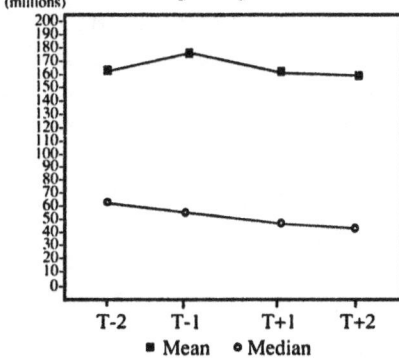

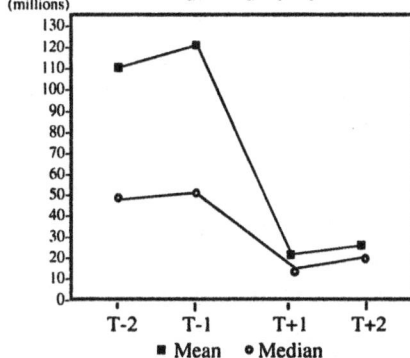

4. EMPIRICAL RESULTS AND INTERPRETATIONS

MANOVA tests using Hotelling's T^2 statistic to incorporate the seven relevant variables show that changes in performance are significant at the .001 level, both in comparison against self and in the industry-adjusted comparisons. The comparison against self, with an F value of 6.57536, shows that the sample entities improved over their past performance. The industry adjusted comparison, with an F value of 5.90416, reflects a similar improvement in comparison to their competitors.

Descriptive data and plots reflecting the mean and the median of major variables for the two T- years and the two T+ years are presented in Tables 3-3 and 3-4. These tables of the means[8] and medians reveal a number of interesting results, many of which are predictable for companies in stable industries that change from equity to debt financing.

Interest expense (on debt financing) increases significantly in the T+ years. Income from continuing operations decreases, although the decrease in income is less than the increase in interest expense. Income tax expense shows a large reduction in the T+ years, primarily the result of increased tax-deductible interest expense. Cash available for debt and interest increases to meet the necessary debt service requirements. Assets decrease, apparently the result of better asset management after the buyout. The decrease in equity reflects the effects of the LBO transaction, that is, the financing of assets with debt.

The decrease in the level of capital expenditures in the T+ years was unexpected. The study was not designed to provide a theory for, or evidence about, capital expenditure behavior. The findings are reported as a matter of interest without attempting to interpret the findings as evidence of acquisition efficiency or of short-term managerial horizons or of some other reason.

The large difference between the mean and the median reflects the inclusion of a few large companies, an artifact of the sample. The smaller companies appear to reflect a greater increase in operating profit after the buyout, but the sample is too small to attempt to draw conclusions about a size effect.

Table 3-5 compares performance for the average of the two T- years to the average of the two T+ years as ratios to comparison companies in the same primary industry. The mean and the median of the sample company variables for the two T- years and for the two T+ years are converted to ratios

Table 3–5
**Comparison of performance of 25 Sample Leveraged Buyouts to industry
performance using averages of the two T- and T+ Years**

Ratios of mean and median performance of leveraged buyouts to industry
performance for T- and T+ Years[a]

Variable	T- Years		T+ Years		Standard Deviation	
	Mean	Median	Mean	Median	T-	T+
Earnings/Beginning Equity	.9193	.7839	3.6520	2.1921	.5958	6.2310
EBIT/Beginning Assets	1.0265	1.0253	1.4138	1.3455	.4014	.5936
Sales/Beginning Assets	1.0918	.8640	1.2640	1.2039	.4299	.4174
Sales	.2002	.1109	.1924	.1181	.2101	.2083
Operating Profit/Sales	1.0699	.9450	1.2144	1.3990	.4283	.5073
Cash Flow/Sales	1.4542	.9745	2.1657	2.0986	1.9800	.9901
Income Tax/Sales	1.1214	1.0080	.7205	.6890	.7150	.6364
Capital Expenditures/Sales	.6386	.5380	.5002	.4051	.4789	.2992

[a]See Appendix 3-1 for adjustments reflected in T- years. Ratio of 1 equals industry performance,
ratio of 2 doubles industry performance, etc.

of the same variables for the same years as reported in *Financial Dynamics*
for the companies that it lists in the same primary industry. Table 3-6 shows
the same data in the form of plots.

Tables 3-5 and 3-6 show that mean performance improved in the T+
years for six of the variables, but the mean of sales dropped in relation to the
industry. The median performance improved for all variables.

The changes in the amounts and the variability of Earnings/Beginning
Equity and Cash Flow/Sales are noteworthy. In the T- years, the mean of
Earnings/Beginning Equity was approximately 92% of the industry (the
median was 78%), and its standard deviation was .5958. In the T+ years,
the mean was 365% of the industry (the median was 219%), but its standard
deviation was 6.231. Both the amount and the variability increased
materially. The Cash Flow/Sales mean also increased from 145% to 217%
(the median from 97% to 210%), but its variability decreased from 1.9800
to .9901. Those statistics, interpreted as evidence of significant change, are
discussed further in Section 5.

Table 3–6
Comparison of performance of 25 Sample LBOs to industry performance using averages of the two T- and T+ years

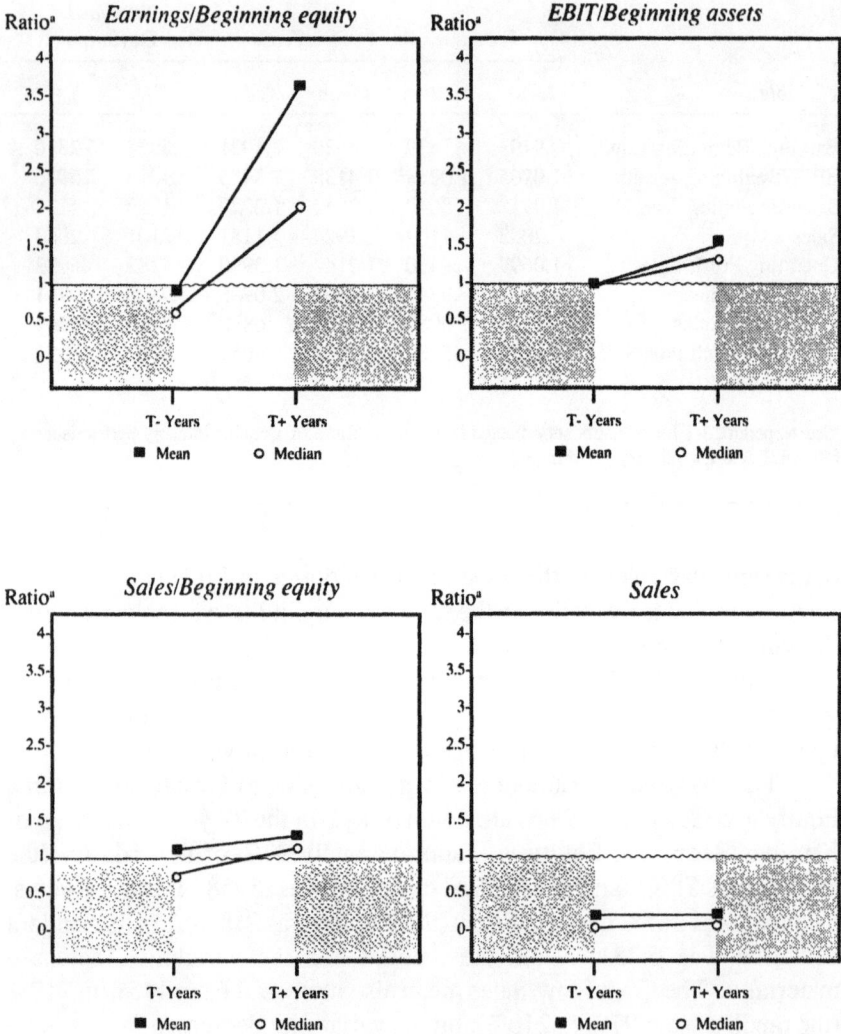

[a]Ratio of 1 equals industry performance, ratio of 2 doubles industry performance, etc.

Table 3–6—continued

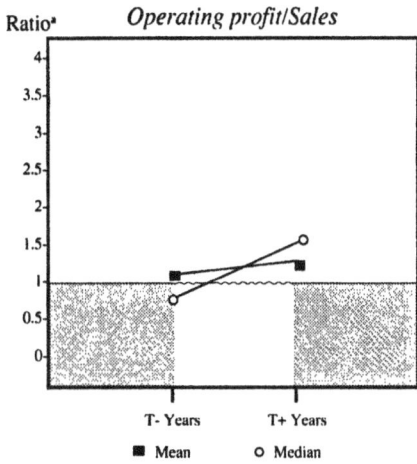

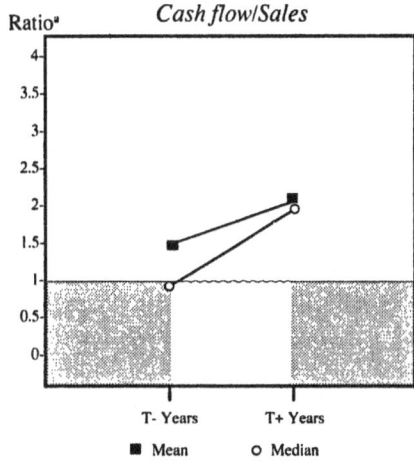

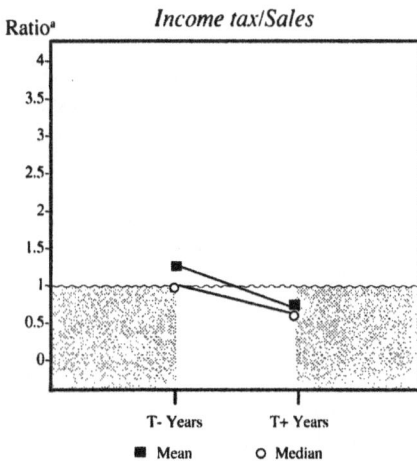

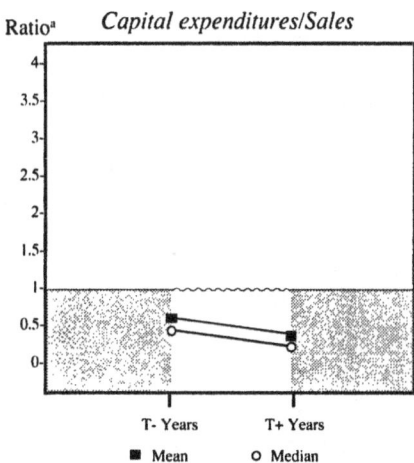

Operating profit/Sales

Cash flow/Sales

Income tax/Sales

Capital expenditures/Sales

[a]Ratio of 1 equals industry performance, ratio of 2 doubles industry performance, etc.

Table 3-7
Paired samples t tests comparing mean performance of the 25 Sample Leveraged Buyouts for the average of the two T+ years to the adjusted mean performance for the average of the two T- years

Variable	Against Self		Industry Adjusted	
	2-tailed t Value	Probability	2-tailed t Value	Probability
Earnings/Beginning Equity	2.39	.025	2.26	.033
EBIT/Beginning Assets	1.58	.128	3.75	.001
Sales/Beginning Assets	.88	.386	3.23	.004
Sales	1.97	.060	- .93	.361
Operating Profit/Sales	.02	.985	1.93	.066
Cash Flow/Sales	5.04	<.001	1.68[a]	.107[a]
Income Tax Expense/Sales	-3.23	.004	-2.16	.041

[a]Eliminating one outlier and then performing the tests with the remaining 24 cases changes the t-value to 3.12 and the 2-tailed probability to .005. The outlier is caused by one ratio where the denominator is approximately zero in amount.

A post-hoc test using Hotelling's T^2 statistic provides evidence about changes in efficiency-type variables. Using only variables that exclude income tax effects, that is, EBIT/Beginning Assets, Sales/Beginning Assets, and Operating Profit/Sales, the comparison against self is marginally significant (F of 2.34976 at .100), while the industry-adjusted comparison reflects an F value of 5.97558 at the .004 significance level. These test results are consistent with the hypothesis that an LBO of the type included in the study leads to an improvement in efficiency and profitability.

A series of post-hoc MANOVA tests omitting one of the seven variables from each test are less informative. Omitting Cash Flow/Sales from the comparison against self reduces the overall F value from 6.57536 at .001 to 4.45413 at the .006 significance level. Eliminating the Income Tax/Sales variable from the industry adjusted comparison reduces the F value from 5.90416 at .001 to an F value of 3.90603 at the .100 significance level. The significance of F is at least .001 for all other six variable comparisons. This series of post-hoc tests using different combinations of six variables demonstrates that no single variable dominates the finding of significance.

Table 3-7 reflects a series of univariate paired sample two-tail t-tests[9] used to determine the significance of change in the means of the individual variables for the average of the two T+ years as compared to the average of the two T- years.

Earnings/Beginning Equity in Table 3-7 reflects a significant increase for the T+ years over the T- years for the comparison against self (p =.025), and also in the industry adjusted comparison (p =.033).

Following are some components:

	T- Years (000)		T+Years (000)	
	Mean	Median	Mean	Median
Beginning equity	$115,756	$47,597	$19,904	$16,727
Earnings	10,132	4,728	4,149	3,016
Return	.0875	.0993	.2085	.1803

Reasons for the change in this statistic appear to be the composite of all the reasons hypothesized for improvement in performance. The increase is also partly due to the restructuring of equity into debt, an increase that could be expected because of the increase in financial risk because of the increase in leverage.

EBIT/Beginning Assets in the T+ years shows an improvement over the T- years. The improvement is marginally significant when compared to self (p =.128). Assets decrease, and EBIT increases. However, the increase in this ratio is highly significant when compared to other companies in the industry (p =.001).

Sales/Beginning Assets shows an insignificant increase when compared to self (p =.386), but a significant improvement in the industry adjusted comparisons (p =.004). This improvement is in spite of a negative industry adjusted comparison of sales means.

Assets appear to have supported higher sales after the buyout and higher earnings when the method of financing and income taxes are ignored. No attempt is made to specifically identify which assets appear to have been reduced, although interviews provided anecdotal evidence of reducing inventories and opportunistically converting idle assets into cash.

The mean of Sales for the sample companies increases, but less than other companies in the same industry. The negative industry comparison (p = .361), which is outside the range normally considered to be significant, might be considered to reflect a decline in performance. One CEO who was interviewed reported a policy change of weeding out unprofitable sales. Discontinued lines of business may account for another part of the decline. Five companies reported discontinued operations in either year T+1 or T+2. The highest percentage for the discontinued business is 3% of total sales for the year of discontinuance, but comparable sales for years T-2 and T-1 could not be determined. Comparing T+ to T- years, three of those five companies reported negative growth in total sales, one reported a 2% positive growth, and one reported substantial growth.

Operating Profit/Sales for the T+ years appears to be unchanged when comparing the T- to the T+ years against self (p =.985). However, industry adjusted comparisons reflect significant improvement (p =.066). Detailed analyses of sales prices or cost of sales are not attempted. One might infer that the sample companies maintained the margins of the T- years, while their competitors did not.

The most dramatic change of the T+ years compared to the T- years shown in Table 3-7 in the Comparison Against Self is reflected by the variable Cash Flow/Sales (p = <.001). The industry adjusted comparison, after elimination of the outlier which results from a tiny denominator in one ratio, is highly significant at p = .005. Cash flow is the one item discussed in some detail by each LBO manager interviewed. The immediate measure of success of an LBO company is meeting its heavy debt service requirements, and the sample companies appear to have been managed with that critical measure in mind.

Even though the change in the variable of Income Tax Expense/Sales does not dominate the finding of significance in the above Table 3-7, the reduction in income tax is clearly substantial in absolute dollars (see Table 3-3). The reduction is also substantial when expressed as a percentage of income tax expense to sales. The difference in the single variable Income Tax Expense/Sales is highly significant (p = .004) in the Comparison Against Self. The same variable is also significant (p = .041) in the industry adjusted comparisons. This finding that income taxes are important but not dominant in accounting for the change in performance seems consistent with the Schipper and Smith (1986) conclusion that premiums and proceeds paid to shareholders in LBOs are only partly explained by tax savings. It also seems consistent with the Gilson et al. (1986) conclusion that the source of acquisition premiums is something other than tax gains uniquely related to acquisitions.

5. CONCLUSIONS

This study has a number of research limitations. These limitations include a concentration of the sample LBOs in the years 1980 to 1983 when the economy was generally considered to be reasonably strong, the non-randomness of the sample, the lack of a uniform degree of available detail in financial statements for the T- years, the shortcomings of accounting variables as performance measurements, and the short two-year measurement period. Lack of uniform detail prevents, for example, specific identification of the sources of improvement such as reduction of labor costs or better utilization of inventories. In spite of these limitations, the data and interview findings are consistent, and two firm conclusions tend to emerge.

First, the evidence is convincing that management does change significantly after an LBO. The management change is interpreted as one of becoming entrepreneurial, subject to the severe constraint that a high level of debt must be serviced. The changes in Earnings/Beginning Equity and Cash Flow/Sales dramatically illustrate the change of management focus to a different end-result, ostensibly from minimizing variability in reported profits to maximizing cash flow. The increase in average return on equity is interpreted as partly due to leverage and partly due to better management. The extreme increase in variability of earnings is interpreted as results of leverage and of opportunistic behavior. Entrepreneurs observe and try to exploit perceived opportunities for gain. Some exploitive actions provide large gains, some result in losses. The more efficient use of assets is also interpreted as entrepreneurial management.

Secondly, income tax savings do not appear to be the driving force behind LBOs. Tax savings are important, and entrepreneurs are not blind to that benefit, but the evidence suggests LBOs would occur with no tax savings at all. The Tax Reform Act of 1986 removes many benefits, and LBOs have continued. Because the value of any investment is the present value of the expected future cash flows, the price paid in an LBO will reflect expected tax savings. However, the significance of the change in the multivariate statistic of EBIT/Beginning Assets, Sales/Beginning Assets, and Operating Profit/Sales provides strong ex-post evidence that expected improvement in efficiency and profitability are important reasons for LBOs. These are "real" gains, they are not tax generated.

Implications of these findings are hard to assess. They might be considered at the levels of both public policy and individual entity. However, neither of the two following implications can be regarded as more than an interesting speculation.

In view of the apparent gains in efficiency and profitability, changing public policy to make LBOs more difficult, a result of some of the 1986 tax law changes, seems hard to justify. It is true that the gains are short term, and that the sample is restricted to the type where the entity continues as an operating unit. The same gain in efficiency cannot be claimed for the type of LBO where business units are treated as inventory items to be repackaged and resold. However, efficiencies such as those observed in this study should surely be encouraged by public policy, not discouraged.

At the level of the individual entity, the implications may be disquieting for some managers. The evidence tends to suggest that entities typically operate at less than optimal efficiency. Assuming that the efficient market prices financial investments at the present value of their expected future cash flows, any existing valuation that is based on a continuation of the present management and a continuation of present nonoptimal operations would seem to place inefficient managers at risk. Assuming further that public policy does not preclude takeovers, entrepreneurs are likely to continue to search out companies that are undervalued in terms of probable improved operations under entrepreneurial management. They are likely to continue takeover activity. Entrepreneurs can share part of the expected rewards with present equity owners in the form of purchase premium for stock and still enjoy high residual benefits. Existing managers should not feel complacent.

APPENDIX 3-1

Adjustments to Accounting Variables for Years T-1 and T-2 Made to Provide Comparisons Consistent with Years T+1 and T+2[a]

	Mean		Median	
	Year T-1	Year T-2	Year T-1	Year T-2
Beginning assets	$139,567	$151,160	$65,894	$57,615
Allocated premium	30,929	30,406	4,663	4,849
Adjusted assets	170,496	181,566	70,557	62,464
Beginning equity	78,978	91,200	42,135	43,546
Allocated premium	30,929	30,406	4,663	4,849
Adjusted equity	109,907	121,606	46,798	48,395
Earnings before interest & taxes	23,673	22,351	9,700	8,354
Amortization of premium	(3,051)	(3,054)	(29)	(38)
Adjusted EBIT	20,622	19,297	9,671	8,316
Operating profit	22,232	21,727	9,700	7,827
Amortization of premium	(3,051)	(3,054)	(29)	(38)
Adjusted operating profit	19,181	18,673	9,671	7,789
Income continuing operations	12,218	10,918	5,200	4,322
Amortization	(3,051)	(3,054)	(29)	(38)
Income tax:				
re amortization	1,624	1,609	0	0
adjusted income	10,791	9,473	5,171	4,284

[a]Beginning asset and beginning equity balances are adjusted to reflect a portion of the premium (discount) paid over book value as shown above. Amortization of that premium (discount) reduces EBIT and operating profit. Income tax expense is adjusted for the T- years for the Earnings/Beginning Equity computation when amortization appears to have been tax deductible in the T+ years.

Adjustments to cost of sales are not attempted even though different inventory valuation methods may be used. Those possible cost of sales adjustments are believed to be immaterial because the major effects on income are reflected in T-0, the year omitted from comparison.

NOTES

1. See Jensen and Meckling (1976) for an extensive discussion of agency costs.
2. Michael C. Jensen and W. H. Meckling, "The Takeover Controversy: Analysis and Evidence," *Midland Corporate Finance Journal*, summer 1986.
3. The year of the buyout (year T-0) is normally 12 months in length. A change in the fiscal year causes T-0 to be more or less than 12 months. Buyouts that are consummated in the last month of a fiscal year tend to "contaminate" both the current and the following year, in which case T-0 usually encompasses two years.
4. In two cases when the primary industry match is not apparent and the company might conceivably be matched against either of two different industries, the match is made on the basis of the closeness of the numerical match of three variables: Operating Income/Sales, Sales/Assets, and EBIT/Assets.
5. It is believed that each source that provided information made all qualifying investments available for analysis, so that within-source bias should not be present.
6. See APB Opinion No. 16, "Business Combinations," for general principles of accounting for a business combination by the purchase method.
7. The most frequent adjustments (a) increase fixed asset and goodwill accounts (most entities were purchased at a premium over book value) and (b) provide for amortization of those increases. The amount of the increases in asset values at transfer date is available or is approximated from data that are available. The proportion of the increase assumed to be applicable to years T-2 and T-1 is the proportion of sales for T-2 and T-1 to sales for year T-0.
8. Note that arithmetic means of account totals give large weight to large totals and therefore assign more significance to large companies than to small ones. Study conclusions are based on the means of ratios of individual companies, whereby a ratio for a small company receives the same weight as a ratio for a large company.
9. One-tailed tests might have been utilized, for performance was expected to improve. However, one could not feel confident that each individual variable would improve nor that industry-adjusted variables would improve. In addition, two-tailed tests present a more conservative approach to measuring and reporting significance.

REFERENCES

Behind the scenes at a leveraged buyout. (1987, July 20). *Business Week*, pp. 120-122.

Do mergers really work? (1985, June 3). *Business Week*, pp. 88-91.

Drucker, P. F. (1986, winter). Corporate takeovers—what is to be done? *The Public Interest, 82*, 3-24.

Financial dynamics. (1985). (14 volumes). Denver: Standard & Poor's Compustat Services.

Gilson, R. J., Scholes, M. S. & Wolfson, M. A. (1986, February). Taxation and the dynamics of corporate control: The uncertain case for tax-motivated acquisitions. (Unpublished manuscript, Stanford Graduate School of Business, Stanford, California).

Gleckman, H. & Weiss, S. (1986, September 22). How tax reform will cool takeover fever. *Business Week*, pp. 83-84.

Halpern, M. (1984, summer). Roundtable: The leveraged buyout market. *Mergers & Acquisitions, 19* (2), 26, 36.

Jensen, M. C. (1986, May). Agency costs of free cash flow, corporate finance and takeovers. *American Economic Review, 76*, 323-329.

Jensen, M. C. (1984, summer). A discussion of corporate restructuring. *Midland Corporate Finance Journal, 2* (2), 62, 65.

Jensen, M. C. & Meckling, W. H. (1976). Theory of the firm: Managerial behavior, agency costs and ownership structure. *Journal of Financial Economics, 3*, 305-360.

Jensen, M. C. & Meckling, W. H. (1986, summer). The takeover controversy: Analysis and evidence. *Midland Corporate Finance Journal*, 6-32.

Kaplan, R. S. (1983, October). Measuring manufacturing performance: A challenge for managerial accounting research. *The Accounting Review, 58 (4)*, 686-705.

Kaplan, R. S. (1984, July). The evolution of management accounting. *The Accounting Review, 59* (3), 390-418.

Kirzner, I. M. (1973). *Competition and entrepreneurship.* Chicago: University of Chicago Press.

Kirzner, I. M. (1980). The primacy of entrepreneurial discovery. *The prime mover of progress.* London: The Institute of Economic Affairs.

Lowenstein, L. (1985, May). Management buyouts. *Columbia Law Review, 85*, 730-784.

Meeks, G. (1977). *Disappointing marriage: A study of the gains from merger.* Cambridge, England: University Press.

Mueller, D. C. (1980). A cross-national comparison of the results. In D. C. Mueller (Ed.) *The determinants and effects of mergers.* Cambridge, MA: Oelgeschlager, Gunn & Hain.

Schipper, K. & Smith, A. (1986, July). Corporate income tax effects of management buyouts. (Working paper, University of Chicago).

Seely, M. (1984, summer). A discussion of corporate restructuring. *Midland Corporate Finance Journal, 2* (2), 78.

Seldon, A. (1980). In I. M. Kirzner, *Prime movers of progress* (Preface). London: The Institute of Economic Affairs.

Sloan, A. (1984, April 9). Luring banks overboard? *Forbes,* pp. 39-43.

ABOUT THE AUTHOR

Ivan Bull is Professor of Accountancy and Finance and the Director of the Office of Business Innovation and Entrepreneurship at the University of Illinois at Urbana-Champaign. He holds a PhD in Accountancy from the University of Illinois and a BS from the University of Iowa. He was the Managing Partner of McGladrey, Hendrickson & Co. from 1966 to 1982. He has served as the Chairman of the Board of the American Institute of Certified Public Accountants, on a number of its committees, and is currently a member of its Council. He has also served as a trustee of the Financial Accounting Foundation. His current research interests include leveraged buyouts, corporate audit committees, and entrepreneurial topics.

CHAPTER 4

SOURCES OF VALUE IN
MANAGEMENT BUYOUTS

Steven N. Kaplan *

There has been a tremendous amount of controversy and criticism about why MBOs have been so profitable. How can buyout investors pay a premium over the market price to take a company private and then earn an additional premium for themselves? In the MBOs of public companies that I have studied, the total premium or added value in the buyouts has averaged 80% net of market movements. My work has tried to answer where this value comes from.* There are four basic views.

One view, supported by Ivan Bull's evidence, is that MBOs combine several powerful incentives that lead to increased efficiency and value creation. Large debt service payments force managers to find ways to generate cash. If they succeed in making the payments, the managers can become rich through their relatively large equity stake in the buyout. On the other hand, if the company does not pay off the debt, the managers' equity will be worthless and their jobs probably gone (see DeAngelo & DeAngelo, 1987). In opposition to this value creation view, critics have charged that the buyouts do not create any useful value at all but rather transfer it from other parties to the buyout investors.

---

*The analysis and results I describe here can be found in Kaplan (1988).

There's the tax view, that all the profits come as gifts from the IRS in the form of interest and depreciation deductions (see Lowenstein, 1985). There's the labor view, that most of the gains come from firing employees.

And there's the underpricing view, that managers and buyout investors know a great deal about the company that public shareholders and other potential bidders do not. Under this view, public shareholders are stuck with a low price while the buyout investors end up with a hidden, but very valuable, "pot of gold" (see Gilson's discussion in Chapter 10).

The empirical evidence in my study favors the value creation views over the value transfer views. This evidence is taken from an analysis of a sample of large MBOs of publicly traded companies completed between 1980 and 1986. These companies were taken private at a cost of at least $50 million.

1. POST-BUYOUT OPERATIONS

The first question I considered was whether operating improvements are present. Supporters of the transfer view would predict that the improvements do not exist.

I found that operating income and operating margins in the first two years after the buyout were significantly higher than they were in the year prior to the buyout. These increases were larger, on average, than the increases for the typical company in the same industry.

The more efficient use of free cash flow within the company is another measure of operating improvements. Jensen (1986) has referred to this as the reduction of agency costs of free cash flow. The data are consistent with a more efficient use of cash within the company.

As a percentage of sales and compared to other companies in the same industry, capital expenditures of the buyouts decreased. This result is consistent with the buyout forcing managers to stop investing in unnecessary and inadvisable projects.

This result is also consistent with the criticism that the buyout companies do not invest enough. Although it is not yet possible to distinguish between these two positions with certainty, one should keep in mind that these companies are not high-tech companies. Instead, they tend to be low-tech companies in mature industries.

Working capital management also improved. Inventory to sales ratios for the buyout companies dropped after the buyout.

The improved operating performance translated into good coverage ratios and steady debt retirement. In fact, the median coverage ratio—the ratio of operating income to interest payments—in the first full post-buyout year was almost 2. Overall, the results suggest that operating improvements occurred and were an important determinant of the returns to the buyout investors.

There is one caveat to these results. I began with 76 buyouts of at least $50 million in size. I have obtained and analyzed post-buyout data for approximately 60% of these. These data come from 10Ks filed because the companies use public debt, from IPO prospectuses, and from 8Ks issued by purchasers of the buyout companies. It is conceivable, however, that those companies without post-buyout financial information performed differently. Nevertheless, the pattern of post-buyout results for the companies in the sample because of 10K filings is similar to that of the other companies in the sample. This is important because the companies that file 10Ks must file regardless of post-buyout performance.

The next question I addressed is whether the value transfer views have any merit. Under the tax view, tax benefits from interest and depreciation deductions should have explained most of the profits to buyout investors. Undeniably, interest deductions from the debt were large. Depreciation write-ups were less important. Only one-half the companies in the sample took them. And when they did, the depreciation was worth approximately one-half as much as the interest deductions. In total, the tax benefits were sizable, but probably not as large as the premium paid to public shareholders. Taxes cannot be the whole story.

In addition, the evidence suggests that the tax benefits themselves would not have been available without a large change in the company's ownership structure. I base this conclusion on the result that the pre-buyout capital structure of the buyout companies was not significantly different from that of other companies in the same industry. The buyouts do not seem to be companies that have unused debt capacity vis-à-vis their industry counterparts.

The second value transfer view is the "take it out of labor" view, according to which I should have found that buyouts are terrible for employment. To my surprise, I found that the number of employees in the typical MBO actually increased. To be fair to the critics, I could not measure whether wages decreased and I could not tell if some employees were fired while others were hired. The fact is that the level increased.

2. POST-BUYOUT RETURNS

The third transfer view is the underpricing view. So called reverse LBOs, in which buyouts go public, have generated huge returns for equity investors—the "pot of gold"—as well as most of the criticism that these returns are unfair. That criticism is off the mark. The returns are reasonable and, in fact, not surprising considering the effects of leverage, market movements, and operating improvements.

It is true that leverage can lead to big profits if the market goes up. For most of the 1980s prior to October 1987, the stock market moved in one direction—up. For example, the total return on the market from early 1985 to the end of 1986 was about 50%. If I had been smart (and I wasn't), I would have taken $10,000 of my own money, borrowed $90,000 from a bank, and invested the $100,000 in the market in early 1985. If I had, I would have ended up with $30,000 at the end of 1986 after repaying interest and principal—triple my money. The large equity returns in buyouts have benefited from this same leverage effect.

I examined whether the total return to all capital (debt and equity) invested in the buyouts beat the return that capital would have earned on the market during the same period. For the companies I could value after the buyout, the answer is a strong yes. The total return from the buyouts beat the market by approximately 80%. (The average is over 109%, the median 57%.)

How was that 80% divided between post-buyout investors and pre-buyout public shareholders? The average return to the post-buyout investors was approximately 40% greater than the market return. So even when controlling for leverage and market movements, the buyout investors did extremely well.

At the same time, the public shareholders also received a return approximately 40% over the market to let the company go private. The two groups more or less split the total gains of 80% in the buyout. Public shareholders got a big slice of the total pie.

The existence of increased value in the buyouts still leaves open the question of what factors drive the returns to the public shareholders and to the buyout investors. It turns out that a $1 increase in the total potential tax benefits was associated with a $0.70 increase in the market-adjusted return to public shareholders. At the same time, $1 of tax benefits was not related to the returns to the buyout investors. The public shareholders effectively captured all the tax benefits in the premium they receive. The buyout investors must earn their market adjusted returns from some other source.

Operating income is one such source. A $1 increase in post-buyout operating income was associated with a $7 payoff to the buyout investors. At the same time, the returns to the public shareholders were unrelated to post-buyout changes in operating income. The buyout investors appear to reap the rewards of implementing operating improvements.

At this point, I still have to address the evidence on underpricing. A value transfer proponent would argue that the company and the public shareholders could have and would have obtained the entire 80% value increase from tax benefits and the operating improvements without the buyout. As I mentioned earlier, the evidence suggests that the tax benefits would not be available without the buyout changes in incentives. However, it is still possible to argue that the operating improvements would have occurred anyway. If this is the case, then the buyout investors would have known about the operating improvements at the time of the buyout, whereas the public shareholders would have been unaware of those improvements.

There are several reasons why I think this is unlikely. First, in most buyouts, managers provide public shareholders with projections of sales and operating income. With the underpricing story, I should have found that the companies routinely did better than the projections. Instead, the opposite was true; the projections were overly optimistic (probably to ensure financing).

Second, underpricing implies that everybody who knows the "true" value of the company will invest in the buyout to get their pot of gold. In fact, many managers and directors sell their shares and leave the company. In my sample, those managers and directors who did not participate in the buyouts owned an average of $22 million or almost 10% of the company. If the public shareholders got a low price, then these managers and directors with big stakes who did not invest in the buyout got a low price and they knew it.

Furthermore, buyouts of public companies are not announced or completed in a vacuum. If a price is low, a buyout announcement will trigger intense interest from other potential bidders. During the same time period as my sample, 46 companies announced large MBOs that were not completed. Of these companies, 34 were taken over by a nonmanagement bidder.

At other times, the interest of other bidders triggers the buyout. Approximately one-third of the buyouts in my sample either defeated a competing offer or announced the buyout after a hostile party had accumulated a 5% (or greater) stake in the company. Since 1986, the buyout market, if anything, has become more competitive.

3. CONCLUSION

Where does all this leave us? I have made five basic arguments about the profitability of the buyouts in my sample. The total returns created by the buyouts for public shareholders and post-buyout investors have been large, approximately 80% above the market return. Those returns have not come from firing slews of employees. The returns do not appear to have come from cheating public shareholders. Tax benefits have been important and were captured by the public shareholders in the premium they received. Finally, operating improvements were made by the buyouts and were strongly related to the returns to the buyout investors.

These results suggest that the combined incentives of a large debt load and a larger equity stake exert a powerful positive force on management efficiency and on corporate value.

REFERENCES

DeAngelo, H. & DeAngelo, L. (1987, May-June). Management buyouts of publicly traded corporations. *Financial Analysts Journal*, 38-49.

Jensen, M. (1986, May). Agency costs of free cash flow, corporate finance and takeovers. *American Economic Review, 76*, 323-329.

Kaplan, S. (1988). Sources of value in management buyouts. (Unpublished doctoral dissertation, Harvard University, Cambridge, MA).

Lowenstein, L. (1985, May). Management buyouts. *Columbia Law Review, 85*, 730-784.

ABOUT THE AUTHOR

Steven N. Kaplan is an Assistant Professor of Finance at the Graduate School of Business of the University of Chicago. He earned his PhD in Business Economics from Harvard University. His research focuses on issues in corporate control and corporate finance. Prior to his PhD studies, Professor Kaplan held positions with Kidder, Peabody & Co. and Booz, Allen & Hamilton. He has also worked at the National Bureau of Economic Research.

CHAPTER 5

OBSERVATIONS ON RECENT DEVELOPMENTS IN LEVERAGED BUYOUTS

Alfred C. Eckert III

I would like to make some brief observations about the history of the LBO phenomenon. I shall present my views about some of the factors that have affected the explosion in the activity and make a brief comment on what I think are widely held myths about the effects of LBOs on the American financial scene.

Six years ago, it would have been very difficult to hold a conference on LBOs since most people didn't know what they were. Now, people in the street see headlines about them on the cover of *Time* magazine. I cannot think of anything in the world of finance that in my lifetime has gone so fast from an obscure sidelight to the front of consciousness, both in society at large and certainly in the business community. Rare is the chief executive of a company of any size today who has not had many LBO analyses done for him by his staff and his investment bankers. Rare is the financial institution that has not either invested in parts of LBOs or considered investing. And rare is the division management of any division of a publicly held company in this country that has not dreamed of becoming rich after reading about Gibson-Greeting and other windfalls.

Before 1981, LBOs were characterized as relatively small transactions, generally less than $50 million, where the purchase price was approximately equal to the assets and the financing was a mortgage. There wasn't anything particularly magical about them. They were called "bootstrap" transactions or "bottom-crawling." They generally involved businesses that weren't very exciting or attractive, that were in effect sold for their net asset value. Their size was restricted by both the convention of financing the transaction within a secured basis tied to the asset value and the lack of the number of participants interested in doing them.

In 1981, this was changed by Kohlberg, Kravis , Roberts & Co. in a transaction called "Houdaille." For the first time a $400 million transaction was done where the financing wasn't tied directly to the amount of assets. The bank financing was the first "cash flow loan," in which the banks decided that, instead of looking strictly at current assets and plant and equipment to determine the amount of senior debt, they would look at the cash flow coverage of the enterprise. This not particularly startling breakthrough in finance does give some indication of the conservative nature of the banking community before that time.

This event ushered in the era of the $500 million LBO. Banks were financing 50% to 60% of the assets. Then there was an explosion in the types of LBOs that could be done: not just mundane businesses, but all types of businesses—television stations that had no assets but very predictable cash flows, Coca-Cola bottling franchises, and a wide variety of other types of businesses. "Mezzanine," or subordinated, debt was generally provided by insurance companies. Now, this became the binding constraint on size, because even if you got Prudential, Equitable, and Metropolitan, for example, it was difficult to arrange for more than about $125 million in subordinated debt. Given the way the numbers worked, that meant it was pretty hard to do more than a $500 million LBO. People talked about it, but the constraint was the private placement of the subordinated debt.

In 1985, the junk bond market exploded, changing from financing for companies that were either in trouble or growing to acquisition financing, as pioneered by Drexel Burnham Lambert. A large number of new players came into the business. Suddenly, there was no $500 million cap. People began talking about transactions of $1 billion. During the first part of 1985, I remember speaking to people at a conference, discussing the chances for a billion dollar LBO someday. I think we all agreed the chances were 50-50. Later that year, people began talking about $5 billion LBOs. The size exploded, because of the junk bond market, $100 to $150 billion market, 75 to 100 very sophisticated players who can put up $50 million for a single transaction, and all publicly financed. All the constraints from the insurance companies disappeared.

That's both the good news and the bad news. The good news is you could do anything. The bad news is you could do anything.

Companies that should not have been LBO'd were being leveraged up. When talking about excesses, we used to say, "Equitable, Prudential, Metropolitan will keep the prices in line." Well, that went away.

At the same time, the whole concept was gaining social acceptability in the board rooms of corporate America. The Macy's transaction was probably the one that people will look to as the breakthrough. There is probably no bigger household name than "Macy's" and the chairman, basically frustrated by the prospects for future stock market-related incentives for key executives, said, "I want to buy that company for $4.5 billion." It wasn't smooth, but it got done. Suddenly, every CEO looked at what Ed Finkelstein stood to make on the transaction and what it had done to his organization to spread stock around to 300 executives, and all those CEOs said, "I want to get in on this." Then we had the start of a runaway train.

But just when you think it is time for the financial market to self-correct and dampen the activity, in 1987 we had the advent of the "junk zero." Then, not only could you do a deal as big as you wanted, you could pay whatever you wanted, because the junk zero simply said "I promise to pay you in the future." There was a liquid market for these securities, and if the lendable value of an enterprise was $100 and you wanted to pay $110, you put $10 worth of "I promise to pay in the future" notes. That is when we saw a dramatic run-up in the multiples of cash flow that were paid in LBOs.

Up until that time, mathematical analyses would show a rough correlation between the level of interest rates and the multiples of pretax, depreciated income. It shot up 25% in 1987. Until the crash came, it looked as though there would be LBOs pricing in the double-digit, pretax multiples. When you think about it, with interest rates where they were, it doesn't take much arithmetic to see that an immense amount of growth in the basic business was required to enable the paying of this level of debt.

So how far have we gone since 1981? From mundane, slow-growth, highly predictable cash flow businesses, conservatively priced, to any kind of business at any kind of price, with the true mortgaging in the future.

Why did this happen? I touched on one of the major factors: the development of the junk bond market. Second were the commercial banks.

Commercial banks were under tremendous pressure after the deregulation of deposits, and they did not have good places to put their money. They loaned all they could to the Third World, they loaned all they could to the oil and gas industry. They needed something new. They had up-front fees and margins over prime, and literally billions of dollars have been placed by commercial banks into these transactions.

I might add that there is speculation these LBO loans are very risky things for banks. I heartily disagree. I think the banks have been very clever this time. These loans are structured on a very secure basis. Unless there is a drop of 30% to 40% in the value of the business, the banks will come out secured. The risk is not being borne by the banks. There is risk being borne, but not by them.

Looking behind the numbers in the investment banking industry to see how much of the revenues have come from LBOs, directly or indirectly, can be startling. The fees provide a lot of money, which provides a strong impetus for this kind of transaction. Currently, $15 billion has been raised from the setting up of LBO funds, by people who are doing it for fees and profit overhead. That's even a better deal than investment banking fees. This money was the fuel for $150 billion in LBOs, in normal 10-to-1 debt construction.

Nothing breeds excess like success. For six years, everything has gone straight up. Unfortunately, people began to believe that the rising stock market was not as important as their own genius in structuring these transactions, and that is dangerous. It is dangerous because the economy is obviously not going to continue up forever. I'm concerned that there are transactions structured right before the decline of business that will be in serious trouble.

I think it is clear that the LBO is not some genie that will be put back into the bottle. This is a fundamental transformation for the long term for financing in this country. There have been and will be more discussions about whether this is good, bad, or indifferent for the country as a whole.

I make two observations. First, it is clear that if you believe in a capitalist system, having the managers be owners rather than having the managers be custodians has got to be a plus. The productivity and cost reduction that have come about in these transactions is staggering. The efficiencies created in the economy by this phenomenon have been overlooked, while what the media and sometimes the regulators focus on is the amount of money being made. Yes, money has been made, but risks have been taken. By and large, the productivity improvements, in my judgment, far offset the social disadvantage of allowing some people to become very wealthy.

Second, from a finance point of view, we have the opportunity to have a financial structure with more options. If we stay with the basics, the mundane, slow-growth businesses to compete for equity should have a large amount of debt because they have less operational risk in the business—that's fundamental finance. It's hard to practice that in a conglomerate where one business should be 10-to-1 debt equity and the other should be "no debt." Decoupling and de-conglomeration is financially efficient as well.

ABOUT THE AUTHOR

Alfred C. Eckert III was graduated from Northwestern University in 1971 and received his MBA from Harvard University in 1973. He joined Goldman, Sachs & Co. in June 1973 and was named a Partner in 1984. Presently he is Chief of Operations, Global Finance Department and serves as Director of Georgia Gulf Corporation.

PART 2

LEGAL ASPECTS OF MANAGEMENT BUYOUTS

CHAPTER 6

REPRESENTING A PUBLIC COMPANY IN A LEVERAGED BUYOUT TRANSACTION

Lawrence Lederman

Barry A. Bryer

1. INTRODUCTION[1]

The level of LBOs, though lower than that reached in the fourth quarter of 1986, remained significant throughout most of 1987. Transactions consummated in 1987 included the $4.4 billion buyout of Borg-Warner, the $3.7 billion LBO of Owens-Illinois, and the $2.1 billion buyout of Lear Siegler. Announced or commenced during 1987 were the $4.9 billion buyout of Southland, owner of the 7-Eleven chain of convenience stores, and the $3.4 billion buyout of Jim Walter, the Florida housing and construction company.

The outlook for the future, however, is uncertain. While it is still too early to adequately assess the long-term impact of the October 19, 1987, stock market collapse on the availability of financing for leveraged transactions, the crash and other economic factors, such as the current weakness of the U.S. dollar, have had a dampening effect on the market's receptiveness toward so-called junk bonds, which are essential to the successful consummation of many such transactions. The steep market decline was widely viewed as the cause for Southland's and Jim Walter's buyout groups' inability to sell the debt necessary to complete the acquisitions.

An additional source of uncertainty is the income tax reform proposal, currently under serious consideration by the House of Representatives, to deny deductibility to interest exceeding $5 million per year (whatever its form) directly or indirectly supporting either (1) the acquisition of a majority of the stock of another corporation or (2) the redemption of a majority of the issuer's stock. If enacted, the proposal would virtually preclude LBOs.

In general, there were fewer landmark decisions in 1987 affecting LBO transactions than in the previous year, when the Delaware Supreme Court and federal appeals courts in New York and Michigan embraced the policy that, once a decision to sell the company has been made, a board of directors must maintain a so-called level playing field and thus may not favor one bidder over another. These decisions are discussed in Section 3. Having thus determined that it is desirable to sell the company, the board assumes an affirmative duty to maximize stockholder values. If the board does not act as a neutral auctioneer, it must be prepared to defend its actions as being in the best interests of the stockholders before a court that has been increasingly willing to substitute its judgment for that of the board's.

The factors relevant to the consideration of an LBO proposal by the board of directors of a publicly held company, in part, are no different from those relevant to the consideration of a proposal for a negotiated sale of the company to an unrelated third party. In either case, the board's paramount obligation is to determine whether the proposed transaction is in the best interests of the company's stockholders. However, because the acquiring group in an LBO typically includes officers, directors and/or major stockholders of the company, special attention must be given to the fairness of the proposed transaction to the company as an entity and to its public stockholders. In addition, in light of the recent judicial pronouncements mentioned above, it can be argued persuasively that the board must be willing, at a minimum, to subject the transaction to free market forces even if it does not affirmatively go out and shop the company.

This chapter examines some of the fairness and other issues to be addressed by the board of directors of a publicly held Delaware corporation and its counsel in connection with the consideration of a proposal for an LBO of the company by a group that includes members of senior management of the company, some of whom are also directors of the company.

2. STRUCTURING THE DECISION-MAKING PROCESS

Weinberger v. UOP, Inc. and the Requirement of Entire Fairness

LBOs almost invariably precipitate stockholder litigation.[2] Indeed, it is not unusual for the first suit to be filed within hours of the announcement of a proposed transaction. Such suits allege, among other things, breach of fiduciary duty by the directors of the target company. In view of the substantial likelihood of litigation, the parties to the buyout must proceed carefully to avoid having the conflicts inherent in the situation taint the "fairness" of the buyout under state law standards.

Except for the recent Revlon, SCM, and Fruehauf cases, most of the relevant precedents regarding the appropriate discharge of a director's fiduciary duties in the context of an LBO transaction have arisen in the context of parent-subsidiary mergers and other forms of going-private transactions. Because such cases rest on concepts of fiduciary duty, it is reasonable to assume that a court applying Delaware law would review the buyout in light of the general principles enunciated by the Delaware courts in the going-private context.[3] The going-private cases establish a procedural framework which must be followed by the board in evaluating the "fairness" of the buyout. The Revlon, SCM, and Fruehauf cases, discussed in Section 3, build on the procedural framework established in the going-private area, embracing the proposition that the board must provide a level playing field for all bidders once it determines that the company is up for sale.

The same conflict of interest and self-dealing concerns inherent in parent-subsidiary mergers are presented by the buyout. The management members of the buyout group have a direct conflict of interest, for they have determined to acquire the company, whether or not the timing of the buyout is in the best interests of stockholders, and the members of the buyout group will be financially best served if they pay the lowest practicable price.[4] Furthermore, the management members of the buyout group will have access to information about the company not available to stockholders generally or to other potential acquirers of the company and will be in a position to influence the nature and scope of the information given to stockholders in the proxy statement. Moreover, as in the case of a parent corporation considering the eventual acquisition of the remaining equity of a subsidiary, the management members of the buyout group might conceivably be in a position to manipulate the company's financial status so as to reduce its apparent value and thus the cost of the buyout.

The leading Delaware case in the going-private area is Weinberger v. UOP, Inc. (457 A.2d 701, Del. Sup. 1983). The Weinberger decision arose out of a stockholders' class action challenging the cash-out of public stockholders of UOP, Inc., through a merger with The Signal Companies, a then 50.5% UOP stockholder. The suit alleged, among other things, that the merger was unfair and that the proxy statement used to solicit the approval of minority stockholders was misleading. Prior to the merger, a feasibility study had been prepared by two Signal representatives on UOP's board concerning Signal's possible acquisition of the balance of the outstanding UOP stock. The study, which utilized UOP internal information, concluded that an acquisition of the remaining shares at any price up to $24 per share would be a good investment for Signal. Nevertheless, Signal initially proposed a price of $20 to $21 per share.[5] The feasibility study was not disclosed to UOP's independent directors or to UOP's minority stockholders when they considered the proposed merger with Signal. UOP retained the investment banking firm of Lehman Brothers Kuhn Loeb, which had previously performed investment banking services for UOP and was familiar with its business, to opine as to the fairness of the proposed merger. After a summary review, Lehman Brothers delivered an opinion that a price of $21 was fair.[6] The independent directors of UOP then approved the merger. A majority of the voting minority of such stockholders subsequently approved the merger.

In holding that the circumstances of the merger failed to satisfy the fairness standards of Delaware law, the Delaware Supreme Court stated:

> Given the absence of any attempt to structure this transaction on an arm's length basis, [Signal] cannot escape the effects of the conflicts it faced, particularly when its designees on [UOP's] board did not totally abstain from participation in the matter. There is no "safe harbor" for such divided loyalties in Delaware. When directors of a Delaware corporation are on both sides of a transaction, they are required to demonstrate their utmost good faith and the most scrupulous inherent fairness of the bargain. The requirement of fairness is unflinching in its demand that when one stands on both sides of the transaction, he has the burden of establishing its entire fairness (Weinberger, p. 710).

As analyzed by the Delaware Supreme Court, the concept of entire fairness resolves into two components: fair dealing and fair price. "Fair dealing," in the court's view, "embraces questions of when the transaction was timed, how it was initiated, structured, negotiated, disclosed to directors, and how the approvals of the directors and the stockholders were obtained." "Fair price," the court noted, "relates to the economic and financial considerations of the proposed merger, including all relevant factors: assets, market value, earnings, future prospects, and any other elements that affect the intrinsic or inherent value of a company's stock."

Although fair dealing does not ensure that a fair price will be realized, the Delaware Supreme Court's implicit view is that it greatly increases the probability of such realization.

Fair Dealing—The Role of the Independent Committee

The decision in Weinberger highlights the importance of structuring the board's decision-making process regarding the buyout with certain procedural safeguards in place. Although no specific requirements have been mandated by the courts or the SEC, certain guidelines for structuring the procedural aspects of the buyout can be formulated based on Weinberger and the disclosure requirements of Rule 13e-3 promulgated under the Securities Exchange Act of 1934, as amended (the Exchange Act).

The Weinberger court placed great weight on the absence of a committee of independent directors, saying, "the result here could have been entirely different if UOP had appointed an independent negotiating committee of its outside directors to deal with Signal at arm's length.... Since fairness in this context can be equated to a theoretical, wholly independent board of directors acting upon the matter before them, it is unfortunate that this course apparently was neither considered nor pursued " (Weinberger, p. 709).

The court's emphasis on the importance of a bargaining process indicates its skepticism as to the protections provided by structuring the merger to require the vote of a majority of the minority stockholders. Such a structure denies the minority the benefits that they might obtain from having informed fiduciaries bargain on their behalf and may result in stockholder approval of what is a second-best alternative. Such a structure, however, does shift to the plaintiff the burden of proving that the merger is unfair. Note the similarity between Weinberger's emphasis on the bargaining process and the emphasis in the Fruehauf case on the auction process.

The Weinberger "entire fairness" analysis was applied by the Delaware Supreme Court in upholding the fairness of the merger of Getty Oil Co. and its publicly held subsidiary Skelly Oil Co. (Rosenblatt v. Getty Oil Co., 493 A.2d 929, Del. Sup. 1985). The court cited the "adversarial" nature of the negotiations and noted with approval the fact that the divergence in objectives ensured the arm's-length quality of the bargaining. Getty, knowing that it would be sued in connection with the merger, assiduously sought to comply with Delaware law, while Skelly persistently sought the highest possible price for its shares.

However, in another post-Weinberger decision, the Delaware Chancery Court in Wilen v. Pollution Control Industries, Inc. (10 Del. J. Corp. L. 357, Del. Ch. Oct. 15, 1984) held that the absence of arm's-length negotiations standing alone does not state a legally cognizable claim.

In the SCM case, discussed in Section 3 the United States Court of Appeals for the Second Circuit stated that in the context of a defensive LBO it would be unreasonable to expect management, having a financial interest in the transaction, to fully represent stockholders' interests; therefore, the independent directors have an important duty to protect stockholder interests. The court stated that although the establishment of an independent committee to negotiate on behalf of the board is not strictly required, such steps would certainly have been appropriate under the circumstances.

Note, however, that in the Fruehauf case discussed in Section 3, the court held that the authorization of a buyout transaction by the disinterested directors, even after complete disclosure, is not sufficient to establish that the transaction is fair and reasonable where such directors, in dereliction of their fiduciary duty to the corporation and its stockholders, merely "rubber stamped" the buyout proposal.

In view of Weinberger's emphasis on the subject, the board's decision-making process should be structured to maximize the role of the independent directors.

If the directors who are members of the buyout group constitute a minority of the board, the disinterested majority can act for the board, with the buyout group members abstaining from both the vote and participation in the deliberations on the buyout. If a majority of the board is not disinterested, the board can delegate to a committee of independent directors (the independent committee) the power to review and/or negotiate the terms of the buyout.[7] The board can then act on the recommendation of the independent committee.[8]

At a minimum, in the context of the buyout, "independent" means a nonmanagement director who will not be investing in the ongoing private entity (Newco) resulting from the buyout. Further guidance as to what constitutes independence may be found in the rules of the New York Stock Exchange relating to the composition of audit committees. The NYSE rules require that an audit committee be "comprised solely of directors independent of management and free from any relationship that, in the opinion of [the] Board of Directors, would interfere with the exercise of independent judgment as a committee member."[9]

In the event that there are only one or two independent directors, the advisability of delegating authority to such a director or directors must be assessed in light of the circumstances. If the one or two independent directors are not sufficiently qualified to adequately review (and, if necessary, negotiate) the buyout, it may be best either to postpone the buyout until the board can be strengthened or to cause such independent directors on their own to select and retain experienced counsel who can advise them appropriately.

It is possible that the buyout group may ask current members of the board (including the members of the independent committee) to stay on after the consummation of the buyout. Counsel should consider the impact on the company's litigation position of a decision by the members of the independent committee to remain on the board of Newco. In this regard, in Radol v. Thomas (772 F.2d 244, 6th Cir. 1985; cert. denied, 106 S. Ct. 3272, 1986), the Circuit Court held that the fact that a target company's board had been requested to remain after a merger did not create a sufficient conflict of interest to undermine the presumption of good faith. In both the Metromedia and ARA Services LBOs, the directors continued on the board after the transaction and no issue was raised in the attendant litigation.

The importance of maximizing the independence of the independent committee is illustrated by the result in the Revlon case, discussed in Section 3. The Delaware Chancery Court, in enjoining a lock-up option granted by the Revlon board to a white knight buyout group, questioned the independence of the Revlon board. According to the court, the Revlon board was "composed of fourteen members, six of whom held prominent positions in Revlon's management, two of whom held significant blocks of stock with most of the remaining nonmanagement directors having an association with entities which did business with Revlon."

The importance of an active independent committee and the committee's role as a surrogate for an arm's-length seller were also recently reaffirmed by the Delaware Chancery Court in Freedman v. Restaurant Associates Industries, Inc. (Civ. Action No. 9212, Del. Ch. Oct. 15, 1987), where the court, in refusing preliminarily to enjoin an MBO proposal or to require the company to accept the terms proposed by a third-party offerer, had the following observations on the place of independent committees in fiduciary duty analyses:

> Heavy reliance is placed upon the acts of specially constituted committees of disinterested directors when Delaware courts are asked to review the propriety of corporate transactions that involve elements or claims of self-dealing. See, e.g., Weinberger v. UOP, Del. Supr., 457 A.2d 701, 709 n.7 (1983). While that reliance may, given the informal relations that may exist between board members, be seen as providing a possible escape-hatch for the unprincipled, cases such as this demonstrate that this technique of negotiation, when pursued in good faith, is a close surrogate for the structure that ordinarily provides protection to shareholders. Here there is no structural reason to doubt the effectiveness of the independent committee—it was appropriately constituted, well advised and active. Moreover, the results it achieved bespeak an aggressive and effective attempt to maximize public shareholder values.

The record in Restaurant Associates indicated that the independent committee bargained assiduously with both management, whose initial offers were rejected out-of-hand as inadequate, and the competing third-party bidder, whose numerically superior but highly conditional offer the Committee ultimately decided not to pursue.

Whether a committee or a disinterested majority of the board is acting, staffing problems will arise. It has been assumed that the chairman and CEO and several other key executives will be members of the buyout group. In addition, the staff accountants, lawyers, and other experts employed by the company who normally provide staff work for the board are likely to have divided loyalties insofar as they may be future employees of Newco. If the independent committee is to function properly, it must be supported by the advice of experts on whom it can rely for guidance and who themselves are independent and free of conflicts. Consequently, once the independent committee is formed, it should promptly retain its own outside legal counsel and independent financial advisor.

The independent committee's legal counsel will, among other things, advise the independent committee with respect to its fiduciary obligations to the stockholders and the other legal ramifications of the buyout, including any litigation that may be initiated, as well as assist in the preparation and negotiation of the acquisition agreement and other relevant documents.

The independent committee's financial advisor will assist in reviewing the financial terms of the proposed buyout and will render an opinion as to whether such terms are fair from a financial point of view to the company's stockholders.

Fair Price—The Financial Advisor's Opinion

The issue of fair price is particularly sensitive in an LBO because the acquired company's own assets substantially provide the financing to purchase the company. Any lawsuit brought in connection with the buyout is likely to challenge the offering price as unfair.

In almost all LBOs, the price to be received by the public stockholders is significantly above the market price immediately before public announcement of the transaction. However, in and of itself, even a large premium will not serve to establish conclusively the financial fairness of the price. On the other hand, the offering price need not be above book value to be fair. Many companies do not earn a reasonable return on their assets and the market price reflects the return on equity. In such a case, a purchase at book value could fairly represent a substantial premium.

Before Weinberger, the Delaware courts had essentially adopted the rule that the valuation method to be used in testing the financial fairness of a transaction was the one traditionally used in determining the fair value to which a dissenting stockholder was entitled when his or her shares were appraised. Under this so-called Delaware block method, market value, book value, and the investment value (including earnings and dividend records) were determined. The appraiser then assigned a weight to each value based on his overall judgment of the prospects and circumstances of the appraised corporation and computed a weighted average of the values.

In adopting Rule 13e-3, the SEC seemed to have had this method in mind. Schedule 13E-3 requires a detailed discussion of the factors on which the issuer's opinion of the transaction's fairness is based. For the most part these factors are similar to those traditionally considered in appraisal proceedings and include (1) current market prices, (2) historical market prices, (3) net book value, (4) going concern value, (5) liquidation value, (6) the price paid in purchases by the issuer or its affiliate over the previous two fiscal years, (7) any report, opinion, or appraisal received by the issuer or its affiliate relating to the fairness of the transaction, and (8) other firm offers during the preceding 18 months for merger, consolidation, or sale of assets of the issuer or for sale of securities of the issuer sought in order to exercise control. In addition, Rule 13e-3 requires a statement of the weight given each of these factors, corresponding to the approach used in the Delaware appraisal cases at the time Rule 13e-3 was adopted. Rule 13e-3 does not explicitly require that an investment banker be asked to render a fairness opinion, but it does require the issuer to disclose any fairness opinions that are prepared by an outside party.

In Weinberger, the Delaware Supreme Court acknowledged that the Delaware block method was "clearly outmoded and mandated that the question of valuation be approached in terms of contemporary financial market theories and practices." The court adopted a more liberal approach, permitting proof of value "by any techniques or methods which are generally considered acceptable in the financial community and otherwise admissible in court." Thus the fairness of the price being offered may be determined by looking at the "economic and financial considerations of the proposed merger, including all relevant factors: assets, market value, earnings, future prospects, and any other elements that affect the intrinsic or inherent value of a company's stock" (457 A.2d at 711). Accordingly, the Delaware Supreme Court decided that the lower court in Weinberger should have considered evidence offered by the plaintiffs of premiums over market price paid in similar acquisitions.

In view of Weinberger's liberalized approach to valuation, it is essential that the independent committee establish a record that the consideration proposed to be paid in the buyout is fair. This objective usually is achieved in large part by having the financial advisor render an opinion as to the fairness of the acquisition price to the company's public stockholders from a financial point of view.[10]

Although a favorable opinion does not itself establish fairness, it would be highly unlikely for the buyout to proceed at a price found unfair by the financial advisor.

All relations between the financial advisor and the buyout group, on the one hand, and the company, on the other, must be disclosed. Such relations may include past service as an underwriter, agent, or broker.

Ideally, the financial advisor's compensation should not be contingent on consummation of the buyout; such an arrangement may be viewed as undermining independence, as discussed below.

The financial advisor will generally be in constant communication with the independent committee and will convey to the independent committee some sense of its conclusions long before any report is finalized. If it is clear that there is a substantial likelihood of an adverse report from the financial advisor, the independent committee will be well advised to undertake negotiations to raise the price to be paid in the buyout to a more acceptable level.

However, even where the financial advisor indicates that the proposed consideration is in a fair range, the independent committee should carefully consider the desirability of conducting negotiations to improve the offer as an intrinsic element of the members' duty to unaffiliated stockholders. Such negotiations should be avoided only when there is a reasonable possibility that they will cause the withdrawal of an offer that the independent committee considers fair and in the best interests of the unaffiliated stockholders. See Section 3.

Weinberger and subsequent cases demonstrate the necessity of establishing a record that the financial advisor conducted a thorough and extensive analysis of the company and the buyout prior to rendering its fairness opinion.

The Weinberger court gave little credence to the Lehman Brothers opinion because it found that it was hastily drawn and based on cursory preparation. Although Lehman Brothers was familiar with UOP from prior engagements, the court was particularly struck by the facts that the opinion was drafted over a weekend after short notice from the Signal board and the price term was left blank until just prior to the execution of the merger agreement. The court was also critical of Signal for not disclosing these facts to the independent directors of UOP and to the minority stockholders. The court's opinion suggests that the minority stockholders should have been informed of the circumstances surrounding the preparation of the fairness opinion to avoid the impression that it had been the result of a careful study.

Another Delaware case, Joseph v. Shell Oil Company (482 A.2d. 335, Del. Ch. 1984), is instructive. Defendant Royal Dutch Petroleum Company indirectly controlled 69.5% of the outstanding common shares of Shell Oil Company and was directly represented on Shell's board of directors. In 1982, Royal Dutch considered acquiring the minority shares of Shell and retained Morgan Stanley & Co., Incorporated, to prepare an estimate of the value of those shares. No such acquisition was made at that time, but early in 1984 Royal Dutch decided to proceed with the acquisition and requested Morgan Stanley to update its 1982 valuation. Eight days later, Morgan Stanley opined that the shares were worth $53 per share and expressly stated in its opinion that its valuation was based only on publicly available information and that it was not furnished with any detailed information on Shell's probable oil reserves. Royal Dutch proceeded to propose a merger in which it would acquire the minority shares at a price of $55 per share. A special committee of Shell directors rejected the offer, based in part on the opinion of its financial advisor, Goldman, Sachs & Co., that the minority shares were worth $80 to $85 per share and the opinion of Shell's president that the shares could be worth as much as $91 per share under certain circumstances. The special committee instead proposed a merger price of $75 per share, which Goldman, Sachs opined was in the "lower range" of a fair price. Royal Dutch responded by withdrawing its merger proposal and commencing a tender offer to purchase all the minority shares at a price of $58 per share.

The Delaware Court of Chancery preliminarily enjoined the Royal Dutch offer on the grounds that Royal Dutch breached its fiduciary duty to the minority stockholders by failing to make full and complete disclosure of all facts pertinent to the transaction. The court was most troubled by the fact that: (1) Royal Dutch withheld from Morgan Stanley essential information concerning the value of Shell's probable oil reserves—the "single most valuable asset of Shell"; (2) Royal Dutch failed to disclose to stockholders that "essential" information had been withheld from Morgan Stanley, upon whose appraisal stockholders had been asked to rely; (3) Royal Dutch's tender offer materials failed to make clear that Morgan Stanley's initial valuation opinion was arrived at after only eight days; (4) there was no disclosure of the fact that estimates of a $91 per share value had been made by some of Shell's management; and (5) there was incomplete disclosure of Shell's recent discoveries in the Beaufort Sea.

Although the court's findings may have been influenced by its belief that the tender offer price was unfair and the conduct of Royal Dutch was coercive, the court was clearly troubled by Morgan Stanley's opinion.

As the Weinberger and Joseph cases dramatically illustrate, the independent committee should make available to the financial advisor all the information which the latter believes is germane to its opinion and should give the financial advisor sufficient time to study such information thoroughly and perform such other analyses it deems relevant.

In Lynch v. Vickers Energy Corp. (383 A.2d 278, Del. Sup. 1977), which preceded Weinberger, the Delaware Supreme Court held that a majority stockholder owed a fiduciary duty of "complete candor" to the minority stockholders when seeking to purchase their shares through a tender offer.

The plaintiff in Vickers was a former stockholder of TransOcean Oil, Inc., who had tendered his shares in an offer made by Vickers Energy Corporation to acquire all outstanding shares of TransOcean. At the time of the tender offer, Vickers owned 53.5% of TransOcean's outstanding common shares. The court held that the plaintiff was not limited to appraisal rights because Vickers and the directors of TransOcean breached their fiduciary duty to the minority stockholders by failing to disclose that (1) a "highly qualified" geologist who was a member of TransOcean's management had calculated that TransOcean's net assets were worth significantly more than disclosed in the offer and (2) that Vickers' management had authorized open-market purchases of TransOcean stock at up to $15 per share immediately prior to its $12 per share offer. The court stated that the appropriate disclosure standard under the circumstances was that of completeness, not adequacy, and that the defendants had the duty to disclose "all germane facts."

In several cases, courts have enjoined directorial actions, faulting directors for relying on hastily prepared or inadequate fairness opinions.

In the SCM case, discussed in Section 3, the court held that SCM's directors breached their duty of care by granting a lock-up option without adequately considering the fairness of the option price. The court criticized the board for relying on the "conclusionary" opinion of its financial advisor.

In Dynamics Corp. of America v. CTS Corp. (794 F.2d 250, 7th Cir. 1986 ["CTS I"]; rev'd on other grounds, 107 S. Ct. 1637, 1987), the court, in enjoining a rights plan adopted by CTS Corporation in response to a partial tender offer by Dynamics Corporation of America, was critical of the fact that CTS failed to evaluate the DCA tender offer in a "dispassionate and thorough fashion." The court questioned how much weight could properly be placed on the fairness opinion of CTS's financial advisor Smith Barney when Smith Barney had been promised a bonus of $75,000 if CTS was successful in defeating DCA's efforts to gain control of CTS.

After the first rights plan was enjoined in CTS I, an independent committee of the CTS board determined that the company should be sold and that, pending the sale, a so-called back-end rights plan should be adopted. Smith Barney was hired to advise the independent committee regarding the back-end plan and to help the committee set an appropriate exercise price for the "rights." In Dynamics Corp. of America v. CTS Corp.

(805 F.2d 705, 7th Cir. 1986 ["CTS II"]), the court, while stating that the basic concept of the rights plan is valid and legal under Indiana and Delaware law, remanded the case due to its concerns regarding the procedure by which the back-end plan was adopted. The court was concerned that the $50 exercise price for the rights was unreasonably high and that Smith Barney's compensation might have been structured so as to bias its analysis in reaching the $50 price. The court was also troubled by the fact that Smith Barney never independently validated management's earnings projects upon which its analysis was based. The court's willingness to look beneath the surface of Smith Barney's analysis, questioning the price earnings multiple and earnings forecasts upon which Smith Barney's analysis was based, is a clear indication of the degree of heightened scrutiny to which fairness opinions may be subject (See CTS II, 805 F.2d, pp. 714-715).

"Entire Fairness"—The Availability of Nonappraisal Remedies

Stockholders of the company who are dissatisfied with the price being offered in the buyout will have recourse to the appraisal procedure specified by Section 262 of the Delaware General Corporation Law.

In Weinberger, the Delaware Supreme Court indicated that while ordinarily a stockholder challenging the fairness of a merger would be entitled to an appraisal proceeding under Section 262, such a proceeding might prove inadequate where there has been "fraud, misrepresentation, self-dealing, deliberate waste of corporate assets, or gross and palpable overreaching" (457 A.2d, p. 714).

Thus, in Jane Joseph v. Shell Oil Co. (498 A.2d 1117, Del. Ch. 1985), the Chancery Court refused to remit the plaintiffs to an appraisal proceeding, stating that a reasonable doubt that an appraisal proceeding would provide an adequate remedy was raised where the defendants had the burden of showing the entire fairness of the transaction, no negotiation as to price occurred, no vote of the subsidiary's directors or stockholders would ever occur and no guarantee existed that a short-term merger would ever take place.

In Rabkin v. Philip A. Hunt Chemical Corp. (498 A.2d 1099, Del. Sup. 1985), the court held that an appraisal remedy for minority stockholders may not be the only recourse where questions of procedural fairness having a reasonable bearing on substantial issues affecting the price being offered are the essential bases of the lawsuit. The court reversed a Chancery Court dismissal of a class action on the ground that, absent deception, Weinberger relegated aggrieved stockholders to the appraisal procedure.

On March 1, 1983, Olin Corp. bought 63.4% of the outstanding shares of common stock in Philip A. Hunt Chemical Corp. at $25 per share pursuant to a stock purchase agreement. The agreement provided that Olin would have to pay the same price if it acquired the remaining Hunt shares within one year. On March 23, 1984, Olin requested a fairness opinion from an investment banker as to its proposed purchase of the minority shares at $20 per share. The price was found to be fair, and a proposal to merge the companies was presented to Hunt's directors. Hunt's board obtained a fairness opinion that found the range of values for the shares to be from $19 to $25 per share and determined to accept the Olin offer despite its conclusion that while it was "fair," it was "not generous." The plaintiffs charged that the price was grossly inadequate because Olin unfairly manipulated the timing of the merger to avoid the one-year commitment, contrary to its fiduciary obligations.

The Rabkin court noted that Weinberger makes clear that appraisal is not necessarily the only remedy for a minority shareholder. The court says that "the trial court's narrow interpretation of Weinberger would render meaningless our extensive discussion of fair dealing found in that opinion."

Fair dealing was defined in Weinberger as embracing questions of when the transaction was timed; how it was initiated, structured, negotiated, and disclosed to the directors; and how the approval of the directors and the shareholders was obtained. In this regard, the Delaware Supreme Court in Rabkin stated: "While this duty of fairness certainly incorporates the principle that a cash-out merger must be free of fraud or misrepresentation, Weinberger's mandate of fair dealing does not turn solely on issues of deception."

The specific act of misconduct alleged was the denial of the $25 price the plaintiffs claim was guaranteed them by the stock purchase agreement. The court noted that the plaintiffs contended that Olin knew all along that it would eventually acquire Hunt, but it delayed doing so to avoid paying the minority $25 per share.

The court found that these are issues of procedural fairness that cannot be addressed by an appraisal nor by a motion to dismiss at this juncture of the proceedings. Noting the defendants' objection that they had no legal obligation to effect the cash-out merger during the one-year period, the court responded that inequitable conduct will not be protected merely because it is legal.

The significance of Rabkin in the context of the buyout is that it would permit the assertion of an "opt-out" class action for money damages, as distinguished from the "opt-in" procedure mandated by the appraisal statute. The uncertainty of the potential liability thus created may cause concern to potential lenders.

The Business Judgment Rule

Broadly speaking, the members of the independent committee properly constituted will enjoy the full protection of the business judgment rule. Under that rule, their obligation as fiduciaries is to act in good faith and on an informed basis in what they reasonably and honestly believe to be in the best interests of the company and its stockholders. If the decision of the independent committee is made in good faith, after due deliberation, and is reasonably based on the facts presented, its members can be confident that there will be no liability for actions taken with respect to the buyout.

In Smith v. Van Gorkom (488 A.2d 858, Del. Sup. Ct. 1985), one of only a few cases ever to impose personal liability upon directors of a major corporation for breach of their duty of care, the Delaware Supreme Court reversed the decision of the lower court and found directors of Trans Union Corporation personally liable for improvidently approving the acquisition of Trans Union by Marmon Group, Inc.

In September 1980, Jerome Van Gorkom, the Chairman of Trans Union, proposed to Jay Pritzker, the Chairman of Marmon, that Marmon acquire Trans Union for $55 per share (a price suggested by an LBO study by Donald Romans, the company's chief financial officer). Three days after meeting with Van Gorkom, Pritzker agreed to make a proposal to acquire Trans Union at $55 per share. His offer was conditioned on Trans Union board action within three days and on the granting of a lock-up option to acquire approximately 8% of Trans Union's outstanding common stock at $38 per share, slightly above the then current market price.

The Trans Union board approved the merger after a two-hour meeting held on one day's notice, which notice had not indicated the subject to be considered. At the meeting, the board heard oral presentations by three officers of the company, including an explanation by Romans of his studies as to the feasibility of an LBO. Romans told the board that his studies did not purport to indicate either a fair price for, or a valuation of, Trans Union. He did say, however, that in his opinion, $55 per share was at the low end of the range of fair prices for Trans Union's stock. No questions were raised by any directors, and no explanation was given concerning the basis for determining the merger price or Van Gorkom's role in proposing it.

The directors received a draft of the merger agreement at the meeting but had no opportunity to review it. Instead, the terms of the agreement were described to them by Van Gorkom, who himself had not read it. No other documentation summarizing the proposed transaction or supporting the adequacy of the price was made available. Moreover, Salomon Brothers, Inc., Trans Union's usual investment bankers, had not been invited to the meeting. Although the majority of Trans Union's senior management, other than Van Gorkom, had opposed the transaction, the board neither asked, nor was it told, about such opposition.

The merger agreement initially approved by Trans Union's board and executed by Van Gorkom prohibited the solicitation by the company of other acquisition proposals. It subsequently was amended to permit such solicitation as well as to provide for the termination of Trans Union's agreement with Marmon upon receipt of a better offer. Trans Union thereafter retained Salomon Brothers to solicit other bids. The Court noted that the press release announcing the engagement of Salomon Brothers also stated that Marmon had exercised the lock-up option and that if a more favorable offer were not received within four months, Trans Union's stockholders would meet to consider the merger.

In January 1981, General Electric Credit Corporation made a preliminary proposal to acquire Trans Union at a price of $57 to $60 a share but terminated discussions when Marmon refused to agree to a postponement of the scheduled stockholders' meeting. Kohlberg, Kravis, Roberts & Co. also made an offer to purchase Trans Union's assets for $60 per share. This offer was withdrawn, however, the same day that it was made.

Trans Union's proxy statement was mailed to its stockholders on January 21, 1981. The court noted that it did not disclose the basis of the merger price or the failure of Trans Union's board to obtain a valuation study. Five days later the board met and, after a lengthy meeting, voted to proceed with the Marmon merger. It also approved for mailing, on or about January 27, 1981, a supplement to its proxy statement. On February 10,

1981, the merger was approved by approximately 70% of Trans Union's stockholders.

The Supreme Court found that the directors had been grossly negligent, citing among other things its view that the Trans Union directors relied entirely on oral presentations and had no written documentation with respect to the proposal or the adequacy of the offering price; the board acted hastily, without prior consideration of the proposal, and had no prior knowledge of the subject of the directors' meeting; the premium over market price in the proposal was accepted without sufficient valuation information (such as a "fairness opinion" by an independent investment banker) and the market price of Trans Union's stock was an insufficient basis from which to measure the appropriateness of the offering price; the directors did not sufficiently provide for competing offers to be obtained; the directors did not make sufficient inquiry of members of management who presented the proposals to them; and the actions of the directors following approval of the merger agreement, including the amendments made to the agreement, did not cure the directors' inappropriate act in approving the acquisition. The court also held that the shareholders' vote approving the merger did not preclude liability and that the shareholders had not been appropriately informed by the proxy material relating to the transaction.

Although no self-dealing on the part of the directors was alleged, the court held that their duty of care was breached when they approved the merger agreement with inadequate information.

The court characterized the business judgment rule as "a presumption that in making a business decision, the directors of a corporation acted on an informed basis, in good faith and in the honest belief that the action taken was in the best interests of the company." The court then stated that the determination of whether a business judgment is an "informed one" turned on "whether the directors have informed themselves prior to making a business decision, of all material information reasonably available to them" (id., p. 872).

Of particular significance is the court's statement that the size of the premium did not justify the directors' determination that the merger price was fair. The court said that while a substantial premium may be one reason to recommend a merger, it could not provide the sole basis on which to assess the fairness of the purchase price. This was especially true because Trans Union's directors testified that they believed that the market price of Trans Union's stock did not adequately reflect the company's inherent value. The court expressly stated that it did not mean to imply an outside valuation is essential to an informed business decision or that fairness opinions are required as a matter of law. Under appropriate circumstances, it said, directors may rely on in-house valuation reports.

The court also rejected the directors' arguments that their provision for a market test and the failure of any other bidder to make a better offer validated their judgment that the merger price was fair. Although the court seemed to indicate that such a test could indicate a fair price, it found that in this case no effective test had been conducted. It noted the prohibition of solicitation included in the acquisition agreement initially approved by Trans Union's board, the grant of a lock-up option to Marmon, and the issuance of press releases that described the terms of its agreement with Marmon but did not disclose the company's right to terminate that agreement in the event that a better offer were made. The court also focused on evidence indicating that the merger agreement did not accurately reflect certain conditions that the board thought it had imposed.

Although Trans Union has been criticized as a major departure from the traditional application of the business judgment rule,[11] the opinion may be read to complement the broad discretion granted to the board of directors under earlier cases.

The Delaware Supreme Court's holding, in effect, is that if a board of directors has the power to formulate strategies that will determine the fundamental structure of the corporation's existence, it must act only after a thorough and reasoned analysis. Indeed, as Trans Union indicates, this responsibility cannot be transferred to the stockholders. The court states that "a director may not abdicate [his] duty by leaving to the shareholders alone the decision to approve or disapprove" proposed corporate action.

Trans Union highlights the importance of careful analysis and review by the board before any action is undertaken with respect to the buyout. Indeed, because of the inherent conflict of interest (which was absent in Trans Union), even greater care must be taken to create an unassailable record that procedures used to analyze the buyout were fair and that studies were done to establish that the price offered was fair.

In Unocal Corp. v. Mesa Petroleum Co. (493 A.2d 946, Del. Supr. 1985), the Delaware Supreme Court resoundingly reaffirmed the applicability of the business judgment rule to the decisions of directors in corporate control transactions when such decisions are taken in good faith after due deliberation. The court, however, introduced a new standard for applying the business judgment rule to actions taken by directors in the context of corporate control transactions. The court stated that in responding to a takeover proposal, directors must analyze the nature of the takeover and its potential effect on the corporation in order to ensure that any defensive measure taken is reasonable in relation to the threat posed (id., p. 955). The Unocal standard has been used by some courts to limit the discretion granted to directors under the business judgment rule.

In AC Acquisition Corp. v. Anderson Clayton & Co. (519 A.2d 103, Del. Ch. 1986), the court held that the directors of Anderson Clayton failed to meet the requirements of the Unocal standard in their efforts to provide shareholders with an economic alternative to a cash bid by Bear Stearns & Co. & Gruss & Co (BSG) for any and all shares.

On August 21, 1986, after Anderson Clayton's initial efforts to implement a recapitalization had been enjoined, BSG announced its intention to make a cash tender offer for all Anderson Clayton shares at $56 per share. On the next day, Anderson Clayton announced a cash self-tender offer for approximately 65% of the outstanding stock at $60 per share. The company announced that in connection with the self-tender it would sell stock to a newly created ESOP in an amount equal to 25% of the shares that would be outstanding after the self-tender. The proposed self-tender was a continuation of the recapitalization that the Anderson Clayton board had approved in February 1986. BSG sued to enjoin the self-tender on the grounds that it was an economically coercive transaction that in effect deprived stockholders of the option of choosing between the self-tender and the BSG offer.

The court held that the board was justified in its desire to present the stockholders with an economic alternative to the BSG offer and that, although the board's financial advisor could not call the BSG offer unfair, the board was fully within its power to seek an alternative transaction. The court concluded, however, that the coercive aspects of the self-tender were not reasonable in relation to the threat posed by BSG. The court acknowledged the legitimacy of an alternative that would provide Anderson Clayton stockholders with an immediate cash distribution plus continued equity participation in the on-going company. The court ruled, however, that in face of an all cash offer at a concededly fair price, the board must allow stockholders to choose between alternatives, at least when the board's proposal is not at a clearly superior price.

The injunctive relief granted by the court permitted Anderson Clayton to proceed with its self-tender but prohibited the company from purchasing shares until stockholders had an opportunity to tender shares under the BSG offer. BSG terminated its offer on September 24, 1986, when Anderson

Clayton announced that it was engaged in negotiations with Ralston Purina Company. Anderson Clayton subsequently agreed to be acquired by Quaker Oats Company for $66 per share.

3. SHOPPING, TERMINATION, LOCK-UPS AND BREAK-UP FEES: SOME FIDUCIARY ISSUES

General

During the period between the public announcement of the buyout and the mailing of a proxy statement, the buyout group will be exposed to competing bids and to substantial fees and expenses, especially in the form of bank commitments.[12] Accordingly, it has been common for the buyout group to seek certain agreements from the company in order to discourage competition and to compensate the buyout group in the event their bid is topped. Such agreements have included (1) an agreement not to "shop" the company, (2) the grant of a stock and/or asset option (a so-called lock-up option) and (3) an agreement to reimburse expenses and/or pay a "break-up fee." The courts, however, have become increasingly skeptical of such devices. Although not all lock-ups and similar devices are invalid per se, their legality has been closely scrutinized by the courts.

The independent committee and its counsel should be mindful of the legal developments surrounding such protective devices. Any protective devices used to entice the buyout group to keep its offer on the table should be narrowly tailored. The reluctance of the buyout group to keep its offer open while the company is being shopped may be overcome by agreeing, as discussed below, to pay the buyout group a break-up fee in the event its offer is topped and to reimburse it for its out-of-pocket expenses. The independent committee may conclude, however, that other devices are necessary to induce the offer and secure consummation of a transaction that they have concluded is in the best interests of stockholders. If no-shop provisions or lock-up options are to be utilized, the independent committee and the board must be satisfied that such devices are necessary to induce a bid that is materially higher than that which would be obtainable without such devices. Otherwise, a court may conclude that the board imprudently shut out the possibility of a higher competing offer. Depending on the circumstances, protective devices may be more easily justified when they are necessary to induce an initial bid for the company or at the end of a bidding contest than when employed in a competitive context. Once the company is the subject of competing bids, it will be difficult for the board to justify the use of protective devices that favor one bidder over another. As discussed below, the courts in Revlon, SCM, and Fruehauf have struck down lock-ups and no-shop clauses granted to bidders at a time when the company was the subject of competing bids.[13]

Must Directors Act as Neutral Auctioneers?

In Revlon, Inc. v. MacAndrews & Forbes Holdings, Inc. (506 A.2d 173, Del. Sup. 1986), the Delaware Supreme Court affirmed a ruling by the Court of Chancery that the Board of Directors of Revlon, Inc., breached its fiduciary duty to its stockholders by agreeing to a lock-up of certain of its assets as part of a takeover defense against Pantry Pride, Inc. The Chancery Court had granted a preliminary injunction that barred Revlon and its "white knight," Forstmann Little & Co., from proceeding with a proposed merger and invalidating a provision giving Forstmann the right to buy valuable assets of Revlon.

In response to a cash tender offer by Pantry Pride, the Revlon directors adopted a note purchase rights plan, caused Revlon to make an exchange offer of senior subordinated notes for 10 million shares of its common stock, and approved a plan to enter into an LBO agreement with Forstmann. Pantry Pride raised its tender offer and stated that it intended to counter any increased Forstmann bid with a nominal raise in its tender offer. The value of the Revlon notes issued in the exchange offer dropped significantly following announcement of the LBO agreement because of the latter's impact on certain protective covenants of the notes, and the Revlon directors came to recognize the "importance of doing something for the noteholders." Forstmann therefore made a revised merger proposal containing several important elements: (1) an increased bid for Revlon that exceeded the then pending Pantry Pride offer; (2) a lock-up option that would allow Forstmann to purchase the Revlon subsidiaries at a price arguably far below their fair value; (3) the placement of a $25 million cancellation fee in escrow to be released to Forstmann if the agreement terminated or if another acquirer purchased more than 19.9% of Revlon's stock; and (4) an offer from Forstmann to exchange a new set of senior notes for all of Revlon's substantially discounted notes issued in the exchange offer. Faced with a no shopping clause in the revised Forstmann proposal, a one-day deadline to respond and a declaration by Forstmann that its offer was "nonnegotiable," the Revlon directors approved the revised Forstmann merger agreement. As promised, Pantry Pride then raised its tender offer price again and also offered to match Forstmann's support of the notes, but it conditioned this new offer on the withdrawal or invalidation of the lock-up option.

The Chancery Court found, among other things, that the Revlon board had acted improperly when, in the face of Pantry Pride's undertaking to top any Forstmann bid, the board agreed to the revised Forstmann merger proposal (including the lock-up option) in order "to rid themselves of a vexing and potentially damaging source of litigation" from noteholders. The court found that in accepting Forstmann's revised proposal, the Revlon directors had acted out of self-interest in order to reduce their exposure to the noteholders and had thus breached their duty of loyalty to the stockholders when, for that reason, they agreed to the lock-up option which precluded any further competitive bids.

The Delaware Supreme Court upheld the Chancery Court decision. The court held that when the Revlon board authorized management to negotiate a merger or buyout with a third party in response to Forstmann's revised takeover proposal, and thus the sale of Revlon became inevitable, the duty of the board changed "from defenders of the corporate bastion to auctioneers charged with getting the best price for the stockholders at a sale of the company" (id., p. 182). In this regard, the court held that when the board entered into an "auction-ending lock-up agreement" with Forstmann, for what the court construed to be impermissible considerations regarding the noteholders at the expense of the stockholders, the directors breached their duty of loyalty. "Concern for non-stockholder interests," the court stated, "is inappropriate when an auction among active bidders is in progress, and the objective no longer is to protect or maintain the corporate enterprise but to sell it to the highest bidder." The court went on to note that while a lock-up option is not per se illegal under Delaware law, the Revlon lock-up was properly enjoined under the Unocal standard because the option put an end to an intense bidding contest without achieving substantial gains for the shareholders. The court noted that

> Current economic conditions in the takeover market are such that a "white knight" like Forstmann might only enter the bidding for the target company

if it receives some form of compensation to cover the risks and costs involved. However, while those lock-ups which draw bidders into the battle benefit shareholders, similar measures which end an active auction and foreclose further bidding operate to the shareholders' detriment.... The Forstmann option had a...destructive effect on the auction process. Forstmann had already been drawn into the contest on a preferred basis, so the result of the lock-up was not to foster bidding, but to destroy it (Id., p. 183).

Similarly, the court held that the no-shop provision, while not illegal per se, "is impermissible under the Unocal standard when a board's primary duty becomes that of an auctioneer responsible for selling the company to the highest bidder." The court upheld the injunction against payment of the cancellation fee, pending resolution of the case on the merits. The dispute over the cancellation fee was later settled with Forstmann receiving $24.4 million in a settlement of all claims.

In Hanson Trust PLC v. SCM Corporation (781 F.2d 264, 2d Cir. 1986), the Second Circuit invalidated lock-up options granted by SCM Corporation to an affiliate of Merrill Lynch & Co., Inc., in connection with Merrill Lynch's "white knight" LBO of SCM. In August 1985, Hanson Trust PLC and certain of its affiliates commenced a $60 cash tender for any and all shares of SCM. SCM subsequently entered into an agreement with Merrill Lynch pursuant to which Merrill Lynch would acquire SCM in an LBO in which SCM management would own up to 15% of the new company and SCM stockholders would receive $70 in cash and debt securities. Hanson responded by increasing its offer to $72, conditioned on SCM not granting any lock-up options. Merrill Lynch, in turn, raised its cash and debt offer to $74 per share. SCM accepted the new Merrill Lynch offer and granted Merrill Lynch lock-up options on SCM's pigments and consumer foods business. Hanson subsequently raised its offer price to $75 conditioned on the termination or injunction of the Merrill Lynch options.

The court held that the SCM directors did not adequately consider the fairness of the lock-up option price. As in the Revlon case, the court was most troubled by its perception that the lock-up option was granted in exchange for only a modest improvement in Merrill Lynch's bid. Whereas in the Revlon case the court held that the board had breached its duty of loyalty in granting the lock-up, the court in the SCM case held that the lock-up options were invalid due to the board's lack of due care in its deliberations. The court criticized the lack of substantial analysis on the part of the board in evaluating the lock-up options. The court stated that the actions of the SCM board did not rise to the level of gross negligence found in the Trans

Union case. Nonetheless, the court stated that the swiftness of the decision making on the part of the SCM board strongly suggested a breach of the duty of care. The court's conclusion was based on its perception that (1) the directors relied on the "conclusory" opinion of the company's financial advisor that the option prices were "within the range of fair value" when the advisor had not calculated a range of fairness; (2) no written opinion as to the value of the optioned businesses was given; (3) there was a lack of discussion as to the top value of the optioned businesses; (4) there was a lack of discussion as to what the company would look like if the options were exercised; (5) there was a lack of adequate discussion regarding the likelihood of the option trigger being exercised; (6) the directors failed to seek any documents to support the financial advisor's conclusions; and (7) the directors considered and approved the options in a three-hour, late-night meeting when no emergency situation existed that necessitated a decision that evening.

In Edelman v. Fruehauf (798 F.2d 882, 886-87, 6th Cir. 1986), the court stated that

> Once it becomes apparent that a takeover target will be acquired by new owners, whether by an alleged "raider" or by a team consisting of management and a "white knight," it becomes the duty of the target's directors to see that the shareholders obtain the best price possible for their stock.... When, in violation of this duty, directors take measures that are intended to put an end to the bidding, those measures may be enjoined.

In February 1986, a group of investors led by Asher Edelman began purchasing Fruehauf stock. The Edelman group made several proposals to acquire Fruehauf which were rejected by the Fruehauf board. On June 11, the Edelman group announced its intention to make an all-cash tender offer for all Fruehauf shares at $44 per share. Fruehauf's financial advisors instructed the board that if the Fruehauf offer was made, stockholders would likely tender their shares. In response, the board instructed management to seek alternatives to the Fruehauf offer. The only alternative that emerged was an LBO proposal from management and Merrill Lynch. Under the LBO proposal, the buyout group would pay $48.50 cash per share for approximately 77% of Fruehauf's stock and the remaining stockholders would receive $48.50 in securities of the new corporation in a second-step merger. A special independent committee of the Fruehauf board approved the LBO proposal which was then authorized by the full board. Among other things, the agreement provided for (1) payment of approximately $30 million to Merrill Lynch for loan commitment and advisory fees and a break-up fee that Merrill Lynch would keep even if the LBO was not consummated; (2) a no-shop clause restricting Fruehauf's ability to negotiate with other bidders; and (3) significant equity ownership of the new company by management. Additionally, the board approved changes to the company's stock option plan, incentive compensation plan, and pension plan to provide that if anyone acquired 40% of the company's stock without board approval, all incentive compensation payments would become immediately payable and the overfunding in the pension plan (between $70 and $100 million), which had been available for corporate uses, would become vested.

The Circuit Court concluded that the board failed to carry its burden of establishing that the LBO was fair and reasonable in light of the circumstances. The court stated that the fact that Fruehauf was on the auction block was not in dispute. Citing Revlon, the court stated that the board's duty was thus to obtain the best price for the stockholders in a sale of the company. Based on its perception of the facts, the court concluded that the Fruehauf board had apparently decided to make a deal with management no matter what other bidders might offer. The court held that since the board had failed to provide for a fair auction, the District Court was correct in granting injunctive relief establishing a framework for an open bidding process. The court criticized the directors' actions, stating that

> They acted as interested parties and did not treat the Fruehauf managers and the Edelman group in an evenhanded way but rather gave their colleagues on the board, the inside managers, the inside track and accepted their proposal without fostering a real bidding process (Id., p. 885).

The injunctive relief granted by the court was structured so as to provide a level playing field between the management-Merrill Lynch bidders and outside bidders. To ensure an open bidding process the court ordered the Fruehauf board

> to refrain from taking any corporate actions which are intended to or have the effect of favoring or advantaging any particular bidder over any other bidder...[and] to make available upon reasonable notice to any potential bidder for Fruehauf all information concerning Fruehauf's business and properties (subject to such bidder agreeing to reasonable provisions to keep such information confidential) and to meet on mutually agreeable and reasonable terms with any potential bidder in good faith (Id., pp. 890-91).

The court also enjoined the board from paying any fees, including legal and investment advisors' fees, in connection with any transaction involving management and Merrill Lynch or from taking any action regarding Fruehauf's stock option plans, incentive compensation plans, and retirement plans, unless the same accommodation was made to all other bidders.

The full ramifications of the Revlon, SCM, and Fruehauf decisions are not yet clear. It is difficult to predict to what extent the policy determination that seems to be driving these decisions (i.e., that a neutral auction is the best means of maximizing stockholder values) will be adopted in future decisions. The decision in Anderson Clayton, discussed in Section 2, can be read as consistent with the policy that competitive bidding must be permitted by a board of directors when a company is up for sale. These recent decisions, however, deal with situations in which the board acted to favor a white knight bid (or a self-tender in Anderson Clayton) in opposition to a hostile bid, and in all three cases the board-favored proposal, at least in the court's perception, did not represent a substantial improvement over the competing bid. By contrast, the decision in Restaurant Associates, also discussed in Section 2, may indicate that greater deference will be afforded to the board's choice of a suitor where the company does not face a hostile bid and the board's choice is thus not seen as an imprudent response to such a bid.

Many questions remain unanswered after Revlon, SCM and Fruehauf. These cases do not directly address whether the board is barred from granting a lock-up option or other inducements and protections to a buyout group in exchange for its initial proposal when no other bidders have yet to appear. Arguably, under Revlon a lock-up or other protective device is permissible if it induces a buyout group to make a proposal when no competing bidders are present, or, even once a bidding contest has begun, if it induces a materially superior bid. This reading of Revlon was recently endorsed by the Delaware Chancery Court in the Restaurant Associates decision:

> The Revlon case recognizes an obligation on the part of a board of directors, once it is clear to the board that the corporation is to be subject to a change in control, to attempt to maximize the amount to be received by shareholders. As a consequence, steps taken to defeat a potential suitor, in such a setting, must be designed to maximize shareholders returns. That is, in such a setting, defensive steps such as lock-up options or asset sales are valid

when designed or intended to promote higher bidding and invalid if designed to favor one bidder and stop the bidding.

In a footnote to this statement, the Chancellor noted the contradiction inherent in this dichotomy, since "even when designed to promote another bid, a good (i.e., effective) lock-up agreement may well end the bidding after that one last bid it induces is on the table." The Texas Air decision, discussed later in this section, arguably supports the proposition that lock-ups and similar steps are valid under Delaware law if they help to secure an attractive initial bid for the company.

In Buckhorn, Inc. v. Ropak Corporation (656 F. Supp. 209, S.D. Ohio 1987; aff'd by sum. ord., 815 F.2d 76, 8th Cir. 1987), the court, applying Delaware law, held that a board may engage in preliminary negotiations with one party concerning the potential sale of the company or its assets without committing itself to sell the company.

On November 24, 1986, after preliminary discussions concerning a possible business combination between Buckhorn, Inc., and suitor Ropak Corporation broke down, Ropak launched a hostile tender offer for Buckhorn shares. Although the Ropak bid was a cash offer for all shares, due to concerns regarding Ropak's ability to secure financing for the entire acquisition the directors treated the offer as a two-tiered bid. The Buckhorn board responded by adopting a back-end rights plan and other defensive measures and authorized management to explore alternatives to the Ropak offer, including a restructuring of the company, a sale of a significant portion of Buckhorn's assets, a business combination with another company, or an acquisition of another company. Management and the company's financial advisors explored several such alternatives, including the sale of the company's crown jewel.

Ropak sued, claiming, among other things, that the Buckhorn board had decided to sell the company, either in whole or in part, and thus had a fiduciary duty to negotiate with Ropak while pursuing negotiations with other companies. The court concluded that the Buckhorn board had not inevitably committed itself to sell the company, even though it had authorized management to continue negotiations concerning a sale of the company's crown jewel, noting that the directors had simply maintained a policy of evaluating potential sales on a case-by-case basis along with other strategic alternatives. The court concluded that throughout the Ropak tender offer the directors' primary objective had been to maintain Buckhorn as a going concern and therefore the directors did not breach a fiduciary duty by refusing to negotiate with Ropak.

Similarly, in Gelco Corp. v. Coniston Partners (652 F. Supp. 829, D. Minn. 1986; aff'd in part and vacated in part on other grounds, 811 F.2d 414, 8th Cir. 1987), the district court held that Gelco's proposed restructuring transaction involving a self-tender and sale of preferred stock to Merrill Lynch did not constitute an irreversible shift of control of the company. The court rejected the argument that merely because Coniston Partners made an all-cash offer Gelco's board was required to assume the role of auctioneer. The court, citing Revlon, noted however that "to the extent the bidding war continues, with offers steadily increasing in value, the transition from corporate defender to auctioneer becomes inevitable" (652 F. Supp. p. 847).

In Ivanhoe Partners v. Newmont Mining Corporation (Nos. 341, 345, Del. Sup. Ct. Nov. 18, 1987), the Delaware Supreme Court declined to upset a series of open market purchases of Newmont stock (a so-called street sweep) by Consolidated Gold Fields PLC (Gold Fields), a 26% shareholder, which transactions increased Gold Fields' ownership to 49.7% and were effected following the signing of a 10-year standstill agreement that limited Gold Fields to 49.9% of the stock and allowed Gold Fields to elect no more than 40% of the Newmont directors. The Newmont board had facilitated the street sweep by the issuance of a special cash dividend of $33 per share. In an important pronouncement, the court held that these steps did not render a sale of the company "inevitable" and, consequently, did not implicate the duties imposed by Revlon:

> First, Newmont was never for sale. During the short period in which these events occurred, the Newmont board held fast to its decision to keep the company independent. Ultimately, this goal was achieved by the standstill agreement and related defensive measures.
>
> Second, there was neither a bidding contest nor a sale. The only bidder for Newmont was Ivanhoe. Gold Fields was not a bidder but wished only to protect its already substantial interest in the company. It did so through the street sweep. Thus, the Newmont board did not "sell" the company to Gold Fields. The latter's purchases were from private sellers. While Gold Fields now owns 49.7% of the stock, its representation on the board is only 40% because of the restrictions of the standstill agreement. These facts do not strip the Newmont board of the presumptions of independence and good faith under the business judgment rule (Aronson, 473 A.2d at 815.). Even though Newmont's declaration of the dividend facilitated the street sweep, it did not constitute a "sale" of the company by Newmont.
>
> On this record we are satisfied that the fiduciary obligations imposed by Revlon to sell a company to the highest bidder are not applicable here. We, therefore, find no merit in plaintiffs' contentions (slip op., p. 24-25).

The court also reaffirmed that, in evaluating a takeover bid, the directors may "under appropriate circumstances consider the inadequacy of the bid, the nature and timing of the offer, the impact on constituencies other than shareholders, the risk of nonconsummation, and the basic stockholder interests at stake, including the past actions of the bidder and its affiliates in other takeover contests" (slip op., p. 15-16).

In Rosenfield v. Becor Western, Inc. (No. 87-C-0988, E.D. Wis. Nov. 5, 1987), the court denied a motion for a preliminary injunction against the consummation of a management-led LBO, affirming the principle that a board of directors' decisions in conducting an auction for its company are protected by the business judgment rule.

The Becor Board initially agreed to present a management-led LBO proposal to shareholders. Before the meeting to consider the bid, a third party made a competing acquisition proposal. The board then announced that it would hold an open auction for the company, published the criteria that it would use to assess the offers and set a deadline for the receipt of bids. After the board agreed in principle to a revised proposal from management, the bidders submitted additional offers. Those offers were then considered at a second board meeting. At that meeting, the board determined to accept the management proposal and to terminate the auction until shareholders could vote on that offer. After this decision was made, one of the bidders submitted yet another acquisition proposal. A shareholder plaintiff in Becor claimed that the board had a duty to consider the late bid and accept it if its terms were superior to the management bid. The Court rejected this claim.

The court's ruling makes clear that so long as an auction is conducted fairly, the board's decision as to how to structure the auction, including when to end it—as well as its determination as to which bid to accept—will be protected by the business judgment rule and will not be disturbed.

Although the independent committee and/or board need not necessarily seek alternative bids for the company before accepting a buyout proposal, its (their) actions must still satisfy the Weinberger standards of entire fairness. In light of recent developments in the case law, the board should be prepared to defend any actions it takes that would preclude other bidders from competing with the buyout group against heightened scrutiny by the courts. In granting protections to the buyout group, the board must be satisfied that such protections are necessary to induce a favorable buyout proposal that the buyout group would otherwise be unwilling to make. At a minimum, the board should be satisfied that the buyout proposal will be subject to free market forces even if the board does not itself affirmatively shop the company.

The view of the independent committee as to the adequacy of the price and the prospects of other bidders willing to pay an even higher price than the buyout group will have a tremendous impact on its ability to accede to any or all of the buyout group's requests for protective devices. Other factors that the independent committee may deem relevant are (1) the status of the financing for the buyout, (2) the length of the time needed to complete the buyout, and (3) the need for regulatory approvals.

The following discussion of various protective devices should be read in the context of the foregoing analysis of the Revlon, SCM, and Fruehauf cases in this section.

Shopping

The buyout group will undoubtedly request a covenant by the company not to solicit or encourage anyone to make a competing bid or to engage in any negotiations with or supply any information to any other person who expresses an interest in acquiring the company.[14] The argument likely to be advanced by the buyout group in favor of such a covenant is that it has expended time and incurred expense in putting together its proposal and does not want to be used as a "stalking horse" to attract other bids for the company. The independent committee must satisfy itself as to whether it has a fiduciary obligation to shop the company.

Fairly plausible arguments can be advanced on each side of the question. The board may, on the one hand, believe that the inclusion of a no-shop provision is a sine qua non of the buyout group's proposal and that an otherwise attractive transaction might not be available as a result of the board's refusal to accede to such a provision. On the other hand, the board may rightfully feel that the enforcement of such a provision would preclude the acceptance of a higher bid and thereby deprive stockholders of the best available price.

The more common view is that an obligation to shop does not exist. The rationale most often articulated to support this view is that the independent committee, with the assistance of the financial advisor, will be able to evaluate the buyout independently of an auction process to determine whether it is in the best interests of stockholders. On such a view, the independent committee may, consistent with its fiduciary obligations, choose to proceed with the buyout, rather than searching for a better offer and risking withdrawal of the buyout. Note, however, that in the Revlon and Fruehauf cases no-shop provisions granted during a competitive bidding contest were enjoined by the court.

On the other hand, the absence of a no-shop covenant creates a record which will make the buyout less vulnerable to attack in litigation. An even better record would exist if the financial advisor were to be directed to solicit other bids or at least to inform inquiring third parties that bids would be welcome. Either set of circumstances would be useful in defending the fairness of the price and the procedural aspects of the buyout in contrast to a directive to the financial advisor by the independent committee that it is not permitted to solicit or encourage any other bids.

It should be noted that the financial advisor might have to refer to such a directive in its fairness opinion. In any event, Item 9(b)(6) of Schedule 13E-3 will require disclosure of any limitations placed on the scope of the financial advisor's investigation.

The independent committee can use its ability to shop the company as a means of negotiating a higher price from the buyout group.

Assuming that the independent committee and its financial advisor have assured themselves as to the fairness of the terms of the buyout, the decision as to whether to agree to the inclusion of a no-shop provision will depend on the independent committee's assessment of the likelihood that the buyout group will withdraw its proposal without such a provision. In this regard, the fact that the buyout group has expended time and expense in organizing the buyout proposal argues against the likelihood that they would withdraw the proposal, especially in view of the fact that without a definitive acquisition agreement the buyout group would be forced to bear its own expenses.

A possible negotiating strategy would be to agree to a bust-up or topping fee or reimbursement of expenses in return for the exclusion of the no-shop provision.

Although the acquisition agreement may restrict the solicitation or encouragement of additional bids, it should in any event permit the independent committee and its advisors to provide information to a potential bidder who contacts the company on its own. Such a provision constitutes an important safeguard, for it permits the independent committee to put an interested third party on an equal footing with the buyout group in terms of information that is available. For example:

The company and its subsidiaries will not, and they will use their best efforts to cause their respective officers, employees and agents not to, directly or indirectly, solicit or initiate any discussions with, or provide any information to, any corporation, partnership, person or other entity or group, other than [the acquirer] and its officers, employees and agents, concerning any merger, sale of substantial assets or similar transaction involving the company or any subsidiary or division of the company or any sale of more than 20% of the capital stock of the company or any of its subsidiaries (all such transactions being referred to herein as "Acquisition Proposals"). Notwithstanding the foregoing, the company may furnish information concerning its business, properties or assets to a corporation, partnership, person or other entity if the company's outside counsel advises the company's board of directors that in the exercise of its fiduciary responsibilities such information should be provided to such other party. The company will promptly communicate to [the acquirer] the terms of any Acquisition Proposal which it may receive.

Some commentators, including former SEC Commissioner Bevis Longstreth, have taken the position that the procedural safeguards provided by an independent committee of directors, a fairness opinion and accurate proxy statement disclosure are insufficient to ensure a fair deal to the public stockholders of a target company involved in an LBO transaction. In particular, Mr. Longstreth has proposed with respect to MBO proposals that members of management be permitted to take their company private only after affording all potential bidders a reasonable opportunity to investigate the company and to make alternative bids.[15]

Even if the company is not shopped, the company has been priced once the buyout is announced, and the absence of a higher third-party bid (particularly if the proxy statement discloses projections) will be at least some evidence that the price is fair. This will be less true if competing bids are deterred by the granting of a lock-up or costly inducements to the buyout group. See "Lock-Ups," below.

In this regard, the Delaware Supreme Court in Trans Union found that the stock lock-up granted to Marmon effectively eliminated the practical utility of the market test. The court noted that its review of the record compels a finding that confirmation of the appropriateness of the (Marmon] offer by an unfettered or free market test was virtually meaningless in the face of the terms and time limitations of Trans Union's Merger Agreement with [Marmon].

In In re Beatrice Companies, Inc. (Litigation, Civ. Action No. 8248, Del. Ch. Apr. 14, 1986), the court approved the settlement of stockholder litigation arising out of the LBO agreement between Beatrice and Kohlberg, Kravis, Roberts & Co. (KKR). The court stated that important benefits had been conferred on Beatrice stockholders due to the fact that the merger agreement between KKR and the company had been revised to exclude a no-shop clause and the company had subsequently canvassed alternatives to the KKR offer. The court noted that while no alternatives to the KKR offer arose, the stockholders at least had the comfort of knowing that no higher offer from a third party was overlooked.

Beatrice agreed to KKR's LBO proposal in November 1985 and as part of the agreement granted KKR lock-up options on certain of Beatrice's businesses and agreed to a no-shop provision and a cancellation fee of $123 million. When KKR sought to modify the terms of its offer in December 1985, the board modified the agreement by eliminating the lock-up and no-shop provisions and reduced the cancellation fee to approximately $19 million.

"Fiduciary-Out" Termination Provisions

Closely related to the issue of whether the company should be shopped is the board's obligation to recommend the buyout to the company's stockholders in the event that a higher offer is received. It is not uncommon in an LBO for the target company to reserve the right to terminate the definitive acquisition agreement if a more favorable offer is received at a later date. For example:

> *Termination.* This Agreement may be terminated...by the Board of Directors of the Company:
>
> (i) if a written proposal to effect an Acquisition Transaction is received by the company's Board of Directors from any person other than [the acquirer] or an affiliate or associate of [the acquirer] which, based on the advice of the company's independent financial advisor, the company's board of directors determined to be more favorable to the company's stockholders than the Merger.

A fiduciary-out termination provision in the acquisition agreement will arguably reduce the need for shopping the company. Conversely, there may be less reason to have a fiduciary-out termination provision if the company already has been shopped extensively. In any event, other factors, such as whether the buyout group already has obtained satisfactory financing, must be considered when deciding whether to demand a fiduciary-out termination provision.

The buyout group's willingness to agree to such a termination provision will usually be conditioned upon the inclusion of a no-shop provision and/ or a covenant by the company to pay a break-up or "topping" fee and to reimburse the buyout group for its out-of-pocket expenses in the event that the company terminates the agreement upon receipt of a more favorable offer. The buyout group's acquiescence to a fiduciary-out termination provision reflects the fact that the company's stockholders will not approve the buyout if a more favorable offer is made. Indeed, the board presumably would take the position under the covenant discussed above that its fiduciary obligations prevent it from recommending the buyout to the stockholders.

Recent cases suggest that there may be limits to the degree in which the acquisition agreement will be binding upon the board prior to stockholder approval, irrespective of the existence of a fiduciary-out termination provision.

In Jewel Companies, Inc. v. Pay Less Drug Stores Northwest, Inc. (741 F.2d 1555, 9th Cir. 1984), the Ninth Circuit Court of Appeals, applying California law, reversed a federal district court's grant of summary judgment for Pay Less Drug Stores Northwest (Northwest) on Jewel's claim of tortious interference with a merger agreement between Jewel and Pay Less Drug Stores [16]

In Jewel, Jewel and Pay Less entered into a merger agreement pursuant to which the two companies would engage in a tax-free merger in which each outstanding share of Pay Less stock would be exchanged for .652 shares of Jewel stock. The merger agreement contained a so-called best efforts clause, pursuant to which each company's board of directors was obligated to "use its best efforts to fulfill those conditions...over which it has control or influence and to consummate the merger." The merger agreement also obligated Pay Less to forbear from selling or transferring any of its properties or assets, or agreeing or committing to make any such sale or transfer, and from entering into or terminating any contract other than in the ordinary course of business. Subsequently, Northwest purchased over 12% of Pay Less's stock in the open market and commenced a tender at $22.50 per share of Pay Less's stock. Two weeks later, Northwest increased its tender offer to $24 per share; Pay Less's board recommended that shareholders accept the Northwest offer; and Northwest and Pay Less, through Pay Less's board, entered into an agreement pursuant to which, among other things, the board agreed to abandon the Jewel merger if the merger was not approved by Pay Less's shareholders and Northwest agreed to indemnify Pay Less and its directors against any alleged breach of the merger agreement with Jewel. On the same date, the Pay Less board signed a merger agreement with Northwest. The Jewel merger agreement was subsequently rejected at a Pay Less shareholders' meeting.

The court concluded that under California law the board of directors of a corporation could agree in a merger agreement to forbear from entering into competing and inconsistent agreements until the stockholders' vote on the merger. Having entered into such an agreement, the Pay Less board was bound by it, and the board's breach of the agreement could not be justified on the basis of its fiduciary duties. The court pointed out:

> Even after the merger agreement is signed a board may not, consistent with its fiduciary obligations to its shareholders, withhold information regarding a materially more attractive offer. While the board can bind itself to exert its best efforts to consummate the merger under California law, it can only bind the corporation temporarily, and in limited areas, pending shareholder approval (Id., p. 1564, citations omitted).

The court declined, however, to address the question of whether a merger agreement could bind the board, in the event of an unsolicited receipt of a more favorable offer after signing the agreement, to continue to recommend to its stockholders that they approve the initial proposal.

In ConAgra, Inc. v. Cargill, Inc. (382 N.W.2d 576, Neb. Sup. Ct. 1986), the court held that a best efforts clause in a merger agreement does not preclude a board of directors from recommending a subsequent superior offer to the stockholders.

ConAgra had entered into a definitive merger agreement to acquire MBPXL. The agreement contained a best efforts clause requiring both corporations' directors and officers to "take all such further action as may be necessary or appropriate in order to effectuate the transactions contemplated hereby including recommending to their respective stockholders that the merger be approved." The clause then continued, "provided, however, nothing herein contained shall relieve either Board of Directors of their continuing duties to respective shareholders." Subsequently, after negotiations initiated by a director-stockholder of MBPXL and then participated in by other directors, Cargill determined to make a tender offer for MBPXL. MBPXL's board ultimately determined that this offer was superior to the ConAgra merger agreement, refused to recommend the merger to the stockholders, and instead recommended Cargill's tender offer. ConAgra sued Cargill for tortiously interfering with the merger agreement and MBPXL for breach of contract and conspiracy with Cargill.

ConAgra prevailed in the lower court. The Nebraska Supreme Court reversed. First, the court read the fiduciary-out proviso to the best-efforts obligation as expressly countenancing the course taken by the target board. But in language that makes clear that the result would have been the same regardless of the terms of the particular merger agreement, the court stated:

> This court should not sanction "agreements which have the effect of removing from directors in a very substantial way their duty to use their own best judgment on management matters.... The directors of MBPXL could not agree to assist ConAgra by pledging their best efforts if by doing so the directors of MBPXL violated their legal duties to the MBPXL shareholders.... Once the directors of MBPXL learned of the competing Cargill offer, the "best efforts" clause in the ConAgra proposal could not relieve the MBPXL directors of their duties to act in the shareholders' best interests (Id., p. 587).

The court also noted that under Delaware law the MBPXL board lacked statutory power to bind the corporation to the ConAgra merger agreement, absent stockholder approval.

The court expressly stated that it was not deciding whether the directors of MBPXL might be personally liable for breach of an agreement with ConAgra. (See id., p. 587.)

An offer to acquire the company at a higher price will not necessarily be a "more favorable" offer. The independent committee and its advisors must evaluate other aspects of each offer, such as whether there are legal or other impediments to completing the proposed transaction, whether there is a "financing out" (and, if there is, the likelihood of the acquirer obtaining satisfactory financing without delay), how quickly the transaction can be completed and payments can be made to the public stockholders for their securities, the value of any non-cash consideration being offered, and the tax consequences of the transaction to the public stockholders.

In lieu of a fiduciary-out termination, the independent committee should seek to have the buyout conditioned on receipt of a favorable opinion of the financial advisor at the time of closing. In the face of a substantially higher offer, it is unlikely that such a favorable opinion would be forthcoming.

Lock-Ups

Lock-ups are generally arrangements that are designed to discourage other prospective bidders by granting a particular bidder a competitive advantage. The purpose of a lock-up is to provide only an advantage, not the certainty of success.

Lock-ups can take two general forms: the stock lock-up and the asset lock-up. The stock lock-up involves the purchase, or the granting of an option to purchase, of authorized but unissued shares of stock of the target company. Stock lock-ups have the effect of making an acquisition of the company more expensive for a competing bidder and/or of enabling the grantee to successfully defeat any corporate action by a competing bidder. Stock lock-ups also have the effect of providing the grantee with a profit in the event a competing bidder is successful in acquiring the company at a price higher than the price paid for the shares pursuant to the lock-up. In several LBOs the buying group has been granted stock lock-ups, at the transaction price, to purchase shares of authorized but unissued stock.

The New York and American Stock Exchanges both impose limitations on the number of shares which may be issued without shareholder approval (18.5% on NYSE and 20% on AMEX). Such limitations will significantly reduce the effectiveness of stock lock-ups.

In an asset lock-up the target agrees to sell, or grants an option to sell, a valuable corporate asset to a bidder. As a result of the sale, the company would be less attractive to a competing bidder. Asset lock-ups in particular have been subject to heightened scrutiny by the courts in recent cases.

One of the factors inherent in the buyout and which may concern the independent committee in granting a lock-up is the fact that the Buying Group has no real commitment to buy. In almost all LBO agreements, the acquiring group's obligation to proceed is conditioned upon obtaining financing. Because the agreements providing for the financing will themselves be subject to conditions within the control of the buyout group, in practical terms the buyout group has been granted an option to buy the company. The question facing the independent committee is why the buyout group should be given a windfall when it has only committed its name to the buyout.

Any lock-up is likely to be a focal point of litigation and its presence is likely to add uncertainty to the buyout. In Delaware, it is likely that the courts would evaluate such lock-ups as part of their analysis under Weinberger of whether the buyout met the requirements of fair dealing. In addition, the lock-up will be subject to the Revlon test and will be sustainable only if it induces a bid materially superior to that which would otherwise be obtainable.

The decision in Mobil Corp. v. Marathon Oil Co. (669 F.2d 366, 6th Cir. 1981), created uncertainty as to the validity of lock-ups under federal law. Marathon, attempting to thwart a tender offer by Mobil, granted U.S. Steel a stock option and an option on Marathon's crown jewel, the Yates Field. The Sixth Circuit held that, by deterring other bids, the lock-up options violated the Williams Act. Other courts have declined to follow Mobil. In Data Probe Acquisition Corp. v. Datatab Inc. (722 F.2d 1, 2d Cir. 1983; cert. denied, 465 U.S. 1052,1984), the Court of Appeals for the Second Circuit reiterated its view, expressed in Buffalo Forge v. Ogden (717 F.2d 757, 2d Cir. 1983; cert. denied, 464 U.S. 1018, 1983), that the Sixth Circuit's decision in Mobil Corp. v. Marathon Oil Corp. was "an unwarranted extension of the Williams Act." In Data Probe, the Second Circuit held that a lock-up stock-option on the equivalent of 200% of the target's outstanding shares granted to a potential acquirer in a bidding competition was not "manipulative" within the meaning of Section 14(e) of the 1934 Act.

Since the issue before the court in Data Probe was limited to the status of the option under the Williams Act, the court did not address questions of fiduciary duty or the validity of the option under state law. Recent decisions, while stating that lock-up options are not per se illegal, have placed substantial limits upon a board's ability to grant lock-up options. The Revlon and SCM cases, which are the leading cases on the legality of lock-up options under Delaware and New York law, respectively, are discussed above. Other significant cases involving lock-up options are discussed following.

In Thompson v. ENSTAR Corp. (Civ. Action No. 7641, Del. Ch. June 10, 1984), the court denied a preliminary injunction against consummation of certain agreements providing for the acquisition of ENSTAR Corp. by Allied Corp. and Ultramar PLC. Under these agreements, Allied and Ultramar were granted the right, operative in the event of a change of control of ENSTAR (including a change of control in favor of a suitor other than Allied and Ultramar), to direct ENSTAR's vote in an oil and gas joint venture in Indonesia in which Allied, Ultramar, and ENSTAR had major interests. The court held that the acts of ENSTAR's directors in approving ENSTAR's agreements with Allied and Ultramar were protected by the business judgment rule and that the directors acted reasonably in granting the voting rights to Allied and Ultramar in order to secure the best available price for the company's stockholders. The court noted, however, that lock-up agreements "often prevent open bidding for assets which, of course, is usually in the best interests of the shareholders" and that such agreements "often infringe on the voting rights of shareholders." Accordingly, the court stated that such agreements "must be given careful scrutiny by a court to see if under all the facts and circumstances existing in a particular case they are fair to the shareholders."

In Keyser v. Commonwealth National Financial Corporation (644 F. Supp. 1130, M.D. Pa. 1986), the court upheld the granting of a stock option to a purchaser in a negotiated bank merger. According to the court's opinion, in connection with a merger Commonwealth granted Mellon Bank Corporation an option to purchase approximately 25% of its common stock under certain circumstances. The conditions to exercise related principally to activities of third parties designed to thwart the merger. At the time of the granting of the option, a prior bidder for Commonwealth (whose offer price was less than the Mellon offer price) had withdrawn its bid. The option exercise price was the market price of a share of Commonwealth common stock on the last trading day preceding the execution of the merger agreement, which was slightly more than $5 less than the merger consideration of $40 per share. The plaintiffs charged that the granting of the option was done in a "hasty" manner without independent evaluation by Commonwealth's board, was designed to prevent competitive bids, and was in breach of the directors' fiduciary duty of care. In upholding the validity of the bank's action, the court noted that lock-up provisions are "very common in bank mergers." It found that were it not for the lock-up, Commonwealth would not have been able to keep Mellon as a competitive bidder. In upholding the exercise of business judgment and finding no breach of the directors' fiduciary duty of care, the court held:

> The warrant and option price were fully negotiated and were a necessary and integral part of a merger agreement with Mellon. A merger with Mellon was considered by the directors to be in the best interests of Commonwealth and its shareholders. Further, the effects of the (lock-up) were fully disclosed to shareholders, who ultimately voted to approve the merger agreement (Id., p. 1147).

The court's opinion makes no reference to the Revlon or SCM decisions.

In Hecco Ventures v. Sea-Land Corporation (Civ. Action No. 8486, Del. Ch. May 19, 1986), a case arising out of CSX's agreement to acquire Sea-Land at $28 per share—which included an alleged lock-up stock option—the Delaware Chancery Court denied a temporary restraining order against the pending tender offer. The court noted that the option was granted at the conclusion of the auction process and that there was no bidder other than CSX, there was no bid other than CSX's, and there was no showing that an injunction would cause a different bidder or a higher bid to materialize (id., pp. 13, 14).

Plaintiffs were unable to support claims of breach of fiduciary duty by Sea-Land's board, by Harold Simmons (who controlled 39.5% of the Sea-Land stock and for $5 per share had sold CSX an option to purchase his position for $28 per share), or by CSX as a conspirator in the Sea-Land board's and Simmons' alleged breaches. The court found that Sea-Land had actively searched for a buyer, had invited Simmons to top CSX, had provided him with the same information given to CSX, had not participated in the Simmons-CSX transaction, and had sold to the highest and only bidder remaining at a price deemed fair by its investment banker.

In Greenfield v. National Medical Care, Inc. (Civ. Action Nos. 7720 and 7765, Del. Ch. June 6, 1986), the court refused to dismiss plaintiff's claim that the directors of National Medical Care, Inc. (NMC) breached their fiduciary duty by granting options to W.R. Grace to purchase shares of NMC at $12.875 per share (the pre-proposal market price) in connection with the company's agreement to be acquired in an LBO transaction at $19.25 per share. Under the options, Grace would be entitled to purchase 1 million NMC shares at $12.875 per share if a third party made an offer to acquire a majority interest in NMC or if the NMC stockholders did not approve the merger of NMC and a holding corporation formed by Grace and other investors. Grace would also be entitled to purchase an additional 2.4 million shares at $12.875 in the event that a third party made an offer to acquire a majority interest in NMC at a price higher than $19.25 per share.

The court stated that although the options only involved a small percentage of NMC's outstanding stock, they would be considered a form of lock-up inasmuch as they would make an acquisition of NMC more costly for a third party.

The court concluded that the complaint sufficiently stated a claim for breach of fiduciary duty against the NMC directors. The court noted that while the complaint did not allege that there were other bidders for NMC, it did allege that the price was unfair and that the lock-up prevented holders from obtaining a higher offer. This, when combined with allegations that the merger was approved by an interested board, was sufficient in the court's view to state a cause of action. The court, however, did dismiss plaintiff's claim against Grace alleging that Grace aided and abetted the directors in the breach of their fiduciary duty.

In Hastings-Murtagh v. Texas Air Corp. (649 F. Supp. 479, S.D. Fla. 1986), the court upheld a lock-up stock option granted by Eastern Air Lines to Texas Air pursuant to a merger agreement which Eastern entered into without soliciting competing offers at a time when Eastern was not subject to competing bids. The court, applying Delaware law, distinguished the Revlon case, stating that lock-up options and no-shop provisions are valid when they serve to attract a bidder and result from arm's-length negotiation and are impermissible "only if they are adopted in a situation where there is a live auction with competing bidders " (id., p. 484). The court noted that plaintiffs failed to cite "any legal authority that obligates a board of directors to jeopardize one bid in order to give a group of employees or anyone else an indefinite amount of time in which to develop and finance an acquisition proposal" (id., p. 484). See also In re Anderson Clayton Shareholders' Litigation (C.A. No. 8387, Del. Ch. June 10, 1986): directors have no duty to delay an otherwise appropriate transaction merely because a competitor shows up at the last minute.

In the Restaurant Associates decision, discussed in Section 2, plaintiff shareholders sought an order compelling the company to accede to a bidder's demand for a stock lock-up, which demand was part of a highly conditional offer for the company ultimately rejected by the board in favor of a numerically inferior management proposal. The plaintiffs contended that, where the board has determined that the company is for sale, Revlon requires the board to take all affirmative steps that are necessary to maximize the return to stockholders. Without opining as to whether the relief sought "would ever be authorized as an extension of the Revlon teaching," the court denied the plaintiff's request, holding that the independent committee's recommendation that the board not accede to the bidder's demand, which recommendation was adopted by the board, was based on plausible and persuasive reasons and was thus protected by the business judgment rule.

It is difficult to draw clear guidelines from the Revlon and SCM decisions. Both opinions state that lock-up options are not per se illegal, but both opinions invalidate the lock-ups there under consideration. Both opinions acknowledge that lock-up options can be beneficial to stockholders when they induce a bidder to compete for control of a company, but they state that options that put an end to the bidding process may be harmful to stockholders. Neither case, it should be noted, addresses the validity of a lock-up option granted to a would-be acquirer in a friendly transaction when no other competing bidders are present.

The legality of lock-up options will likely depend upon the stage at which they are granted and a court's perception of the facts in each case. As the Revlon and SCM cases suggest, if a lock-up induces a new bidder to compete at a bid materially higher than the existing offer, its legality may be sustainable. Legality of a lock-up may be more easily sustainable where, as in Texas Air, the lock-up is granted at a time when the company is not subject to competing bids. The principal factors that the Delaware court would likely consider in making this determination are the terms and effect of the lock-up and the circumstances under which the lock-up was granted. Among the relevant circumstances are (1) the price being paid to the public; (2) whether the company had been "shopped" prior to the granting of the option; (3) whether there are any competing bidders and the price being offered by any such bidders; (4) the status of the buyout group's financing; (5) the option price; and (6) the size of the block of stock or asset in comparison to the value of the buyout.

It is important to note that the use of lock-ups in the LBO context had been severely criticized long before Revlon and SCM. Former SEC Commissioner Longstreth, in a 1984 address before the American Bar Association's Section of Corporation, Banking and Business Law, noted, among other things, that the use of the corporate machinery for defensive maneuvers such as lock-ups "seem[s] entirely out of place in a management buyout" where their only purpose is to prevent a third-party bid. Mr. Longstreth urged that lock-ups be prohibited completely in MBOs.[17]

Reimbursement of Expenses and Break-Up Fees

The members of the buyout group are likely to request that the acquisition agreement provide that they be reimbursed by the company for their out-of-pocket expenses if the transaction is not consummated.

The justification likely to be put forward is that the consummation of the buyout will benefit the company's stockholders and therefore the payment of expenses incurred in an attempt to achieve that result is permissible.

The receipt by the independent committee of preliminary advice by the financial advisor as to the fairness of the consideration to be offered in the buyout should suffice to justify the payment of expenses under the business judgment rule.

It may be appropriate for the independent committee to consider limiting the company's obligation to reimburse the buyout group for its expenses (particularly in situations where such expenses cannot be accurately predicted due to the possibility of protracted litigation or for other reasons) or otherwise to maintain some control over the amounts payable by the company under such provisions.

In addition to seeking reimbursement of its expenses, the buyout group may request the company to agree to pay it a fee if the buyout is not completed for certain reasons. The demand for "break-up" fees may be especially strong given the legal questions surrounding other protective devices. Once it is determined to agree to make such a payment, the independent committee must focus on the circumstances under which this break-up fee will be payable—a factor that will help to determine how much the fee should be.

The payment of a break-up fee is most easily justified in situations where the acquisition agreement is terminated by the company pursuant to a fiduciary-out termination provision. In such a situation it can be said that the buyout group has served as a stalking horse to attract a more favorable offer for the company's stockholders and merits compensation for its efforts. In addition, a break-up fee may be justified if the buyout cannot be completed, or cannot be completed in a timely manner, because another person has acquired or proposed to acquire a substantial portion of the company's stock or assets. Under such circumstances, the buyout group's inability to complete the buyout is due neither to its failure to perform its obligations nor to a determination by the independent committee or its stockholders that the buyout group's offer is unsatisfactory. Acquirers typically insist that they be compensated for their time and trouble in that event.

The following is an example of a typical covenant to pay a break-up fee and to reimburse the acquirer for its out-of-pocket expenses:

If this Merger Agreement is terminated by the company without the consent of the Purchaser for any reason other than (1) pursuant to Section 7.1(b)(ii) [failure of the Purchaser to deliver fully executed and binding Definitive Financing Agreements to the company by a specified date], where such termination is not due to the Purchaser being unable to deliver fully executed and binding Definitive Financing Agreements primarily because a representation or warranty of the company is not then true and correct in all material respects, (2) pursuant to Section 7.1(b)(iii) [failure to consummate the transaction by a specified date], where such termination is not primarily because the condition set forth in Section 6.3 [the company's representations and warranties shall be true and correct in all material respects and the company shall in all material respects have performed each of its obligations] shall not have been satisified or (3) pursuant to Section 7.1(d) [United States federal or state court or governmental order or decree prohibiting the transaction or the company's stockholders do not approve the transaction]; or (ii) if this Merger Agreement is terminated after such time as an entity or person (as defined in Section 13(d)(3) of the Securities Exchange Act of 1934, as amended) other than the Purchaser or any of its affiliates, acquires beneficial ownership of 25% or more of the sum of (1) the number of Shares then outstanding and (2) the number of Shares issuable upon conversion of the Preferred Shares and pursuant to the option and employee benefit plans of the company, the company will, within five days after such termination of this Merger Agreement (i) pay the Purchaser a fee equal to $7.5 million and (ii) reimburse the Purchaser for all reasonable out-of-pocket expenses and fees incurred by it or on its behalf in connection with the Merger and the Financing, or incurred by financial institutions and assumed by the Purchaser in connection with the negotiation, preparation, execution and performance of this Merger Agreement, the financing commitments referred to in Section 2.3 and the Definitive Financing Agreements.

In Revlon, Pantry Pride sought to enjoin the payment of a $25 million cancellation fee placed in escrow for Forstmann, claiming that such payment was a waste of corporate assets because the fee was in addition to the payment of Forstmann's expenses. Although noting that the timing of the escrow of the cancellation fee along with the lock-ups granted Forstmann was disturbing, the Chancery Court acknowledged that cancellation fees per se were not unusual in transactions of the magnitude of the Forstmann-Revlon transaction. Since the record before the Chancery Court did not permit a ruling on the merits and in view of the injunction against lock-up, the court determined that it would be appropriate to preclude distribution of Forstmann's cancellation fee until the merits of the claim could be resolved.

In the Fruehauf case, the court enjoined Fruehauf from paying any fees in connection with any buyout transaction involving management and Merrill Lynch unless similar accommodations were made to all other bidders. The court specifically noted that its treatment of the commitment and related fees in its injunctive order did not suggest that under the business judgment rule it was never permissible to use corporate funds to encourage bidders or even to encourage buyout proposals. The court stated that in some instances, "where the neutrality and objectivity of the board is clearly present," the payment of commitment, legal and other similar fees would be permissible. The court noted that "obviously some marginal costs to finance the flow of information are necessary, and advisory fees for lawyers and investment bankers to structure and conduct the bidding process will have to be paid." The court held, however, that the size of the commitment fees Fruehauf granted, when added to the other benefits granted management and Merrill Lynch, was disproportionate to such costs.

In Samjens Partners I v. Burlington Industries, Inc. (663 F. Supp. 614, S.D.N.Y. 1987), the court, in an opinion by Judge Kram, denied the request of a hostile bidder controlled by Asher Edelman and Dominion Textile, Inc., for a preliminary injunction against a merger agreement between Burlington Industries and a white knight LBO group led by Morgan Stanley. The court, interpreting the Delaware Supreme Court's holding in Revlon, stated that it is permissible for a target to enter into a negotiated merger agreement with a white knight containing a break-up fee and a no-shop provision, provided the transaction is approved on a proper record. The court stated that lock-up agreements, break-up fees, and no-shop agreements granted to a white knight are permissible if such strategies enhance the bidding, noting that "[s]uch arrangements may also be legitimately necessary to convince a 'white knight' to enter the bidding by providing some form of compensation for the risks it is undertaking" (id., p. 624). The court concluded that granting Morgan Stanley a break-up fee and a no-shop provision was such a strategy. The court stated:

> [A]lthough Morgan might have been Burlington's white knight, it was not Burlington's patron saint. Morgan was involved in negotiations with Burlington because it saw an opportunity to make money.... [I]t wanted a response to its bid quickly, it wanted compensation for the risk it was undertaking in tying up its capital, and it did not want to serve as a 'stalking horse' and have its bids shopped around (id., p. 625).

Judge Kram also rejected the hostile bidder's claim that the board had an obligation to offer the hostile bidder a break-up fee of the sort offered to Morgan Stanley, noting that

> [The bidder] has purchased approximately 13 percent of Burlington shares in the pre-tender offer market at an average price of $50 per share. Thus, [the bidder] enters the bidding process with a nearly $80 million advantage over other prospective bidders who must pay at least $78 per share for all outstanding shares. Denying [the bidder] a break-up fee thus helps to even the playing field (id., p. 626).

The court noted that the board, though not happy with the break-up fee, "realized that such a fee was standard, and that the amount of the fee was fair and within the normal range" (id. , p. 625). Overall, the court concluded, the merger agreement the board signed, rather than ending the auction, provided a starting point for further bidding.

The enforceability of a break-up fee will depend on its size in relationship to the size of the transaction. The larger the fee, the more likely it is that a court will categorize it as corporate waste or a disguised lock-up.

4. SOME DISCLOSURE ISSUES

Initial Announcement

Having received the buyout group's proposal, and having retained its advisors, one of the initial issues to be confronted by the independent committee relates to the timing and scope of the initial public announcement of the buyout. The dilemma presented in this regard is no different from that presented in the discussion stages of any proposed acquisition transaction. On the one hand, failure to disclose that a premium offer has been made harms selling stockholders, who lose the opportunity to participate in the premium. On the other hand, premature disclosure when no terms have been agreed upon may be misleading under the circumstances. The nature and timing of announcements to be made concerning the buyout should be considered carefully from the standpoint of federal and state securities laws and, if applicable, stock exchange regulations. Joint preparation of press releases by the company and the buyout group will eliminate confusion as to the responsibility for publicity and will provide a stable basis for the consistent flow of accurate information.

Federal Securities Issues

As a general matter, it is widely accepted under the federal securities laws that a company is not affirmatively obligated to disclose ongoing preliminary merger negotiations and may elect to say nothing whatever even if such information would be material to investors. See Levinson v. Basic Inc. (786 F.2d 741, 746, 6th Cir. 1986; cert. granted, 107 S. Ct. 1284, 1987) and Staffin v. Greenberg (672 F.2d 1196, 1203-06, 3d Cir. 1982). A duty to disclose arises only in special circumstances, such as (1) where the company is responsible for rumors of the discussions leaking into the market (see State Teachers Retirement Bd. v. Fluor Corp. [654 F.2d 843, 850, 2d Cir. 1981], which found that "a company has no duty to correct or verify rumors in the marketplace unless those rumors can be attributed to the company''; (2) where the company is trading in its own stock (see Jordan v. Duff and Phelps, Inc. [815 F.2d 429, 435, 7th Cir. 1987]; or (3) where SEC rules specifically require disclosure.

Disclosure is specifically required under SEC rules when negotiations are undertaken in response to a tender offer. Any target making a solicitation or recommendation with respect to a tender offer is required to file Schedule 14D-9 with respect to such a solicitation or recommendation and to mail this schedule to its stockholders. Schedule 14D-9 requires the target to disclose, among other things, whether any negotiation is being undertaken or is underway by the target company in response to the tender offer that relates to or would result in certain types of transactions, including a merger or a transfer of a material amount of assets by the target company. If no agreement in principle has been reached, however, the possible terms of any transaction or the parties thereto need not be disclosed if in the opinion of the target's board of directors such disclosure would jeopardize continuation of the negotiations. In that event, disclosure that such negotiations are being undertaken or are underway is sufficient, subject to the company's ongoing obligation to update its prior disclosures in the event of a material change in the information previously published or given to the stockholders. See In re Revlon, Inc. (Sec. Exch. Act Rel. No. 23,320, 35 S.E.C. Dkt. 1541, June 16, 1986), which found that where a previously filed Schedule 14D-9 indicates that no merger negotiations are underway, the company is required to file an amendment disclosing their subsequent commencement.

The stance taken by the SEC in In re Allied Stores Corporation and

George C. Kern (Sec. Exch. Act Rel. No. 24,648, June 29, 1987) suggests that negotiations undertaken in response to a tender offer may present special problems for company counsel. In its administrative complaint, the SEC has alleged that Allied Stores did not promptly amend the Schedule 14D-9 that it filed on September 24, 1986, in response to a tender offer by Campeau Corporation (this schedule stated that the Allied Board had determined to "continue to explore and investigate, with the assistance and advice of Goldman, Sachs," certain transactions, including the acquisition of Allied or of certain of its assets by another company or person) to disclose that (1) in response to Campeau's tender offer, negotiations were underway on September 25, 1986 with representatives of The Edward J. DeBartolo Corporation that would result in the transfer to DeBartolo of a material amount of Allied's assets (six shopping centers for $405 million); (2) in response to Campeau's amended tender offer, that negotiations were underway with another party (a partnership comprised of DeBartolo and a private investor) relating to an acquisition of Allied through a merger; and (3) an agreement in principle had been reached and a board resolution had been passed on October 3, 1986, directing Allied's management to execute a merger agreement, subject to the partnership's obtaining the necessary financing. Allied did not file its first amendment to the Schedule 14D-9 until October 8, 1986, one day after the agreement was executed.

In an unprecedented action, the SEC also brought an administrative enforcement proceeding pursuant to Section 15(c)(4) of the Exchange Act against Allied's principal outside counsel, George C. Kern, a Sullivan & Cromwell partner and a director of Allied. The SEC alleged that Mr. Kern "and other members and associates of Sullivan & Cromwell working under his supervision drafted and reviewed Allied's Schedule 14D-9"; that Mr. Kern either participated in or was aware of the meetings and discussions between Allied and the DeBartolo entities, and that, after considering whether to amend Allied's original 14D-9 filing to disclose such meetings and discussions, Mr. Kern "decided that such an amendment would not be made." In the SEC's view, Mr. Kern's decision rendered him a "cause" of Allied's failure to comply, in a material respect, with Section 14(d)(4) of the Exchange Act and Rule 14d-9 thereunder, due to an act or omission that he knew or should have known would contribute to the company's failure to comply. The SEC's apparent position is that the disclosure requirements set forth in Schedule 14D-9 are not qualified by the materiality of the disclosure or the probability of consummation of any alternative transaction. The SEC's action against Mr. Kern suggests that, in its view, for an attorney to advise any different interpretation of the regulations constitutes grounds for the entry of an order against the attorney pursuant to Section 15(c)(4). Although Allied has settled the administrative proceeding, Sullivan & Cromwell has stated that it will oppose the SEC's position. This would be the first litigated proceeding under Section 15(c)(4).

Even when a company is not affirmatively obligated under the federal securities statutes to disclose the pendency of merger negotiations in the first instance, the rules of the exchange in which the company's stock is traded may require that the company promptly deny or clarify rumors or issue a statement that it knows of no corporate developments to account for unusual market activity. See New York Stock Exchange Listed Company Manual § 202.03. In the event of unusual market activity, an exchange official routinely will request the company to issue an explanatory statement pursuant to the Exchange's rules. See Note, Rule 10b-5 and the Duty To Disclose Merger Negotiations in Corporate Statements, 96 Yale L.J. 547, 551 & n.25 (1987). If the company makes such a statement, or otherwise undertakes to speak about corporate events while merger negotiations are pending and its statement does not disclose such negotiations, the company may be held liable under settled Rule 10b-5 doctrine if its statement is, under the circumstances, materially untrue or misleading. See SEC v. Texas Gulf Sulfur Co. (401 P.2d 833, 862, 2d Cir. 1968, en banc), which states that "Rule 10b-5 is violated whenever assertions are made [by a company]...in a manner reasonably calculated to influence the investing public...if such assertions are false or misleading or are so incomplete as to mislead" (cert. denied, 394 U.S. 976, 1969). Also see First Virginia Bankshares v. Benson (559 F.2d 1307, 1317, 5th Cir. 1977) which states that "[a] duty to speak the full truth arises when a defendant undertakes to say anything" (cert. denied, 435 U.S. 952, 1978). The Courts of Appeal are divided on the issue of when merger negotiations become sufficiently material that a company's denial of new corporate developments during the pendency of such negotiations warrants the imposition of liability under Rule 10b-5. The issue is currently before the Supreme Court.

The Third Circuit has adopted the so-called price and structure test. Under this test, a company is under no duty to disclose its discussions with a prospective merger partner until an agreement in principle—that is, a "fundamental agreement on the price and structure of a merger"—has been reached. See Greenfield v. Heublein, Inc. (742 F.2d 751, 759, 3d Cir. 1984; cert. denied, 469 U.S. 1215, 1985); Staffin v. Greenberg, (672 F.2d 1196,

1207, 3d Cir. 1982). In Heublein the court applied the price and structure test to exonerate a company which, in response to a request by the New York Stock Exchange, issued a "no-corporate-development" statement during the pendency of merger negotiations. The Heublein court reaffirmed its earlier holding in Staffin that "preliminary merger discussions are immaterial as a matter of law" (Heublein, 742 F.2d, p. 756) and went on to hold that, as a matter of law, where a company has no information indicating that the pendency of preliminary talks has been leaked or that insiders are engaged in trading on the basis of such information, a no-corporate-development statement is not false, inaccurate, or misleading.

The Seventh and Second Circuits have adopted the Third Circuit's price-and-structure test to govern pure silence/nondisclosure situations. See Flamm v. Eberstadt (814 F.2d 1169, 1178-79, 7th Cir. 1987); Kronfeld v. Trans World Airlines, Inc. (No. 86-7330, slip op. at 5817, 5833-35, 2d Cir. Nov. 2, 1987); Reiss v. Pan American World Airways, Inc. (711 F.2d 11, 14, 2d Cir. 1983) which notes that merger negotiations "are inherently fluid and the eventual outcome is shrouded in uncertainty. Disclosure may in fact be more misleading than secrecy so far as investment decisions are concerned..." In Flamm, Judge Easterbrook, while explicitly declining to decide the extent to which "firms may deny the existence of ongoing negotiations or shade the truth," had the following observations concerning the effectiveness of a "no comment" response:

> The conclusion of Greenfield is supported by the fact that unless the firm is entitled to conceal the negotiations, a demand by the Exchange to confirm or deny a rumor may flush out the truth no matter what the firm says, even though the firm is entitled to be silent and most investors would want it to be. Suppose a firm is engaged in negotiations that are best kept quiet, and the Exchange asks whether new developments account for activity in its stock. If the firm says yes and says why, the cat is out of the bag; if the firm says no, it faces liability for fraud; if the firm says "no comment" that is the same thing as saying "yes" because investors will deduce the truth. No corporation follows the CIA's policy of saying "no comment" to *every* inquiry; every firm regularly confirms or denies rumors, as the securities laws and the stock exchanges' rules require. The exchanges' rules require a response, not a refusal to respond, to inquiries. When a firm suddenly says "no comment," the inquisitor will realize that his suspicions have a foundation—yet the response may sow confusion all the same. If by hypothesis silence is the best course for investors, then it may be necessary to condone evasive answers, as the Third Circuit did in Greenfield, to put pursuers off the scent for a time.

The foregoing authorities would appear to allow the company to defer a public announcement while the independent committee explores feasibility and negotiates price and structure, provided the company receives no inquiries concerning the pendency of negotiations and provided there are no leaks and knowledge is limited to a few insiders who refrain from trading. Developments must be closely monitored. As a practical matter, experience has proven that the likelihood of leaks is substantial, thus encouraging early disclosure through an appropriate press release. In any event, a specific proposal setting forth the price and other material terms of a buyout, and requesting the board of directors to set in motion the necessary corporate machinery to consider the proposal, would seem to require disclosure at the time the proposal is made.

In In re Carnation Co. (SEC Exch. Act Rel. No. 22214, July 8, 1985; reprinted in [1984-1985 Transfer Binder] Fed. Sec. L. Rep. [CCH] ¶83, 801), the SEC indicated that an issuer that states that there is no corporate development to account for "unusual market activity" in its securities may violate the antifraud provisions of the federal securities laws if the statement is made while acquisition discussions are underway.

The report was issued in connection with an investigation into public statements made during confidential discussions regarding Nestle S.A.'s acquisition of Carnation Co. during the summer of 1984. According to the SEC, Carnation's major stockholder had undertaken activities aimed at the sale of the company and Carnation executives were involved in negotiations when the company's treasurer—who was not informed of the prospective merger—on two occasions told reporters there was no corporate development to account for recent upward movement in Carnation's stock. On the second occasion, he specifically denied the acquisition rumors. Two weeks later, Carnation agreed to be bought out at more than $20 per share from where its stock had been trading at the beginning of the negotiations.

The SEC concluded that Carnation's first public statement had been materially misleading and that Carnation's second public statement had been materially false and misleading. In the SEC's view, the omissions and misstatements were material because, had Carnation disclosed in those statements the contacts with Nestle and the activities of the major stockholder, "the reasonable Carnation shareholder would have considered that information to be significant in deciding whether to buy, sell or hold the stock" (id., p. 87, 597). In coming to this conclusion, the SEC stated:

> Whenever an issuer makes a public statement or responds to an inquiry from a stock exchange official concerning rumors, unusual market activity,

possible corporate developments or any other matter, the statement must be materially accurate and complete. If the issuer is aware of non-public information concerning acquisition discussions that are occurring at the time the statement is made, the issuer has an obligation to disclose sufficient information concerning the discussions to prevent the statements made from being materially misleading. See Shlanger v. Four-Phase Systems, Inc., supra (issuer statement denying knowledge of any corporate development which would account for market activity in its stock at a time when the company was engaged in preliminary merger discussions could be materially misleading).

When an issuer makes a public statement, information concerning preliminary acquisition discussions is material and must be disclosed if the information assumes "actual significance in the deliberation of" and significantly alters "the total mix of information available [to]" the reasonable shareholder (TSC Industries, Inc. v. Northway, 426 U.S. 438, 1976). Thus, in the Commission's view, an issuer statement that there is no corporate development that would account for unusual market activity in its stock, made while the issuer is engaged in acquisition discussions, may be materially false and misleading (Id., 87,595-87,596).

The SEC acknowledged the contrary result in Heublein, stating that it believed Heublein to have been "wrongly decided" (id., 87,596, Note 8). The SEC conceded that "in appropriate circumstances," a no comment response may be given to press inquiries regarding unusual market activity or rumors. However, the SEC report emphasized that "no comment" would not be appropriate where subsequent events have made an issuer's previous statements misleading or where market rumors are attributable to issuer leaks. The SEC indicated that it will take "appropriate enforcement action against issuers which fail to comply with these requirements."

In October 1987, Carnation agreed to pay $13 million to settle a shareholder class action suit relating to its public statements during its negotiations with Nestle, although it continued to deny all claims and contentions of the plaintiffs.

In Levinson v. Basic Inc. (786 F.2d 741, 6th Cir. 1986; cert. granted, 107 S. Ct. 1284, 1987), the court adopted the SEC's position in Carnation. The court held that, although Basic had no duty to speak in the early stages of merger negotiations between Basic Inc. and Combustion Engineering, once Basic voluntarily chose to make a statement, Basic had a duty "to disclose sufficient information so that the statement made is not 'false or misleading...or so incomplete as to mislead' " (Basic, 786 F.2d, p. 746 [quoting SEC v. Texas Gulf Sulfur Co., 401 F.2d 833, 862, 2d Cir. 1968; cert. denied, 394 U.S. 976, 1969]).

Beginning in September 1976 representatives of Combustion Engineering and Basic Inc. held informal discussions concerning a possible acquisition of Basic. In November 1976 the Combustion board authorized management to pursue a possible acquisition of Basic and Basic was informed of this authorization. While informal discussions continued, there were periods of unusual trading activity in Basic stock. In October 1977, after several days of high volume trading, the president of Basic released a statement that "the company knew no reason for the stock's activity and that no negotiations were underway with any company for a merger." Contacts between Basic and Combustion continued through December 19, 1978, when Basic approved Combustion's tender offer. On several occasions between July 1978 and December 15, 1978, Basic was contacted by the New York Stock Exchange inquiring about unusual trading in Basic stock, and on each occasion the company denied that any undisclosed merger or acquisition plans or other significant corporate developments existed. On September 25, 1978, Basic issued a press release stating that "management is unaware of any present or pending corporate development that would result in...abnormally heavy trading activity and price fluctuations in the company shares," and made a similar statement in its quarterly report to stockholders released in the beginning of November. It was not until December 18, 1978, when Basic asked the NYSE to suspend trading in its stock, that the company disclosed that it had been approached concerning a possible merger.

The Sixth Circuit recognized the general rule that a corporation has no obligation to disclose information concerning preliminary merger negotiations unless the corporation is trading in its own stock or is responsible for rumors leaking into the market. The Court stated, however, that once the corporation chooses to speak, it must speak truthfully. The Court held that Basic's denial of any knowledge regarding corporate developments that would cause unusual trading activity in its stock was "misleading, if not totally false" and thus in violation of § 10(b) of the Exchange Act and Rule 10b-5 promulgated thereunder.

The court specifically rejected the Third Circuit's opinion in Heublein. In so doing, it stated:

> When a company whose stock is publicly traded makes a statement, as Basic did, that "no negotiations" are underway, and that the corporation knows of "no reason for the stock's activity," and that "management is

unaware of any present or pending corporate development that would result in the abnormally heavy trading activity," information concerning ongoing acquisition discussions becomes material *by virtue of the statement denying their existence*. The "reasonable investor," having been informed that Basic knew of no corporate development that would result in the high trading activity, would, without doubt, have thought that disclosure of the fact that acquisition was being discussed "significantly altered the 'total mix' of information made available " (Id., 748; emphasis in original).

The Basic court thus endorsed the view expressed by the SEC in Carnation that a company engaged in secret preliminary merger negotiations must limit its public statements to "no comment."

Basic is currently on review by the Supreme Court, having been argued on November 2, 1987. In an amicus brief, the SEC has urged the Supreme Court to reject the price-and-structure test and to hold that "the materiality of merger discussions must be judged in each case on its facts" under the test for materiality first announced in TSC Industries, Inc. v. Northway, Inc. (426 U.S. 438, 449, 1976) which holds that a fact is material "if there is a substantial likelihood that a reasonable shareholder would consider it important" in making an investment decision. The SEC has also argued that while the Sixth Circuit was correct in rejecting the price-and-structure test, its decision should be vacated because the court improperly suggested that any false statement, regardless of how trivial, is per se material.

The Sixth Circuit's decision in Basic and the SEC report in Carnation emphasize the need for the company to be particularly careful when making public statements while it is engaged in preliminary discussions regarding the buyout. The company should take steps to assure that a system is in place for monitoring developments and dealing with press calls and stock exchange inquiries and that the people most likely to receive the calls are cognizant of what is happening or at least are instructed to respond with "no comment."

In addition to securities laws concerns regarding full and accurate disclosure, the board must also be cognizant of state law fiduciary duties that affect disclosure obligations. In order to create a level playing field and to permit fair and open bidding, the board should disclose that it has received a buyout proposal once it determines that it is interested in pursuing the buyout. Early disclosure will provide other bidders a fair opportunity to formulate competing offers.

The key elements of the initial press release will be (1) the price; (2) the form of the buyout; (3) that the buyout will be subject to the approval of the independent committee and stockholders, and (4) to any other material conditions. If the buyout involves the issuance of securities, the press release must contain only the information permitted by Rule 135 under the Securities Act of 1933.

Once the buyout has been publicly disclosed, the company and the buyout group should ensure that adequate disclosure of material developments concerning the buyout continues until it is closed.

Projections, Appraisals and Valuations

It is particularly important that all appraisals and valuations of the company be disclosed. In Weinberger, Signal possessed a valuation of UOP acquired by virtue of Signal's control of UOP. The Court found Signal's failure to disclose the report violated the requirement of fair dealing.

In light of the Fruehauf decision, the board should make sure that any information provided to the buyout group is also made available to other bidders. See "Must Directors Act as Neutral Auctioneers?" in Section 3.

The Joseph case, discussed in Section 2, suggests that when an appraisal or valuation is disclosed, all material circumstances surrounding such documents must also be fully disclosed. In Joseph, Royal Dutch's offer to purchase was found defective in that it failed to disclose the fact that Royal Dutch's investment banker did not consider the value of Shell's probable oil reserves in opining on the fairness of the offering price. In Weinberger, failure to disclose the cursory preparation of the Lehman Brothers opinion was considered misleading. Similarly, in Trans Union, the company's proxy material was found deficient because, among other things, it failed to disclose that the $55 price was predicated on an LBO study.

In connection with obtaining the financing for the buyout, the buyout group will, in all likelihood, have prepared some type of offering circular using the company's financial information and non-public projections—a situation analogous to Weinberger. Such information should be disclosed to the independent committee and, in the proxy statement, to the company's stockholders.

In Flynn v. Bass Brothers Enterprises, Inc. (744 F.2d 978, 3d Cir. 1984), the United States Court of Appeals for the Third Circuit set forth factors to be considered in determining, on a case-by-case basis, whether asset valuations must be disclosed.[18] Many of the factors articulated by the Court in Bass Brothers to be considered in determining whether a particular valuation need be disclosed relate to the reliability of the information. The factors to be considered are as follows:

> The facts upon which the information is based; the qualifications of those who prepared or compiled it; the purpose for which the information was originally intended; its relevance to the stockholders' impending decision; the degree of subjectivity or bias reflected in its preparation; the degree to which the information is unique; and the availability to the investor of other more reliable sources of information   (Id., p. 988).

In Starkman v. Marathon Oil Co. (772 F.2d 231, 6th Cir. 1985; cert. denied, 106 S. Ct. 1195, 1986), the court held that projections and asset appraisals must be disclosed in tender offer materials only if they are based on predictions regarding future economic and corporate events which are substantially "certain to hold"—the reported values must be "virtually as certain as hard facts." If a company voluntarily discloses projections or appraisals that do not rise to this level of certainty, then it must disclose the basis for and limitations on the projected values.

Rule 175 under the Securities Act of 1933 and Rule 3b-6 under the Exchange Act of 1934 provide a safe harbor from liability for projections contained in documents filed with the SEC. The safe harbor rule was adopted to encourage the disclosure of projections and forward-looking information and covers statements containing projections of revenues, income (loss), earnings (loss) per share, capital expenditures, dividends, capital structure or other financial items. The safe harbor would not, however, be available for projections that lacked a reasonable basis or that were not made in good faith.

Projections generally suffer from the fact that they are usually prepared to sell the transaction and it is difficult to put the information in appropriate perspective. Accordingly, any presentation of projections in the proxy statement require numerous disclaimers and the enumeration of underlying assumptions. In this regard, in Goldman v. Belden (754 F.2d 1059, 2d Cir. 1985), the Second Circuit, reversing the District Court, refused to permit the dismissal of a class action complaint against a company and certain of its officers that alleged violations of §10-b and Rule 10b-5 based on overly optimistic statements about the company's prospects contained in reports to shareholders and in public statements by its Chairman. In Walker v.

Action Industries, Inc. (802 F.2d 703, 4th Cir. 1986; cert. denied, 107 S. Ct. 952, 1987), the Fourth Circuit held that Action Industries had no duty to disclose financial projections based on orders it had received for the next fiscal year, noting that because of the uncertainty of such projections investors could be misled.

With the proliferation of LBOs in which so-called junk bonds are issued to public shareholders, the importance of accurate projections and their disclosure has greatly increased. In the event such securities are to be offered in the buyout, important subjects for disclosure will include the pro forma ratio of earnings to fixed charges, the resulting capitalization of the company after the buyout, the terms of any subordination provisions, the terms of any senior indebtedness incurred to finance the buyout, and any tax consequences (in the case of a discount instrument).

Schedule 13E-3

In connection with the buyout, particular attention should be paid to the disclosures required by Items 7, 8, and 9 of Schedule 13E-3 of the Rule 13E-3. These disclosures are designed to ensure that the conflicts inherent in the buyout are fully displayed and the advantages to the insiders are fully noted. The items seek disclosure, among other things, as to whether third parties have been given a chance to bid for (and thereby compete to acquire) the company.

Item 7(b) requires an expression of whether other alternatives were considered and, if so, the reason for their rejection.

The instruction to Item 8 states that firm offers by unaffiliated persons during the preceding 18 months must be disclosed. Consideration would have to be given to disclosing, based on materiality standards, an offer at a higher price than the buyout, even if outside the 18-month period.

Item 9(b)(6) requires disclosure of whether there was a limitation placed on the financial advisor limiting the scope of the investigation.

5. OTHER ISSUES

Financing

As indicated above, the buyout group will condition its obligation to close upon obtaining the financing necessary for the buyout. One of the threshold matters to which the independent committee should address itself is the terms and conditions of the financing of the buyout.

Ideally, the independent committee should receive a detailed commitment letter from the buyout group's lending institutions prior to execution of the Acquisition Agreement.

In lieu of such a commitment, the independent committee or its representatives should receive oral assurances from the proposed lenders.

The Acquisition Agreement should condition the mailing of the proxy statement upon receipt of definitive financing agreements, and should provide for termination of the buyout in the event that definitive financing agreements are not received within a specified period of time.

Drafts of the financing agreement should be reviewed by the independent committee and its counsel to determine the acceptability of the conditions to the financing. Material conditions should be disclosed in the proxy statement.

"Neutral" Voting Requirements

As a matter of "fair dealing," the acquisition agreement will often require, in addition to any stockholder vote required by law, that the buyout be approved by holders of a majority of the shares of voting stock of the company that are not beneficially owned by the buyout group or any of its affiliates. Although not specifically required by law, such a requirement will help to eliminate the possibility that the buyout will be approved over the objection of most of the company's unaffiliated stockholders and, under Delaware law, to shift the burden of proving unfairness to any potential plaintiffs. It should be noted that Item 8(c) of Schedule 13E-3 requires disclosure of whether the buyout is structured so that approval of at least a majority of unaffiliated securityholders is required.

There are three principal types of neutralized voting procedures:

1. Requiring the buyout group to vote for the buyout only if a majority of other shares voted at the meeting vote in its favor.
2. Requiring the buyout group to vote its shares for or against the buyout in the same proportion as other shares voted at the meeting vote in favor of or against the buyout.
3. Requiring the buyout group to vote its shares for or against the buyout if some super-majority of the other shares voted at the meeting, although greater or less than the required statutory majority, voted in favor of the buyout.

In the face of a competing bid for the company by a bidder with substantial holdings of the company common stock, the company may exclude such competing bidder's shares from the vote of disinterested stockholders. For example, in connection with Multimedia's recapitalization, approval of the transaction required approval by a majority of the outstanding shares of Multimedia common stock other than those held by anyone who had made an acquisition bid for the company.

Litigation-Outs

Depending on the circumstances, the buyout group and/or independent committee may seek a provision in the acquisition agreement providing for its termination in the event of litigation. At one end of the spectrum, the acquisition agreement would terminate if any litigation is commenced. At the other end of the spectrum, absent an injunction, there would be no termination because of litigation. A moderate position would differentiate between private and governmental actions.

Indemnification of Directors and Officers

Because of the likelihood of litigation in connection with the buyout, the company's directors will be concerned about the availability of indemnification. Counsel should seek the following protection for the directors and officers of the company in the acquisition agreement:

1. Newco should agree to maintain officers' and directors' liability insurance in force at specified levels (typically on terms no less favorable than the terms of the insurance presently maintained by

the company) for an agreed-upon period of time (usually three to six years). Because most officers' and directors' liability policies are written on a "claims made" basis, directors will have no protection against claims made after the closing of the transaction if the policy is allowed to lapse.

2. Newco also should agree not to amend or repeal any provision in the company's charter or bylaws that authorizes the indemnification of directors or officers of the company for an agreed-upon period of time (typically three to six years) after the closing of the buyout.

3. Finally, Newco should agree to cause the company, after the closing of the buyout, to indemnify the directors and officers of the company to the fullest extent permitted by law against any liability not covered by the company's officers' and directors' liability insurance policy.

ADDENDUM

Since the time that this chapter was written, there have been many developments in the legal and business environment for leveraged buyouts. Certain cases that were pending appeal at the time of writing have been decided, most notably the Supreme Court's decision in Levinson v. Basic Inc. A number of other important decisions subsequent to the date of writing have addressed the processes used in the auctioning of large corporations, some of which cases directly address the use of lock-ups, break-up fee and expense provisions, and rights plans as tools in LBO transactions. In particular, the Delaware Supreme Court in 1988 spent a great deal of time trying to clarify its decision in Revlon, Inc. v. MacAndrews & Forbes Holdings, Inc., discussed at length in this chapter. The 1988 cases are required reading in order to understand the current legal framework for leveraged buyouts.

As to the business environment for LBO transactions, 1988 laid to rest suspicions—still widely held at the time this chapter was written—that the October 1987 market crash would chill buyers' interest in pursuing large leveraged acquisitions or would eliminate the market's receptiveness to junk bonds. Actually, 1988 proved to be a record-breaking year for so-called megadeals, and there is no reason to believe that 1989 will show any slowdown of the takeover boom. Despite the significant developments that have occurred since the date this chapter was written, it nevertheless presents the basic legal framework within which LBOs came to be and are conducted.

NOTES

1. The information in this chapter is current through April 27, 1988.
2. In addition to stockholder suits, a company may also experience suits by bondholders and other creditors. The Delaware courts, however, have consistently refused to recognize the existence of fiduciary duties owed by a company to its creditors. See Anadarko Petroleum Corp. v. Panhandle Eastern Corp. (521 A.2d 624, 629-30, Del. Ch. 1987) (position of holders of "when-issued" rights is analogous to that of convertible debenture holders, to whom no fiduciary duties are owed prior to the exercise of the conversion right); Katz v. Oak Industries Inc. (508 A.2d 873, 879, Del. Ch. 1986) (relationship of corporation to bondholder is purely contractual); Norte & Co. v. Manor Healthcare Corp. (Civ. Action Nos. 827 & 6831, Del. Ch. Nov. 21, 1985) (convertible debentureholders lack standing to maintain an action for breach of fiduciary duty).

   In the event of a bankruptcy, a company's former stockholders might, under certain circumstances, be sued by the company's unpaid creditors in a fraudulent conveyance action for recovery of cash payments received by such stockholders for their stock. See United States v. Gleneagles Investment Co., Inc. (565 F. Supp. 556, 584-85, M.D. Pa. 1983; aff'd on other issues sub nom United States v. Tabor Court Realty Corp. 803 F.2d 1288, 3d Cir. 1986 [holding that certain mortgages given to finance leveraged acquisition were fraudulent conveyances]; cert. denied, 107 S. Ct. 3229, 1987).
3. Indeed, the fiduciary obligations of officers and directors to a corporation and its stockholders are more firmly established than the fiduciary duty owed by a majority stockholder to the minority.
4. Such conflict of interest has been described by Bevis Longstreth, a former commissioner of the Securities and Exchange Commission, as follows:
   Management is acting on both sides of the transaction. In its fiduciary capacity, management is seeking to sell the corporation and, therefore, must have

concluded that a sale is in the best interests of the shareholders. In its proprietary capacity, management is seeking to purchase the corporation, and must have concluded that it can do so at a price favorable to it. In short, management is dealing with itself. (B. Longstreth, Fairness of management buy-outs needs evaluation, *Legal Times of Washington,* October 10, 1983, p. 15.)

5. The market price for UOP stock at the time the proposal was made was $14.50.

6. Lehman Brothers spent three days preparing the opinion. The only prices Lehman Brothers apparently evaluated were the range from $20 to $21.

7. Even where a majority of the directors are independent, delegation of negotiating or review functions to a committee of the board may make sense as a practical matter.

8. In Delaware, a committee of the board does not have the power or authority to adopt an agreement of merger (Del. Gen. Corp. Law § 141[c]).

9. New York Stock Exchange Listed Company Manual § 303.00. The rule was adopted in March 1977. See SEC Release No. 34-13346 (March 9, 1977).

10. For a discussion of valuation techniques typically used by investment bankers in rendering fairness opinions, see Investment bankers' fairness opinions in corporate control transactions, *Yale Law Journal, 96,* pp. 119, 137-139.

11. See, for example, Herzel & Katz, Smith v. Van Gorkom: The business of judging business judgment, *Business Law, 41,* 1187; Manning, Reflections and practical tips on life in the boardroom after Van Gorkom, *Business Law, 41,* 1.

12. Many of the announced leveraged buyouts involving public companies are not completed because of a higher bid by a competing offerer. For example, Stokely Van Camp, Esmark, Royal Crown, Scott & Fetzer, and Multimedia.

13. For a critique of the Revlon, SCM, and Fruehauf decisions, see Lipton, In defense of white knight LBOs, *Legal Times* (August 18, 1986), in which it is argued that a neutral auction is not always the best means of maximizing shareholder values in a contest for corporate control.

14. See generally Bryer and Vlahakis, Enforcement of no-shop clauses, *New York Law Journal,* (December 10, 1984), p. 33, column 6.

15. B. Longstreth (1983, October 6). Remarks to the International Bar Association, Toronto, Canada, Management buyouts: Are public shareholders getting a fair deal? SEC News Release.

16. Pay Less and Northwest were entirely unrelated parties prior to the events described in Jewel, despite the similarity of their names.

17. See also L. Lowenstein, Management buyouts, *Columbia Law Review, 85* (May 1985), 730-784.

18. The Court in Bass Brothers declined to apply the factors to the case, choosing instead to analyze the alleged nondisclosure claims under prior standards: namely, whether the information had "sufficient indicia of reliability to require disclosure" (id., p. 988).

ABOUT THE AUTHORS

Lawrence Lederman and Barry A. Bryer are partners in the law firm of Wachtell, Lipton, Rosen & Katz in New York City. Lederman is also an Adjunct Professor at the New York University School of Law. Both have a particular expertise in mergers and acquisitions and corporate restructuring transactions.

CHAPTER 7

LEVERAGED BUYOUTS: FEDERAL INCOME TAX CONSIDERATIONS

Robert N. Macris

1. INTRODUCTION

An LBO is characterized by a general substitution of debt for equity in the capital structure of the acquired entity. In essence, an LBO is a transaction in which a buying group consisting generally of outside investors, members of management, other employees (usually through an ESOP), and certain substantial shareholders, or some combination thereof, acquires ownership of a corporation or a subsidiary or division of a corporation. An MBO is a form of LBO in which members of management are often the driving force behind the buyout.

An LBO is financed primarily through borrowings from one or more lenders, including, in some instances, from the members of the selling group in the form of deferred purchase price. The lenders will look to the assets and/or the cash flow of the business as the source of repayment of the debt. The magnitude of equity capital contributed by members of the buying group is relatively small, despite the fact that, following the buyout, the members of the buying group will own all the residual equity of the acquired entity. However, because of the large-scale substitution of debt for equity, this residual equity represents only a minor portion of the value of the former equity of the acquired entity. The members of the buying group generally will have no commitment to invest any additional funds.

Current tax law provides a major incentive for leveraged acquisitions, primarily as a result of the deductibility of interest on indebtedness against income. Thus, despite the separate tier corporate and shareholder level of tax schema embodied in our tax system, current tax law in effect sanctions an ad hoc integration of corporate and shareholder taxation.

The financial structure of an LBO is the result of negotiations on behalf of the members of the selling group, the various members of the buying group and the lenders. Consideration of tax consequences, priority of debt and need for collateralization, cash flow analysis, desire for participation in earnings and appreciation versus a fixed yield, as well as management and employee incentives, all play an important role in determining the structure of the buyout. Capital for an LBO generally consists of the following: (1) senior debt that is usually fully collateralized and is provided by banks or insurance companies; (2) so-called mezzanine financing, which is subordinated debt, often with equity kickers, or sometimes preferred stock, usually provided by risk-oriented outside investors, but sometimes by the members of the selling group; and (3) equity capital provided by the members of the buying group. Senior debt is designed to be secured by the assets of the acquired entity, and thus is typically extended to a transitory merger corporation in single-tier acquisitions or to a transitory subsidiary of the acquiring entity in two-tier acquisitions. Senior financing may be in the form of a term loan (generally amortizing over no longer than a 10-year period) or a revolving credit (so-called evergreen financing), which may be asset-based so that the revolver increases as asset values increase. Usually, acquisition and resort to mezzanine financing will be necessary. Risk-oriented outside investors and members of the selling group may provide a portion of mezzanine financing through the receipt of high-yield junior subordinated debentures (that is, junk bonds that are not rated as investment grade). These junk bonds may be in the form of zero coupon postacquisition cash flow of the acquired entity. Mezzanine financing may also be sold to institutions as part of a "strip," consisting of junior indebtedness, as well as to investors, including investment banks structuring the transaction, who provide for short-term "bridge" financing pending the placement of mezzanine financing. Equity capital may be provided in whole or in part by venture capital investors or by former shareholders of the acquired entity who are cashed-out of a large portion of the value of their stock but who risk the remaining portion of the value of such stock in the new enterprise. Furthermore, management investors generally purchase some equity capital in an LBO and receive additional equity incentive in the form of stock options or rights or restricted stock. Employees may provide significant equity capital through investment by an ESOP.

2. TAX ADVANTAGES OF A LEVERAGED STRUCTURE

Deductibility of Interest

Although the corporate entity resulting from an LBO does not enjoy tax advantages unavailable to other corporations, the substitution of debt for equity positions this leveraged entity so that it may utilize such tax advantages to a much greater degree. The major tax advantage associated with a leveraged structure is the deductibility of interest on indebtedness as contrasted with the general nondeductibility of dividends paid on equity. This interest deduction shelters otherwise taxable corporate income and thereby minimizes the penalty of the double-tax corporate schema, in effect creating an ad hoc integration of corporate and shareholder taxation. The typical leveraged buyout candidate is a high-effective-rate taxpayer that enjoys a substantial cash flow. By channeling such cash flow to the deductible repayment of debt interest, income that would otherwise be subject to tax becomes sheltered. The sheltering effect becomes magnified by the utilization of zero-coupon or deferred-interest debentures, which generate current deductions (and interest income to the holders) without requiring current payment of cash. Hence, the buying group can maximize the use of pretax cash flow and, by virtue of the compounding of return on capital, achieve substantially greater growth of net worth than would be the case absent this tax law subsidy.

Investor Rollovers

Oftentimes, certain former shareholders of the acquired entity, including members of management, will be members of the buying group. Generally, it is possible to structure the buyout transaction so that such shareholders may cash out a portion of their existing equity in the acquired corporation at capital gains rates and reinvest or roll over the remaining portion of their equity on a tax-free basis. The creation of a highly leveraged structure permits a cash-out of a relatively large proportion of the value of the existing equity and, at the same time, permits the conversion of the remaining value of the existing equity into a relatively substantial equity position in the newly leveraged entity.

Management Cheap Stock

As a consequence of high leverage, the aggregate value of the equity in the leveraged entity will be considerably reduced relative to the aggregate value of the equity prior to the buyout. Although this stock contains a substantial "option" element, its fair market value at the outset is arguably based primarily on book value. Hence, it may be possible for management to purchase at book value (or at such premium thereto that reflects the option element) a significant equity position in the acquiring entity so that future appreciation will be taxed as capital gain rather than as ordinary compensation income. This would be true even if the stock purchased by management were unvested stock, as long as an election under Section 83(b) of the Internal Revenue Code of 1986, as amended (the Code), were effectively made.

Step-Up in Tax Basis

Prior to the Tax Reform Act of 1986 and the abrogation of the General Utilities doctrine, if the value of an acquired corporation's depreciable assets exceeded their tax basis, it was possible to structure an LBO transaction so that a step-up in the tax basis of the assets resulted (with the only tax cost being recapture income). Therefore, tax deductions would be increased and a greater amount of pre-tax corporate income could be sheltered. Now, with full corporate-level gain recognition in a step-up transaction, any advantage in stepping up tax basis is generally eliminated.

An exception is an acquisition of assets of a standalone corporation that is an S corporation or that has a large loss carryover to absorb gain on the asset sale. In addition, a sale of assets by a subsidiary within a consolidated group, either directly or through an election under Section 338(h)(10) of the Code, would be advantageous, as long as the inherent asset gain is not substantially greater than the inherent gain that would have resulted from a sale of the subsidiary's stock.

As an alternative to a full step-up in "inside" asset basis, a step-up in "outside" stock basis may be desirable if it is expected that various business segments of the acquired corporation will be sold following the LBO. Prior to the Omnibus Budget Reconciliation Act of 1987 (the 1987 Act) this could have been achieved through what was commonly known as a "mirror liquidation" structure. Such a structure permitted the sale of various appreciated business segments in the acquired corporation to different buyers without recognition of corporate level gain. The technique involved the funding at fair market acquisition value of several mirror analogs to the business segments of the acquired corporation with the mirror analogs effecting the acquisition by collectively purchasing (directly or by merger) the stock of the corporation which was subject to the LBO. Thereafter, the acquired corporation would have been liquidated under Section 332 of the Code[1] into the mirror analogs, each of which could then have been sold without recognition of gain. (The 1987 Act eliminates the applicability of Section 1.1502-34 of the Treasury regulations in this context.[2]) Hence, the mirror liquidation technique survives only in a so-called 80/20 structure where 80% or more of the acquired corporation's stock is held by only one mirror subsidiary and where the inherent asset gain in the assets of the acquired corporation to be distributed to the other mirror subsidiary or subsidiaries is relatively small.

A step-up in the outside stock bases of the various business segments of the corporation which is subject to the buyout may be achieved even after the 1987 Act if such business segments are incorporated and distributed to two or more unrelated corporate acquirers pursuant to Section 355 of the Code. This technique may be available if each of the acquirers owns less than 80% of the acquired corporation stock and holds such stock for a sufficient period to establish shareholder status (in this regard, the acquirers should not have a fixed plan for the utilization of Section 355). Thereafter, if the requirements of Section 355 of the Code are otherwise satisfied, the acquired corporation could distribute an incorporated business segment to each acquirer without tax and with a step-up in outside stock basis.

3. TAX CONSIDERATIONS IN FINANCING THE ACQUIRING ENTITY

Debt vs. Equity

The distinction between debt and equity is of utmost importance in an LBO. As discussed above, the substitution of debt for equity in the capital structure of the acquired corporation is the primary tax advantage arising from the buyout.

Characterization of an instrument as debt or equity is based upon a case law "facts and circumstances" analysis.[3] Some of the principal factors in the determination are (1) intent of the parties; (2) name of instrument; (3) proportionality of "debt" and "equity" holdings; (4) debt to equity ratio; (5) fixed obligation to pay principal on definite maturity date and interest on definite payment dates; (6) ability of debtor to meet obligations; (7) subordination; (8) convertibility; (9) voice in operation of entity; (10) rights in default. Generally, straight debt instruments held by nonshareholders are relatively immune from reclassification as equity. Thus, junior subordinated debentures which are employed in highly leveraged buyouts should not be characterized as equity. Debt with equity features—for example, convertible debt that is designed to be converted into equity—may be subject to greater risk of recharacterization in a highly leveraged entity.[4]

Disallowance of Interest Deductions—I.R.C. Section 279

Section 279 of the Code is designed to restrict the use of certain acquisition indebtedness by disallowing some or all of the interest deductions with respect to such debt. In practice, Section 279 is easily avoided. Debt is subject to Section 279 only if *all* the following tests are satisfied: (1) the debt is issued to provide consideration for the acquisition of stock or assets of "another corporation" (I.R.C. Section 279(b)(1)); (2) the debt is either subordinated to the claims of trade creditors of the issuing corporation generally or expressly subordinated in right of payment to the payment of any substantial amount of unsecured indebtedness of the issuing corporation (I.R.C. Section 279(b)(2)); (3) the debt is either convertible into stock of the issuer or issued as part of an investment unit that includes an option to acquire stock of the issuer (I.R.C. Section 279(b)(3)); and (4) on defined dates, the debt-to-equity ratio of the issuer exceeds 2:1 or its projected earnings do not exceed three times annual interest expense (I.R.C. Section 279(b)(4)). If Section 279 of the Code applies, interest deductions on the indebtedness will be denied to the extent that such interest exceeds (1) $5 million reduced by (2) interest paid on any other debt issued to provide consideration for the acquisition of stock or assets of another corporation (whether or not such debt is acquisition indebtedness limited under Section 279) (I.R.C. Section 279(a)).

Generally, in a highly leveraged acquisition, the Section 279 debt-to-equity ratio test will be satisfied. However, the other three tests are easily avoided, as in the following examples: (1) Section 279 does not apply to indebtedness issued in redemption of the stock of the issuer (e.g., debt issued in a recapitalization/redemption LBO); (2) Section 279(b)(2) is generally avoided in a holding company LBO in which the acquisition debt is issued by the holding company, although such debt provides effective subordination with respect to debt of the acquired company; (3) debt issued as part of an investment unit with common stock skirts Section 279(b)(3).[5]

Original Issue Discount

If a debt instrument is issued with a stated maturity amount that exceeds its issue price, the difference is original issue discount (OID). OID is taxed to the holder (and is deductible to the issuer despite the fact that cash is not currently paid) as interest income on a yield to maturity amortization over the life of the debt.[6]

Preferred Stock: Constructive Stock Dividends

If preferred stock has an issue price (i.e., fair market value) less than its redemption price, the difference, to the extent that it constitutes an "unreasonable redemption premium," will be treated as a constructive stock dividend to the holder over the period during which the preferred stock cannot be called for redemption.[7] It is possible that this problem may be avoided by making the preferred stock immediately callable.[8]

4. TAX CONSIDERATIONS RELATING TO MANAGEMENT INCENTIVES

Section 83

Section 83 of the Code provides that the excess of the fair market value of property (including stock) transferred in connection with the performance of services over the amount, if any, paid for such property constitutes ordinary compensation income.[9] It is important to note that fair market value is determined without regard to restrictions on the property that may lapse with the passage of time.[10] The employer corporation obtains a tax deduction for compensation paid equal to the compensation income recognized to the employee, provided that applicable withholding requirements are satisfied.[11]

Often, it is desirable that management's ownership of stock be contingent on the performance by management of services for a specified time period or on the attainment of certain performance goals. If the property transferred under Section 83 is subject to a substantial risk of forfeiture, compensation income is recognized (and the employer is entitled to a corresponding deduction) only when the forfeiture restrictions lapse and is measured by the excess of the then fair market value of the property over the amount, if any, paid for the property.[12] This is true even if full value had been initially paid for the property.[13] If property is subject to a substantial risk of forfeiture, the employee may elect under Section 83(b) of the Code (by filing an election within 30 days after the transfer of property) to recognize income based upon the excess of the fair market value of the property at the time of transfer over the amount, if any, paid. Thus, no additional ordinary income would be recognized when the forfeiture restrictions lapse.

Junior Stock Arrangements

Valuation is the key issue in determining the compensatory element of management purchased equity in an LBO. Sometimes, the capital structure chosen is one in which management receives a "junior" stock with the other investors receiving a stock with "senior" rights and preferences. A senior stock could take the form of a convertible preferred stock or a second class of common stock with special dividend rights and liquidation preferences. Alternatively, the junior stock could be a stock that is callable and/or putable upon the occurrence of certain events (e.g., termination of employment), with the call or put price being based on a fixed differential (or formula price) from the appraised value of the senior stock at such time. Another possibility is the transfer to management of a junior common stock that becomes convertible into regular common stock upon the occurrence of a specified event (e.g., attainment of performance goals or public distribution). At the time of the LBO when the prospects of the business are uncertain, the compensation element to management inherent in the junior stock may thus be reduced or eliminated. It is important, though, for management to obtain a competent appraisal of value to support its tax position.

It should be noted that the Internal Revenue Service (IRS) has indicated that it will carefully scrutinize junior stock arrangements. For example, with respect to junior common stock that is convertible into regular common stock, there is a risk that such stock would be viewed either as (1) containing a lapse restriction so that valuation would be based upon the regular common stock fair market value or (2) a junior stock plus a nonstatutory option to purchase regular common with respect to which compensation income would be recognized upon conversion of the junior stock in an amount equal to the excess of the fair market value of the regular common stock at the time of conversion over the amount, if any, paid for the junior stock. In addition, at least in the context of publicly traded senior stock, the IRS has indicated displeasure with fixed price differential stock (in particular, where the formula price may not be a true nonlapse restriction).

Stock Options and Stock Appreciation Rights

Rather than compensating management by transfers of stock, compensation could take the form of grants of nonstatutory stock options or stock appreciation rights. No income would be recognized by the holder of an option or right at the time of grant.[14] Instead, compensation income would be recognized (and the employer would be entitled to a corresponding deduction) at the time the option or right is exercised (or six months later in the case of a person subject to Section 16(b) of the Securities Exchange Act of 1934) measured by the then spread between the fair market value of the stock and the exercise price, if any. As a supplement to nonstatutory options, management could be granted "incentive stock options" (ISOs) pursuant to Section 422A of the Code. Unlike a nonstatutory option, no income is recognized in respect of an ISO until the time of disposition of the stock received upon exercise (however, the spread between the fair market value at time of exercise and exercise price is an item of "tax preference" for purposes of the "alternative minimum tax"—see I.R.C. Section 57(a)(10)). If the stock received is held for more than two years from the date of grant and more than one year from the date of exercise, capital gain or loss will result upon disposition. See I.R.C. Section 422A(a). Otherwise, ordinary compensation income up to the amount of gain on disposition will result to the extent that such income would have been recognized upon the exercise of a nonstatutory option and any remaining gain will be long-term capital gain.[15] ISOs are subject to strict requirements for qualification as set forth in Section 422A of the Code, including a requirement that the option price not be less than the fair market value of the stock at the time of grant and that the aggregate fair market value of stock (determined at the time of grant) with respect to which incentive stock options become exercisable for the first time by an individual during any calendar year cannot exceed $100,000.[16] Moreover, assuming retention beyond 1988 of the uniform tax rate on individual ordinary income and capital gains, the tax advantage of ISOs (i.e., deferral) is outweighed by the corporate tax cost (i.e., loss of the compensation deduction, absent a disqualifying disposition). Hence, the utility of ISOs is somewhat limited.

Loans to Purchase Stock

Often, management participants in an LBO may not possess resources sufficient to purchase stock. In such a case, the necessary funds may be loaned to the members of management by the corporation. However, it is crucial that the loans be fully recourse (otherwise the borrower will be viewed as having only an option to purchase shares—see Treasury Regulations Section 1.83-3(a)(2). Further, any management loan would be subject to the market rate interest rules of Section 7872 of the Code.

Cash-out or Rollover of Options, Rights and Restricted Stock

Management participants in an LBO may hold unexercised stock options and stock appreciation rights or restricted stock in the corporation to be acquired. The untaxed compensation element or appreciation inherent in these may be cashed-out to provide funds, for example, necessary to purchase stock or may be preserved through the grant, in substitution therefor, of new options, rights or restricted stock in the acquiring entity.[17] It should be noted that if an ISO is cashed out, it will nevertheless continue to be considered "outstanding" for purposes of the ISO sequential exercise rule (see I.R.C. Section 422A(c)(7) as it existed prior to elimination by the Tax Reform Act of 1986 with respect to post-1986 ISOs).

Golden Parachute Tax

One concern with respect to arrangements for executive compensation in connection with an LBO is the impact of the golden parachute tax rules that are applicable to payments or benefits received in connection with a change of control of a corporation excluding payments or benefits received pursuant to a contract entered into on or before June 15, 1984 (and not amended or renewed after June 14, 1984).[18] Under these rules, such tax may result if the aggregate present value of all payments in the nature of compensation to a "disqualified individual" that are "contingent on a change in control" equals or exceeds three times the "base amount" of the disqualified individual. The "base amount" is the average annual compensation of the disqualified individual for the five years preceding the year in which the change of control occurs. A "disqualified individual" is an individual who performs services for the corporation and who is highly compensated, an officer or a shareholder. A payment is considered "contingent on a change in control" (referred to herein as a "parachute payment") if the payment is made because of the change in control (e.g., a payment is made in connection with the change of control or because of termination of employment resulting from the change of control). Payments that are reasonable in amount and for services rendered following a change of control are not considered to be parachute payments. In connection with an LBO, parachute payments may include payments in cancellation of stock options or other employee benefits and payments pursuant to accelerations in time of payment or vesting of employee benefits (excepting perhaps accelerated payments that do not give rise to an increase in present value). If the aggregate present value of all parachute payments equals or exceeds three times the disqualified individual's base amount, the golden parachute tax will be triggered with respect to "excess parachute payments"—that is, the excess of the total present value of parachute payments over the greater of (1) the base amount or (2) "reasonable compensation" for services actually rendered prior to the change of control. Excess parachute payments are subject to a 20%, nondeductible excise tax payable by the disqualified individual and are not deductible by the corporation. Therefore, it is important that these rules be carefully monitored. It should be noted that elective relief from the golden parachute tax is available for certain closely held corporations.

5. THE USE OF ESOPs IN LBOs

The Nature of an ESOP

An ESOP is a qualified employee benefit plan designed to invest primarily in employer stock. ESOPs are subject to stringent requirements under both the Code and the Employee Retirement Income Security Act of 1974, as amended (ERISA). A leveraged ESOP is an ESOP that borrows cash, generally from or on the guarantee of the employer corporation, and utilizes such cash (or a purchase money note) to purchase "employer securities" from the employer. Subject to applicable limitations, the employer will contribute cash annually to the ESOP in an amount sufficient to amortize the principal and interest on the ESOP loan. A leveraged ESOP provides a tax advantaged means of financing an LBO and transferring a significant equity stake in the acquiring corporation to employees.

As a qualified plan, employer contributions to an ESOP are tax deductible.[19] The ESOP is not subject to taxation.[20] Employee participants are not taxed until they receive distributions from the ESOP.[21]

Thus, utilization of a leveraged ESOP as a member of the buying group in an LBO permits the repayment of the ESOP debt to the institutional lenders on a pretax basis. The cost is a substantial reduction in the equity ownership of the other members of the buying group.

General Requirements Relating to ESOPs

Fiduciary Standards

A leveraged ESOP, like all qualified plans, is subject to the fiduciary responsibility provisions of ERISA and the Code. The ESOP must be for the "exclusive benefit" of the ESOP participants.[22] The ESOP fiduciaries must discharge their duties "solely in the interests of the participants...and for the exclusive purpose of providing benefits to participants."[23] In addition, investments of ESOP assets made by the ESOP fiduciaries are subject to a "prudent man" standard.[24]

A fiduciary of a plan, generally, is any person who exercises any discretionary authority in administering, managing or investing on behalf of the plan.[25] It should be noted that where an ESOP is inappropriately created, fiduciary status may arise with respect to the design and implementation of the ESOP.[26]

Generally, with respect to an ESOP, these standards should be applied by taking account of the purpose for which the ESOP is designed, namely, to invest primarily in employer stock. At the same time, however, the implementation of the ESOP and the investment in employer stock must be "prudent."[27] This is of critical importance in an LBO in which the ESOP is purchasing illiquid shares of a highly leveraged entity. In particular, the Department of Labor will closely scrutinize any leveraged buyout transaction in which an extant pension plan converts its assets into employer securities.[28] The fiduciary standards of ERISA will not be violated merely because parties other than the ESOP participants, including the employer, derive an incidental benefit from the implementation or ongoing functioning of the ESOP.[29] However, in establishing and maintaining an ESOP, the primary emphasis must be on the best interests of the ESOP participants.

In addition to the rules relating to fiduciary standards, certain provisions relating to "prohibited transactions" under ERISA are of considerable importance with respect to a leveraged ESOP. Section 4975 of the Code imposes a penalty tax on so-called prohibited transactions, unless an exemption is available.

Although a loan between a plan and an employer (including an extension of credit by way of guarantee by an employer) would normally be prohibited, a specific exemption exists for a leveraged ESOP, provided the loan is primarily for the benefit of the ESOP participants, the loan is at a reasonable rate of interest, and any collateral given consists only of employer securities.[30] In general, this requires that the loan be utilized to effect the purpose of the leveraged ESOP—that is, the purchase of employer stock—and that the terms of the loan be as favorable to the ESOP as terms resulting from arm's-length negotiations between independent parties.[31]

Furthermore, any sale of assets, including employer securities, between a leveraged ESOP and the employer will constitute a prohibited transaction unless the purchase price represents no more than "adequate consideration" and no commission is charged with respect to the purchase transaction.[32] The term "adequate consideration" is defined in the case of traded stock as the prevailing market price and in the case of nontraded stock as fair market value determined in good faith—for example, by obtaining an independent appraisal of valuation from an investment banking firm.[33] Accordingly, in an LBO where the ESOP is to purchase stock in a closely held LBO investment vehicle, a valuation obtained from an investment banker acting on behalf of the ESOP would be advisable. Such a valuation would be particularly important in an LBO in which an ESOP's equity is diluted through the use of a second class of stock. It would not be unusual for the Department of Labor to examine and criticize the basis for such valuation and, if it determines that the ESOP paid more than adequate consideration, to force a modification in the terms of the transaction.[34] In this regard, it is extremely important that an ESOP purchasing a second class of stock be represented by competent advisors both to negotiate on behalf of the ESOP the terms of its participation in the LBO and to advise the ESOP trustee as to the fairness of the structure to the ESOP and the prudence of the ESOP's investment. The payment of a market premium by an ESOP for shares purchased from a person other than a party in interest need not be at the market (for example, a premium tender offer by an ESOP as part of the LBO), but such payment must be prudent.

Employer Securities
A leveraged ESOP, by its terms, must be designed to invest primarily in qualifying employer securities.[35] Generally, with respect to a leveraged ESOP, a "qualifying employer security" will be common stock issued by the employer (or an affiliate of the employer) that is readily tradable on an

established securities market.[36] If no readily tradable common stock exists, then such stock must be common stock possessing a combination of voting and dividend rights equal to the classes of common stock, respectively, having the greatest voting and dividend rights.[37] Noncallable preferred stock may constitute a "qualifying employer security" if the preferred stock is immediately convertible at market into any such common stock.[38]

Two additional requirements must be satisfied by a leveraged ESOP. First, a participant must have a right to demand that his or her benefits from the ESOP be distributed in employer securities and, if such securities are not readily tradable on an established securities market, must have a right to require employer repurchase under a fair valuation formula.[39] Such put option must be exercisable for a period of 60 days subsequent to the distribution and, if not exercised during such period, for an additional 60-day period in the following plan year.[40] Second, if the employer has a class of securities required to be registered under Section 12 of the Securities Exchange Act of 1934 (or a class of securities that would be required to be so registered but for an exemption under Section 12(g)(2)(H) of the Securities Exchange Act), then each participant must have a right to direct the ESOP as to the manner in which employer securities that are entitled to vote and are allocated to the employee's account are to be voted. If the employer does not have a registration-type class of securities, each participant must have a right to direct vote on major corporate transactions.[41] Unallocated shares held in the "suspense account" may be voted by the ESOP fiduciary. Partial diversification elections are required with respect to accounts of participants who attain age 55 with 10 years of ESOP participation.[42]

Suspense Account
The employer securities acquired with the proceeds of an ESOP loan must be placed in a "suspense account" awaiting allocation to the ESOP participants' individual accounts. Securities are released from this suspense account under one of two methods. The first, the "principal and interest" method, provides for release of the stock based upon the ratio that the amount of principal and interest paid on the ESOP loan in that year bears to the total principal and interest projected to be paid in that year and future years. The second, the "principal only" method, provides for release of employer stock from the suspense account based upon the ratio that the principal payment made in a given year bears to the total principal to be paid

in that year and all future years. The principal-only method may be used only if the term of the loan is 10 years or less and the loan provides for repayment of principal at least as rapidly as on a level annual basis over 10 years. Each year, securities are withdrawn from the suspense account in accordance with these rules and are allocated (subject to certain limitations discussed below) to the individual accounts of the ESOP participants. This allocation is generally based on each participant's proportionate share of the compensation paid to all participants; however, it may be based on other factors as long as the allocation method does not discriminate in favor of highly paid employees.[43]

Contributions

Section 401(a)(16) of the Code provides that an ESOP must satisfy the requirements under Section 415 of the Code relating to limitations on contributions and allocations of benefits. Under Section 404 of the Code, certain limitations apply to the deductibility of employer contributions to the ESOP. The deduction under Section 404 of the Code is subject to a cap equal to the maximum limitation under Section 415 of the Code.[44] Otherwise, there is no limitation on the deductibility of employer contributions that are utilized by the leveraged ESOP to amortize the interest component of the ESOP loan and, with respect to the deductibility of contributions to the ESOP that are utilized to amortize the principal component of the ESOP loan, such contributions are limited to a maximum of 25% of participants' covered compensation.[45] Under Section 415, allocations to a participant's individual ESOP account are generally limited to the lesser of $30,000 (as adjusted beginning in 1988) or 25% of the participant's compensation.[46] For this purpose, allocations include employer contributions, certain employee contributions, and forfeitures.[47] However, if no more than one-third of annual employer contributions are allocated to the group of participants consisting of officers, 10% or greater shareholders of the employer and employees whose compensation is in excess of $60,000 (as adjusted beginning in 1988), then the allocations are generally limited to the lesser of $60,000 or 25% of the participant's compensation and, more importantly, for this calculation, allocations exclude forfeitures and employer contributions used to pay interest on the ESOP loan.[48]

Tax Advantages of Using an ESOP to Finance an LBO

Deductibility of Principal Repayment

A principal advantage of using an ESOP in an LBO is that a tax deduction is available for payments to the ESOP indebtedness. This deductibility generates a tax shelter by permitting such principal to be repaid in pretax dollars.

Interest Exclusion

Another advantage obtained by the use of an ESOP in an LBO is a reduction in the effective rate of borrowing to finance the buyout. Section 133 of the Code permits a qualified lender to exclude 50% of the interest received by it on a "securities acquisition loan," which is a loan to an ESOP or an employer the proceeds of which are used to purchase employer securities for the ESOP. The qualifying lender must be either a commercial bank, a casualty or life insurance company, a regulated investment company, or a "corporation actively engaged in the business of lending money." A qualifying lender cannot be a member of the same controlled group of corporations that includes the employer corporation. An employer may borrow from a qualified lender and relend to the ESOP for the purchase of employer securities. However, if the terms of the two loans are not "substantially similar," a question arises as to whether there is sufficient connection between the two loans so that the loan to the employer qualifies as a securities acquisition loan.

6. ACQUISITION MECHANICS AND OTHER TAX CONSIDERATIONS IN LBO STRUCTURES

Forms of Buyout Transactions—Acquisition Mechanics

Single-Tier Recapitalization/Redemption/Dividend Transactions

A single-tier LBO transaction is an LBO in which the corporation that is subject to the buyout (T) remains structurally intact. Such a transaction may be effected by a merger of a transitory corporation (S) that is created solely for the purpose of effecting the acquisition with and into T. As a result of the merger, the T shareholders, other than S, will receive the transaction consideration in exchange for their T stock; and the shareholders of S, who are the members of the buying group, will then generally own all the equity of T. Such an LBO may be structured as a two-step acquisition in which a tender offer by S for shares of T precedes a second-step freezeout merger. The transaction may be structured as a public LBO in which the transaction consideration received by the T public shareholders will consist of equity of T as well as nonequity consideration. This may be accomplished without a merger by having a mandatory share recapitalization under applicable state corporate law. Alternatively, instead of a recapitalization transaction in which old T shares are exchanged for new T shares plus nonequity consideration, T could exchange (in either a pro rata or non-pro rata redemption transaction) a portion of an old T share for non-equity consideration, or (in a pro rata transaction) merely declare a dividend of nonequity consideration with respect to each old T share. Although economically these different forms of transaction are similar, the tax consequences of these differing forms, as discussed below, can vary significantly.

Two-Tier or Holding Company Transactions
A second form of leveraged buyout involves the merger of a transitory subsidiary (S) of an acquiring corporation (P) with and into the corporation subject to the buyout (T). As a result of the merger, the T shareholders, other than P, will receive the transaction consideration (which may consist, in part, of P stock if the transaction is structured as a public LBO) in exchange for their T stock. P, which is owned by the members of the buying group, will then own all the equity of T.

Tax Consequences

Single-Tier Recapitalization/Redemption/Dividend Transactions
Where this form of buyout is effected by merger of S into T, such merger will be ignored for tax purposes. In all cases, other than a dividend transaction, the public shareholders of T, assuming they receive no T equity in the transaction, will recognize capital gain or loss with respect to their T

shares.[49]   Installment reporting of gain with respect to installment notes received is no longer available for publicly traded stock.[50]   It is also possible for members of the buying group who are shareholders of T (including the public in the case of a public LBO) to receive cash or debentures or notes in exchange for some of their T shares.   If the transaction is pro rata, the receipt of such consideration may give rise to dividend income rather than capital gain.   While some of the significance of this distinction has disappeared with the unification of capital gain and ordinary income tax rates in 1988, characterization as a dividend in a redemption transaction as contrasted with a recapitalization transaction will affect the amount of income recognition.[51]   Furthermore, basis recovery and, thus, the amount of gain recognized differs in a recapitalization versus a redemption form of transaction.[52]   In addition, loss is not recognized in a recapitalization form of transaction (unlike a redemption form of transaction).[53]   In order to be certain that capital gains treatment will result in either a recapitalization or redemption form of transaction, a shareholder must have an equity ownership in T subsequent to the transaction that is both below 50% and less than 80% of the equity ownership of such shareholder in T prior to the transaction.[54]   Alternatively, capital gains treatment should result if such shareholder sells T shares in the open market prior to proxy solicitation or, in certain cases, to members of the buying group.[55]   In the case of a public LBO, capital gains treatment could also result to public shareholders under Section 302(b)(1) of the Code (i.e., any reduction in interest of a small, minority shareholder who exercises no control over corporate affairs will meet this test—see Rev. Rul. 76-385, 1976-2 C.B. 92 and Rev. Rul. 81-289, 1981-2 C.B. 82).   It should be noted that in the context of a public LBO, all the public shareholders will be receiving recapitalized equity or retaining old equity following a redemption in the same relative proportion to each other.   Hence, in order for the public to meet one of the Section 302 tests with respect to the transaction, it will be necessary to assure the issuance of sufficient new equity to members of the buying group who are not public shareholders.   Such equity must be issued in a transaction that is integrated with the LBO.[56]   Of course, a distribution of a dividend to all shareholders in a dividend form of transaction would be treated as ordinary dividend income (to the extent of T's earnings and profits).

At the corporate level, the tax attributes of T will generally survive (excluding net operating loss and other carryforwards, the utilization of which would be substantially diminished if there were a shift in ownership of more than 50% of T's equity). Tax incidents of T generated after the transaction may be generally carried back to prior T tax years.

Two-Tier or Holding Company Transaction

No gain or loss will be recognized by any member of the buying group who exchanges T stock solely for stock of P.[57] The merger of S into T will be disregarded and treated for tax purposes as an acquisition by P of T stock.[58] The public shareholders of T, assuming they received no equity of P in the transaction, will recognize capital gain or loss with respect to their T shares.[59] As in the case of a single-tier transaction, shareholders of T who are members of the buying group and who receive cash or debentures in the merger generally must have an equity ownership of P that is both below 50% and less than 80% of their former T equity ownership in order to be assured of capital gains treatment.[60] Although the tax rate differential between capital gain and dividend income has lost significance in 1988, the amount of gain recognized will be affected by capital gain versus dividend characterization.[61] Again, capital gains treatment should also result from open market sales prior to proxy solicitation or, in certain cases, from sales to members of the buying group.[62] Alternatively, provided that there is less than a 50% overlap of equity ownership (by value or vote) between T and P, capital gain treatment should result to shareholders of T who are members of the buying group if they receive stock and cash or debentures of P.[63]

Asset Transactions

In a partial sale of T's assets, T will recognize gain or loss upon such asset sales. The consideration received for the assets will be allocated in accordance with Section 1060 of the Code ("residual valuation" required for goodwill—i.e., excess of purchase price over actual fair market value of identifiable assets is attributable to goodwill).

In the event of a sale of all T's assets followed by a liquidation of T, absent recharacterization as a "liquidation reincorporation," all the shareholders of T, including P, will recognize capital gain or loss upon the liquidation of T with respect to their entire T shareholdings.[64]

At the corporate level, with the repeal of *General Utilities* by the 1986 Tax Act, T will recognize all built-in gains associated with its sold assets and P (or S) will take such assets with a step-up in tax basis.[65] Thus, all the tax attributes of T will be lost (including net operating loss carryforwards, if any) and P (or S) would not be able to carry back any of its tax incidents, such as net operating losses, to prior T tax years. As discussed above, the recognition by T of all inherent asset gain will generally make disadvantageous an LBO constructed as an asset transaction followed by a liquidation.

If an asset transaction were viewed as a liquidation-reincorporation, the tax attributes of T (excluding loss and other carryforwards which would be substantially curtailed if there were a shift in ownership of more than 50% of T's equity) should generally survive without recognition of corporate gain or loss, and tax incidents of P (or S) generated after the transaction would generally be available for carryback to prior T tax years. A former shareholder of T who receives both P stock and cash, debentures, or notes in the transaction may be subject to dividend income unless the shareholder's equity ownership in P is both below 50% and less than 80% of the equity ownership of that shareholder in T prior to the transaction.[66] Under present law, liquidation-reincorporation characterization should not occur unless former T shareholders own 50% or more of the equity of P (by vote or value).[67]

NOTES

1. See Treas. Reg. Section 1.1502-34.
2. See I.R.C. Section 337(c).
3. See also I.R.C. Section 385.
4. See, e.g., Rev. Rul. 83-98, 1983-2 C.B. 40 (adjustable rate note convertible into a fixed number of shares, the fair market value of which shares is highly likely to exceed the principal amount of the debt, thereby causing a "very high probability" of conversion, recharacterized as equity). Cf. Rev. Rul. 85-119, 1985-2 C.B. 60 (mandatory convertible debt, the conversion of which at maturity is based upon the then value of the stock and which must be redeemed in cash at the holder's option, respected as debt).
5. Note that debt issued with convertible preferred stock would run afoul of Section 279(b)(3) because the convertible preferred stock is regarded as an option to acquire common stock. (See Treas. Reg. Section 1.279-3(d).)

6. See I.R.C. Section 1272.
7. See I.R.C. Section 305(b)(4); Treas. Reg. Section 1.305-3(b).
8. See, e.g., Ltr. Rul. 8430002.
9. Section 83(a).
10. Treas. Reg. Section 1.83-5(c).
11. Section 83(h); Treas. Reg. Section 1.83-6(a)(2).
12. Section 83(a).
13. See Alves v. Comm., (734 F.2d 478, 9th Cir. 1984).
14. See I.R.C. Section 83(e)(3).
15. See I.R.C. Sections 422A(c)(2) and 421(b).
16. See I.R.C. Section 422A(b)(4) and (b)(8).
17. See I.R.C. Section 425(a); Treas. Reg. Section 1.425-1(a) (requirements for substitution of ISOs); Treas. Reg Section 1.83-1(b)(3) (substitution of restricted stock for restricted stock).
18. See I.R.C. Sections 280G and 4999.
19. See I.R.C. Section 404(a).
20. See I.R.C. Section 501.
21. See I.R.C. Section 402.
22. See I.R.C. Section 401(a).
23. ERISA Section 404(a)(1)(A).
24. ERISA Section 404(a)(1)(B).
25. ERISA Section 3(21)(A).
26. See Eaves v. Penn, (587 F.2d 453, 10th Cir. 1978) (conversion of existing profit-sharing plan to ESOP).
27. Ibid. See also H.R. Rep. No. 93-1280, 93rd Cong., 2d Sess. 302 (1974).
28. See Department of Labor letter to Charles R. Smith, November 23, 1984, reprinted at 12 Pens. Rep. (BNA) 52 (January 7, 1985).
29. See Donovan v. Bierwirth, (680 F.2d 263, 2d Cir.; cert. denied, 459 U.S. 1069, 1982).
30. See also ERISA Sections 406(a)(1)(B) and 408(b)(3).
31. Department of Labor Regulations Section 2550.408b-3(c).
32. See I.R.C. Sections 4975(c)(1)(A) and 4975(d)(B). See also ERISA Sections 406(a)(1)(A) and 408(e).
33. See ERISA Section 3(18). See also Donovan v. Cunningham, (541 F. Supp. 276, D.C.S.C. Tex. 1982) (independent appraisal in "good faith").
34. See 11 Pens. Rep. (BNA) 1974 (November 19, 1984).
35. See Treas. Reg. Section 54.4975-11(b).
36. See I.R.C. Sections 4975(e)(8) and 409(1).
37. Ibid.
38. Ibid. See also Treas. Reg. Section 1.46-8(g)(1).
39. See I.R.C. Section 409(h).
40. Ibid.
41. See I.R.C. Section 409(e).
42. See I.R.C. Section 401(a)(28).
43. See Treas. Reg. Section 54.4975-7(b)(8).

44. See I.R.C. Section 404(j).
45. See I.R.C. Section 404(a)(9).
46. See I.R.C. Section 415(c).
47. Ibid.
48. See I.R.C. Séction 415(c)(6).
49. Section 302(a).
50. See I.R.C. Section 453(j).
51. Cf. I.R.C. Sections 302(d) and 356(a)(2).
52. Cf. I.R.C. Sections 302(a) and 356(a).
53. Ibid.
54. I.R.C. Section 302(b)(2).
55. See Estate of Appelstein v. U.S., (531 F.2d 1343, 6th Cir. 1970) and I.R.C. Section 1001; but see Schneider Estate v. Comm., (88 T.C. 906, 1987).
56. See Zenz v. Quinlivan, (213 F.2d 914, 6th Cir. 1954); Rev. Rul. 75-447, 1975-2 C.B. 133 and Rev. Rul. 84-114, 1984-2 C.B. 90.
57. I.R.C. Section 351(a).
58. See Rev. Rul. 73-427, 1973-2 C.B. 301.
59. I.R.C. Section 1001.
60. I.R.C. Sections 302(b)(2) and 304(a)(1).
61. See I.R.C. Section 304(a) and (b)(2).
62. I.R.C. Section 1001.
63. See I.R.C. Section 304(c)(2)(B) (public shareholders of T who are not members of the buying group do not count in testing overlap of ownership).
64. I.R.C. Section 331(a).
65. I.R.C. Sections 336(a) and 1012.
66. I.R.C. Section 302(b)(2).
67. See I.R.C. Section 368(a)(1)(D); Davant v. Comm., (366 F.2d 874, 5th Cir. 1966) and Reef Corp. v. Comm., (366 F.2d 874, 5th Cir. 1966). See also Telephone Answering Service Co., Inc., (63 T.C. 423, 1974; aff'd, 546 F.2d 423, 4th Cir., 1976; cert. denied, 431 U.S. 914, 1977).

ABOUT THE AUTHOR

Robert N. Macris is a Partner in the law firm of Wachtell, Lipton, Rosen & Katz in New York City and an Adjunct Professor at the New York University School of Law. He has a particular expertise in the federal income tax considerations relating to the structure of mergers, acquisitions and leveraged-buyout transactions. Mr. Macris has taught several courses, including Federal Income Taxation of Corporations and Shareholders, and has lectured extensively in various professional seminars.

CHAPTER 8

MANAGEMENT BUYOUT PUZZLES

*Roberta Romano**

Lawrence Lederman (with Barry A. Bryer) and Robert Macris have provided superb comprehensive surveys of the fiduciary and tax law of MBOs. Their chapters map the legal regimes that implicate the two principal explanations of the gains from MBOs: agency cost reductions and tax savings.[1] Lederman's and Macris's careful detailings of the institutional terrain offer an excellent opportunity to explore some of the peculiar puzzles presented by MBOs.

The first puzzle involves the capacity to replicate MBO tax savings: Why are MBOs necessary to reduce taxes when the tax advantages associated with MBOs are available to all firms regardless of the MBO ownership structure? I'll take up seriatim the three major tax savings of MBOs detailed by Macris: interest deductions, ESOP stock purchases, and asset writeups.

The major tax reduction achieved by an MBO, at least since 1986—increased interest deductions—is obviously available to all corporations. For example, instead of undertaking an MBO, a corporation could recapitalize; it could buy back its stock, pro rata, and replace it with debt (as

---

*I have benefited from a conversation with Alan Schwartz.

some firms have done in the so-called public LBO). In this way the corporation would obtain the tax savings from increased interest deductions just as in an MBO. There is the problem of dividend treatment for the public shareholders in a pro rata redemption, as Macris notes, which increases the cost of a recapitalization compared to an MBO, in which the public shareholders unambiguously receive redemption treatment. But this cost is not likely to be large enough to negate the gain from interest deductions, particularly now that capital gains are taxed as ordinary income so that the difference is only the amount of gain taxed (the gain from a redemption is reduced by the stockholder's basis, whereas a dividend is taxed in full to the extent of the firm's earnings and profits account).

One possible solution to the puzzle of why an MBO is needed to realize the tax savings of increased leverage would be if lenders accept a lower yield on their capital when a corporation's shareholders are its managers. That is, the tax savings and agency cost reduction explanations of the gains from MBOs may be connected and not separate value sources of MBOs. A high debt-equity ratio may be acceptable to lenders at interest rates coverable by cash flows only if corporate managers face the incentives that substantial stock ownership provides. This would make it more costly for a publicly held firm to achieve the leverage of the MBO firm, which is consistent with the well-documented observation that debt-equity ratios after an MBO are much higher than those pre-MBO (Smith, 1988) and those of public corporations in general,[2] and that firms with greater stock ownership of insiders have more debt than those with diffuse stock ownership (Kim & Sorensen, 1986). Of course, such an explanation simply creates another puzzle: Why should this be the case? Is it psychological? Do people work hard only if they are significant residual claimants? Or do lenders view debt as more secure if management's wealth is as undiversified as it is in the MBO setting, where management's wealth is tied intensively to the firm in salary and stock ownership in conjunction with minimal diversification at the operating firm level? Even if we find psychological explanations inadequate,[3] they suggest a further question, of why there is a compensation contract failure for public corporations, that limits debt capacity, preventing managers from minimizing taxes.[4]

If management ownership is crucial for obtaining the high debt tax shield, there is plainly a further puzzle of why there are any straight LBOs as opposed to MBOs. The source of repayment for a highly leveraged takeover bid is also the purchased assets, approximating an MBO's financial structure even though the bidder's own debt-equity ratio does not come close to that of the MBO firm. However, if key characteristics of the firm's assets—in particular, their capacity for being redeployed in other uses and the degree of firm-specificity of the human capital of managers—differ for public LBO as opposed to MBO firms, that could enable lenders to assume greater risk without management ownership in public LBOs (see Williamson, 1988). This is of course speculative, and we need to study the differences between MBOs and public LBOs to determine whether this is really a puzzle. Comparing outsiders' financing arrangements where there are auctions between management and third-party bidders might provide additional data on this point.

ESOP tax advantages are also not exclusively available to MBOs. They apply to ESOP purchases undertaken in the absence of a bid or allied with a third-party bidder, as well as those allied with a bid by management. The airline takeover battles come to mind here, where employee unions have sometimes sided with third-party bidders as well as made their own bids. One response to this conventional puzzle—that the tax benefits are independent of the MBO—again links agency issues with the availability of the tax savings. Namely, we could adopt the story of Andrei Shleifer and Lawrence Summers (1988) that the source of takeover gains is the abrogation of implicit labor contracts, to maintain that MBOs have a higher tax shield value because ESOPs will align with managers and not outsiders, for only incumbent managers uphold such contracts against the shareholders' interest. The data on employment effects of MBOs presented in Chapter 4—that the post-MBO increase in the number of employees is less than that of the industry—does not unambiguously support this version of the Shleifer-Summers hypothesis; data comparing employment levels after third-party bids are necessary to resolve the issue.

Finally, the repeal of General Utilities in the Tax Reform Act of 1986 and the more recent closing of mirror transactions, as Macris mentions, reduced the tax benefits associated with MBOs from obtaining asset basis step-ups without gain recognition. But it may also have increased the "value" of MBOs from management's perspective. To the extent that an MBO is a defensive tactic, the repeal of General Utilities made direct asset restructuring (in which target management disposed of assets and achieved the tax advantage without buying out the public shareholders) a less viable response to a third-party bid, thereby increasing the importance of capital structure restructuring (the MBO).

Restating the first puzzle concerning the availability of tax savings of MBOs from Why don't public companies increase their debt? to Why can't public companies do so? underscores a second important puzzle: If MBO gains are due to a change in ownership structure that reduces agency costs and not simply from tax savings, why do some MBO firms go public again, and at higher prices than the buyout price? This puzzle implicates the fiduciary issues detailed by Lederman and Bryer.

The legal paradigm for evaluating management's conduct in an MBO is insider trading and not the third-party takeover. Rule 13e-3 that regulates going-private transactions, and hence MBOs, imposes stricter disclosure requirements on buyer valuations than rule 14d-1, which regulates takeover bidders and recognizes, albeit weakly, that third parties are entitled to their discovery values concerning the target firm (see Oesterle & Norberg, 1988). For instance, a statement on the fairness of the transaction is required, and material valuations or appraisals of the offer obtained from outside parties must be disclosed (although as Lederman and Bryer detail, courts do not always follow this distinction and have not always required third-party bidders to disclose outside valuations). Moreover, the two leading fiduciary duty cases involving disclosure issues discussed by Lederman and Bryer, Smith v. Van Gorkom and Weinberger v. UOP, involve the bidder's use of inside information to formulate a bid price without revealing that information to the target shareholders, the rightful owners of that information. The conventional property rights or misappropriation explanation of the regulation of insider trading—which guards shareholder-sellers from buyers who are trading on information obtained through their official position within the issuer—prohibits such actions. Such information is the property of the shareholders and not the managers, whose employment contract specifies, often with great detail, their compensation. Otherwise, the rationale for corporate law is stood on its head and the manager, rather than the shareholder, is the residual claimant.

An auction rule for MBOs, implied by Revlon v. MacAndrews & Forbes, as Lederman and Bryer discuss, advocated by commentators (e.g., Lowenstein 1985), and endorsed by the ALI reporters (as outlined in Chapter 10), is a mechanism for policing the insider-trading prohibition, by ensuring that the lion's share of the gains from an MBO go to the shareholders and not the managers. An auction rule, as well as the strictness of disclosure, will, however, reduce the number of MBOs, for managers will be compensated less for the risk they assume in the restructured MBO firm (see Chapter 1; Schwartz, 1986). While the efficacy of rules promoting auctions for third-party takeovers has been extensively analyzed and debated (e.g., Bebchuk, 1986; Schwartz, 1986), there are important differences in the MBO context. First, whereas target shareholders may not have clear property rights to share the gains of third-party takeovers (Schwartz, 1986) for obvious reasons implicated by the insider-trading prohibition, they have unambiguous property rights to MBO gains. Second, we can distinguish two classes of MBOs where mandating auctions have different consequences. In the first class, where the MBO is a defensive response to a third party bid, there is, of course, already an ongoing auction independent of a legal rule. More important, if the MBO is a preemptive defense (i.e., a response to management's fear that a hostile bid will materialize in the future), then mandating an auction increases the cost of that defense (management risks losing to a competing bidder) and thus should decrease the probability that the defense will be undertaken. As a consequence, third-party bidders' search costs will be reduced as they face less competition, which is a goal of the critics of auctions in the general takeover context. Furthermore, the insider-trading problem is less pressing when the MBO is a defensive response to an outside bid, because there is then less concern that management's offer is premised on private information, for management has to reveal what it knows to ensure the success of its bid.

In the second class of MBOs, management-initiated offers made without regard to the possibility of a hostile takeover, where no third party would emerge with its own restructuring plan in the absence of the MBO, the situation is more complex. An auction may not be likely to produce a competing bidder under these circumstances, and shareholders, who benefit substantially from such transactions, might not want them to be deterred. Although we might not want a rule distinguishing managers from third parties as initiators of efficiency-enhancing acquisitive transactions, the property rights issue looms larger in this class of cases. It seems sensible to maintain that shareholders should be entitled to choose whether they wish to trade off the decreased likelihood of an MBO offer against a potentially higher premium, should an offer occur, by adopting charter provisions facilitating or hindering auctions. Resolving the efficacy of the auction rule for MBOs thus depends on the source of MBO gains and their capacity to be duplicated by third parties, as well as on empirical evidence of shareholders' *ex ante* preferences regarding the tradeoff created by auctions. There is evidence of the duplicative quality of MBO gains to the extent that

MBOs are responses to takeover bids or the threat thereof,[5] as well as evidence suggesting that not all shareholders prefer a higher premium to less frequent bids.[6]

The insider-trading gloss on MBOs dispels the "puzzle" of the MBO firm that goes public at a premium by taking a harsh view of the transaction. Variously termed in this volume as the asymmetric information or exploitation explanation of MBOs, it suggests that the managers who take the firm private and later take it public again knew something about the firm's future projects that was not, and perhaps could not be, disclosed in the market at the time of the buyout. After developing those opportunities in the private entity, the increase in value is captured by the managers upon going public again. From this perspective, such an MBO is a breach of fiduciary duty toward the prior public shareholders.[7]

To determine if this malevolent characterization of the puzzle of premiums upon going public is apposite, we need better data concerning the characteristics of MBO firms that go public and those that do not, and in particular, information more precisely identifying the source of the value enhancement of the public offering price over the buyout price. The division of gain between tax savings and operating profitability identified in Chapter 4 does not resolve this issue, for the insider trading paradigm allocates all such gain to the former shareholders. Evidence that the public offering premium is related to gains derived from responses to new business conditions developing after the MBO transaction[8] or to the gains obtained from increased liquidity (Chapter 1) would be more appropriate data for negating the claim that certain MBOs involve breaches of fiduciary duty. Alternatively, we would not need to isolate sources of gain if we could specify why there is a compensation-contract failure in the public corporation, for in such a situation management could legitimately share in MBO gains within the insider trading paradigm.

If the MBO gain does not involve a reduction of agency costs, then of course the puzzle of the premium upon going public after the buyout is also dispelled. But this apparent resolution simply poses another puzzle. For the pertinent—and equally puzzling—question is then, Why are there situations in which the means to maximize firm value requires removing the firm temporarily from the discipline of the market for corporate control? It is difficult both to articulate the circumstances requiring such a guarantee— perhaps it might be a variant of the Shleifer-Summers concern for protecting implicit labor contracts—and to understand why the many devices besides going private that insulate firms from control changes, such as shark-repellent amendments, dual class stock, poison pills, golden parachutes, and the like, are inadequate for the task. As this volume shows, it is also difficult to identify the source of MBO gains if they are not due to increased profitability from agency cost reductions.

I therefore find myself concluding on a cautionary note. We cannot intelligently advocate reforming the law regarding MBOs when we do not have a good working understanding of the gains produced by these transactions. The two principal explanations of the gains from MBOs, tax savings and agency cost reductions, that parallel the legal regimes affecting MBOs discussed in this book contain puzzles that seriously weaken their explanatory power. Although we have learned a great deal about MBOs, in my estimation, we are still groping in the dark. Given these circumstances, we are as likely to make matters worse as to improve them by tinkering with the law pertaining to MBOs.

NOTES

1. Several of the explanations treated separately in the other chapters of this volume, such as eliminating free cash flows or the costs of being a public company, are best grouped together as agency cost explanations because they originate in the separation of ownership and control.
2. Whereas debt-equity ratios range from 6:1 to 12:1 in post-MBO firms (Shleifer & Vishny, 1988), for most corporations the debt-equity ratio is less than 1:1 (Ross & Westerfield, 1988, pp. 379-382).
3. For MBO participants' views that support the "psychological" explanation, see Chapter 3.
4. For data suggesting a contracting failure, see Jensen and Murphy (1988), who find that management compensation varies insignificantly with stock performance and contend that political factors prevent optimization of management compensation contracts.
5. See Shleifer and Vishny (1988). Approximately 30% of Kieschnick's sample MBO firms (Chapter 2) had been the target of a hostile bid, which is a greater proportion than those in the control sample. It would be difficult, and Kieschnick does not try, to estimate what percentage of MBO firms were following the maxim, the best defense is a good offense, and reacting to the possibility that a hostile bidder could emerge in the future.

6. Shark-repellent charter amendments and certain management defensive tactics such as poison pills are vigorously opposed by institutional investors and have been found to have negative stock price effects (Office of the Chief Economist, 1986 & 1985).
7. Kaplan's claim that managers systematically overstate their future performance in MBO proxy materials (Chapter 4) suggests that private information is not withheld, mitigating insider-trading concerns. But it generates another puzzle: why would shareholders accept less for their shares than the publicly stated projected capitalized value of the future earnings stream? If they do not and the MBO price is the expected value of management's projected income stream, then this result is very hard to interpret because it is difficult to identify the source of an additional premium for going public when the firm has not done as well as projected. Moreover, if the public shareholders accept a buyout price based on the projections in the proxy, if management systematically overstated expected cash flows, it would be risking a substantial loss on the transaction. The explanation offered in this volume, that management deliberately overstates its earnings projections to facilitate the MBO's debt financing, is in my opinion unsatisfactory: why wouldn't rational MBO financiers anticipate this tactic? If rational shareholders understood this tactic, they would not be accepting too "low" a price if the buyout price was less than the capitalized value of management's projections. The premium upon going public would indicate that the old public shareholders had applied too high a discount rate to management's projections. It is unlikely that such a situation would constitute insider trading, unless the discount was a function of management conduct (for instance, the proxy omitted important information upon which management's earnings projections were based).
8. Ivan Bull suggested to me the possibility of gain resulting from the receipt of evidence of management's ability to adapt to change.

REFERENCES

Bebchuk, L. (1986). The case for facilitating competing tender offers. *Journal of Law, Economics, and Organization, 2*, 253-271.
Jensen, M. C. & Murphy, K. L. (1988). Performance pay and top management incentives. Harvard Business School [Working paper].
Kim, W. S. & Sorensen, E. H. (1986). Evidence on the impact of the agency costs of debt on corporate debt policy. *Journal of Financial and Quantitative Analysis, 21*, 131-144.
Lowenstein, L. (1985). Management buyouts. *Columbia Law Review, 85*, 730-784.
Oesterle, D. A. & Norberg, J. R. (1988). Management buyouts: Creating or appropriating shareholder wealth? *Vanderbilt Law Review, 41*, pp. 207-260.

Office of the Chief Economist, Securities and Exchange Commission. (1986, October 23). The effects of poison pills on the wealth of target shareholders.

Office of the Chief Economist, Securities and Exchange Commission. (1985, July 24). Shark repellents and stock prices: The effects of antitakeover amendments since 1980.

Ross, S. A. & Westerfield, R. W. (1988). *Corporate finance.* St. Louis: Times Mirror-Mosbey College Publishing.

Schwartz, A. (1986). Search theory and the tender offer auction. *Journal of Law, Economics, and Organization, 2,* pp. 229-253.

Smith, A. (1988). Corporate ownership structure and performance: The case of management buyouts. [Working paper].

Shleifer, A. & Vishny, R. W. (1988). Management buyouts as a response to market pressure (pp. 87-102). In A. Auerbach (Ed.), *Mergers and acquisitions.* Chicago: University of Chicago Press.

Shleifer, A. & Summers, L. H. (1988). Breach of trust in hostile takeovers (pp. 35-56). In A. Auerbach (Ed.), *Corporate takeovers: Causes and consequences.* Chicago: University of Chicago Press.

Williamson, O. (1988). Corporate finance and corporate governance. *Journal of Finance, 43,* 567

ABOUT THE AUTHOR

Roberta Romano is Professor of Law at the Yale Law School and School of Organization and Management. She is co-editor of the *Journal of Law, Economics, and Organization,* and a member of the executive council of the American Law School Association section on business associations. She received her JD from Yale, and was a law clerk to Judge Jon O. Newman, United States Court of Appeals for the Second Circuit. Her research has focused on state competition for corporate charters, the political economy of takeover laws, and directors' liability to shareholders.

PART 3

POLICY AND LEGISLATION

CHAPTER 9

LEGISLATIVE VIEWS ON MANAGEMENT BUYOUTS

The Honorable Edward J. Markey

Many of you will be pleased to know that the Telecommunications and Finance Subcommittee is not presently considering legislation relating to LBOs. We have, however, been studying these transactions from the standpoint of public policy. Our inquiry has focused on several issues including the following:

1. Have LBOs been fair financially to shareholders?
2. Have they been fair financially to bondholders?
3. Have they been the basis for incurring prodigious levels of debt on our corporate books, and concomitantly, how will the debt be serviced during a recession or other slowdown?
4. More broadly, have LBOs been beneficial to the health of our economy? Do they serve any economic purpose beyond enriching management, underwriters, and lenders?
5. Since the market crash, have LBOs helped to attract investors back to the market, or have they worked to keep investors on the sidelines?

Many believe that on all these questions, the jury is still out.

1. FAIRNESS TO SHAREHOLDERS

The value that LBOs have generated for shareholders of publicly held companies has been substantial, often averaging a premium of between 30% to 40% over market price. Yet, even at these levels, critics contend that the shareholders may not be fairly compensated where (1) management disposes of components of the company for considerably more than the shareholders received or (2) the company goes public after a short period of time, with management receiving several times what the shareholders were originally paid.

To some, LBOs are, by definition, a mismatch. They are founded on an offer made by one party having complete knowledge to a second party that has only such information that the offerer provides. In the words of its critics, an LBO is an offer from an insider who knows to an outsider who is kept guessing.

It is difficult to keep the role of management straight in a management-led LBO. On the one hand, management is representing itself in trying to purchase the company at the lowest price. On the other hand, management has a fiduciary duty to try to obtain the highest price for the shareholders.

Management has sought to accommodate these disparate interests in part by obtaining "fairness letters" from investment banks. These opinion letters have been used in many cases to convince shareholders that they are receiving fair compensation for their shares. However, these letters rely almost exclusively on limited information supplied by management and typically state that the firm has made no independent verification of the information. In these circumstances, such letters are of questionable value.

Moreover, I have a special concern about the two-tiered pricing for many of these fairness letters. An investment bank may receive $1 million to write a fairness letter, but $1.5 million if the deal goes through. Under those conditions, the impartiality of the investment bank's fairness letter must at least be subject to question.

During the last session of Congress, Senator Arlen Specter introduced a bill designed to deal with fairness letters as they presently exist (S. 634, March 3, 1987). The bill makes it unlawful for officers, directors or employees of a publicly-held company to do an LBO of the company's shares unless the company has obtained a report on the proposed acquisition by an independent appraiser appointed by a federal district court. The appraiser must review the terms of the proposed acquisition and report to the company and its shareholders regarding the fairness of the valuation used in the proposed acquisition. Under the bill, the costs of conducting the review and preparing the report are paid by the party proposing to acquire the shares (S. 634).

This opportunity for a truly independent appraisal may gain support in Congress. It has been suggested that the "weak link in the protections afforded shareholders in management buyouts is the misuse of fairness opinions from investment advisors."[1]   Some believe that because management wants the investment advisor to legitimize low bids as fair, management could be tempted to pay handsomely for such letters.

Access to honest and fully informed valuations of the corporation by recognized experts is the shareholders' single most important protection. It is important that this access be as unobstructed as possible. In my judgment, it is not unreasonable, therefore, that all buyout proposals "be accompanied by at least one fairness opinion, drafted by reputable financial advisors who are paid without respect to the success of the buyout and who have no financial stake in the buyout itself." [2]

2. FAIRNESS TO BONDHOLDERS

In addition to seeing that shareholders are fairly treated, we have to assess realistically the effects of most LBOs on bondholders of the target company. Because of the additional debt burden assumed by the company to carry out the transaction, corporate bonds have become riskier and their value has been diluted. Most recently, downgradings by Moody's have included Allied Stores, Borg-Warner, and Jim Walter Corporation—all of which took on heavy new debt burdens as a result of LBOs.

As the LBO process becomes more refined, and bondholders become more assertive—especially in the aftermath of the 1987 stock market crash—transactions are likely to include more equity and have tougher covenants to protect bondholders.

3. CORPORATE DEBT IN AMERICA

This brings me to a third area of concern with regard to LBOs—the buildup of excessive corporate debt in our economy. It is properly the role of Congress to safeguard the vitality of companies that comprise key portions of our nation's economic base. As Revco learned recently, the LBO of today is the staggering debt payment of tomorrow.

As many of you know, about 18 months ago, Revco went private in a $1.3 billion management-led LBO. It financed the transaction with a heavy junk-bond debt. Now, Revco has announced that it will miss its June payment of $45 million in interest on this debt and that it must arrange further refinancing.

Here is a company that will probably have a 1988 cash flow of $125 million, but interest payments on its junk bond debt amount to $140 million.

In 1987, Alfred Malabre of *The Wall Street Journal* wrote a book entitled *Beyond Our Means*. Mr. Malabre makes a compelling case for the proposition that our nation is awash in corporate debt. Worse, it is not the kind of debt that can be a positive factor on our national balance sheet. Much of it is not debt for new plants, new equipment, new technology, new jobs. Rather, it is LBO debt that is taken on to buy off the existing shareholder in the hope of generating spectacular profits for a few managers and investment banks. Indeed, it is the kind of debt that most affects a company's creditworthiness and prevents it from financing additional plant, machinery, and technology investments.

No one has yet repealed the business cycle. Although we can quibble over the timing of the next recession, one will surely come. And when it does, there may be many more Revcos on America's balance sheet.

A clear answer is not apparent at this time, but the mountain of debt certainly is. The annual accumulation of close to $40 billion in often low-rated, questionably backed debt cannot be swallowed endlessly without choking.

To help cope with levels of debt in society, some have suggested that Congress establish industry-by-industry schedules of acceptable levels of debt to equity ratios, and eliminate the interest deduction for companies whose debt to equity ratios fall outside these standards. Although this strikes me as a rather interventionist approach by the public sector, it is a point of view that has its adherents.

As Shakespeare wrote following the death of Julius Caesar, "Ambition's debt is paid." Reckless buildups of LBO debt could lead someday to a similar eulogy for some of our finest and most productive companies.

Finally, on my list of concerns, there is a most fundamental one. Shareholders—small investors—see management making millions, in some cases hundreds of millions, from these transactions. They think that as shareholders they know the company, but they learn that management knows it better. Although they gain a modest premium on their stock, they lose much more faith in the integrity of the process.

This may be part of the reason why the small-to-medium investor has retreated from the market since the October 1987 crash. He thinks that a

140-pound freshman football player doesn't belong on the same field with a 280-pound NFL lineman.

So, at bottom, I am concerned that shareholders be treated fairly so that they will continue to participate in our markets. Without them, it will be tough going in the years ahead.

America's economic hopes are pinned in large measure on the successes of our public corporations. Those companies can source their capital from either equity or debt. We already have too much of the latter. But if shareholders continue to abandon the market, corporate debt will continue to surge, or corporate America will stagnate. Neither result is desirable.

So it is critical that we prove to shareholders that they will be treated fairly and honestly. Often, perception is reality. We must not only be certain that shareholders are fairly treated but also that we freely disclose corporate information to them so that they recognize that they are fairly treated, and want to continue to participate in our markets.

4. THE FUTURE OF LBOs

One can discern three rough stages in the evolution of LBOs. The first stage, which lasted into the mid-1980s, saw the entrance into the market of investment banks and "boutique" financing sources; new financing techniques, such as junk bonds; new groups of participants, such as ESOPs; and enormous profits reaped by quick "reverse LBOs."

The second stage, which lasted from the mid-1980s until October 1987, saw the emergence of "mega" LBO deals; still more new financing techniques such as bridge loans and LBO funds; mandatory sale of assets to service debt; and an even more rapid reverse-LBO cycle.

The third, but of course not necessarily final, stage of LBO activity began with the October 1987 market crash. The crash seems to have caused only a temporary reduction in LBO activity. Comparatively lower stock prices may now be luring more investors into this market. The Fed's policy of trying to keep interest rates low may also be a boon to the LBO market.

And two final points. First, continuing volatility in the public securities markets may cause a diversion of investment to the private and LBO market. Second, one must anticipate significant merger activity generally throughout 1988 because a change of administrations in

Washington could signal stricter antitrust enforcement. So there may be a tendency to get deals done now.

In conclusion, I will tell you that the Subcommittee will likely bring LBOs into sharper focus as they account for an ever increasing share of total merger and acquisition activity, both in terms of actual transactions and total dollar value.

NOTES

1. Oesterle & Norberg, 1988, Management buyouts: Creating or appropriating shareholder wealth? *Vanderbilt Law Review, 41,* 207, 249.
2. Ibid., 251.

ABOUT THE AUTHOR

Edward J. Markey is a Member of the United States House of Representatives representing the Seventh District of Massachusetts since 1976.

As a member of the House Energy and Commerce Committee, in 1987 Chairman Markey was elected Chairman of the Telecommunications and Finance Subcommittee. In his first two years as Chairman, the Subcommittee considered a broad range of finance issues including mergers and acquisitions, tender offer reform, Glass-Steagall, insider trading, Securities and Exchange Commission budget, arbitration, financial market reform in light of October 19, 1987, and leveraged buyouts.

CHAPTER 10

MARKET REVIEW OF INTERESTED TRANSACTIONS: THE AMERICAN LAW INSTITUTE PROPOSAL ON MANAGEMENT BUYOUTS

Ronald J. Gilson *

The American Law Institute's Corporate Governance Project[1] was born out of controversy. Commencing in 1980, it emerged against a background of various efforts—for example, judicial extension of Rule 10b-5 to matters of corporate governance, the enactment of the Foreign Corrupt Practices Act, and the growing political pressure for federal chartering of public corporations—to federalize corporate law. A strong restatement of first principles, it was thought, was a necessary step to temper calls for increased federal regulation.[2] More quickly than anyone expected (and for reasons having nothing to do with the American Law Institute), the pressure for federal action diminished. The controversial character of the project, however, did not. Restating first principles, it turned out, was controversial,

*I am a Reporter of the American Law Institute's Corporate Governance Project, whose proposal concerning the treatment of management buyouts is the subject of this paper. The view expressed here are solely my own and do not reflect those of my fellow Reporters. Additionally, because the proposal has not been approved by the Council or the members of the American Law Institute, it does not represent the position of the Institute.

even when undertaken by an old-line, establishment law reform organization with a goal, among others to be sure, of strengthening state law as a bulwark against federal encroachment.

While one well might question whether the substance of those parts of the project that have generated the most hostile debate—Part IV's formulation of the business judgment rule is the best example—really warranted the reaction they received, Part VI of the project, dealing with transactions in control, is appropriately controversial. Whatever else may be said about the conduct of transactions in control, legal rules do influence their outcome, especially in hostile transactions. And whatever else may be said about whether transactions in control result in the *creation* of wealth, they do result in *transfers* of wealth among those affected. An effort to alter any legal rule that has significant distributional consequences is a prescription for controversy.

Interestingly, the Reporters' proposal for standards governing the conduct of MBOs, now contained in §5.15, has been one of the least controversial aspects of Part VI.[3] In general, the Reporters' goal in dealing with MBOs has been to substitute market for judicial review of the fairness of MBOs. The results of this effort to short-circuit expensive and, in the end, inevitably indeterminate judicial search for an Aquinian "just price," and the effort's justification, are set out in §5.15 and the extensive commentary that accompany the "black letter" of the section. Both are reproduced as an Appendix to this chapter. Rather than restate that material, in what follows I will try to place MBOs in the general context of the corporate governance structure, to describe the Reporters' overall outlook on the range of appropriate techniques available to those crafting a governance structure, and to anticipate two objections to the Reporters' proposal on MBOs. With that introduction, §5.15 and its commentary should stand on their own.

1. MBOs IN THE CONTEXT OF CORPORATE GOVERNANCE

From the perspective of corporate governance, an MBO—the acquisition, typically highly leveraged, of a corporation by an investment group that includes members of the target's senior management—presents some troublesome characteristics. First, one must recognize from the outset that the claim of increased efficiency from MBOs is more difficult to analyze than the more general claim that third-party acquisitions lead to efficiency gains. An MBO simply cannot achieve either of the two most familiar sources of the efficiency gains commonly ascribed to acquisitions: synergy[4] and displacement of inefficient management.[5] Because an MBO makes no additional resources available to a target company, the absence of synergy is virtually tautological. Similarly, because a central characteristic of an MBO is to *retain* existing management, *displacement* of inefficient management is hardly a likely source of efficiency gains from the transaction.

That is not to say that there has been a shortage of explanations proffered for the source of the high premiums being paid in MBOs. But because of the very nature of the transaction, all of these explanations share a common characteristic. Since an MBO brings no new resources— whether operating, financial or managerial—to the target company, each of the potential sources of gain from the transaction is at least theoretically available to the target company even without an MBO.

So, for example, it is claimed that the gains from MBOs result from tax benefits, particularly a step-up in the basis of the target's depreciable assets and the deductibility of interest on the borrowed funds, available through the transaction.[6] Gilson, Scholes, and Wolfson have argued, however, that in the period prior to the Tax Reform Act of 1986, an MBO was not the only way that these benefits could be achieved.[7] The step-up in basis also was available (though to a lesser extent) through a sale and leaseback, and interest was deductible regardless of the use to which the borrowed funds were put. Thus, the tax hypothesis does not explain why target management would have chosen to achieve the tax gains through a control transaction, such as an MBO, rather than through a noncontrol transaction such as a sale and leaseback of appreciated assets or a leveraged recapitalization.[8]

In turn, Michael Jensen argues that the obligation to service the debt associated with an MBO has the beneficial effect of eliminating management's opportunity to misinvest the target company's free cash flow.[9] Again, however, precisely the same results can be achieved without a control transaction, as the success of defensive restructurings have demonstrated.

Finally, it is argued that the increase in the diversifiable risk borne by management after an MBO, as a result of both management's increased ownership and the increased risk to the manager's human capital associated with the company's increased leverage, provides a heightened incentive to managerial performance.[10]   But no claim is made that the increased incentive could not have been achieved—for example, through stock options and self-leveraging—without a control change.

The clear implication of this analysis is that management always has a choice of means to secure the gains claimed to be available through an MBO. Imagine that management discovers a favorable business strategy— say increased after-tax cash flow through a step-up in the tax bases of depreciable assets—that could be implemented in two ways. It could be implemented through a sale and leaseback, the gains from which management would participate in to the extent of its existing equity interest in the company. Alternatively, it could be implemented through an MBO, with the result that management would substantially increase its ownership and, therefore, its share of the value created by the new strategy. Put this way, management's preference for implementing the new strategy through an MBO is not surprising. There is simply more in it for management with an MBO.

Nonetheless, it is too easy to treat management's preference for an MBO as simply an expression of greed. However implemented, the substance of the new strategy involves the company's borrowing the amount by which the market value of its depreciable assets exceeds their tax bases. Thus, by increasing the company's leverage, both strategies also increase the risk associated with the managers' undiversified human capital. A sale and leaseback causes the managers to bear this risk without compensation. In contrast, an MBO compensates management for the increased risk with the potential for an increased return.[11]

Thus, one can understand the selection of an MBO rather than other means of securing a generic gain as a way by which management is compensated for altering the structure of the company in a fashion that results in gains for shareholders but, in the absence of increased managerial compensation, losses for management.

So considered, MBOs pose a familiar corporate governance problem. Many circumstances arise in which a transaction between management and the company may be more beneficial to both than an alternative transaction between the company and an unrelated third party. The governance problem is how to police the division of the gains from the interested transaction. In transactions with third parties, management acts on behalf of shareholders in negotiating the division of the gains. In MBOs, in contrast, no one negotiates on behalf of shareholders because management is on both sides of the transaction.

Based on the evidence reported by Steven Kaplan in Chapter 4, an empirically inclined observer might be tempted to treat this inherent conflict of interest as just another example of lawyers creating a hypothetical problem which they then feel obligated to expend real resources to solve. Kaplan reports that the excess return earned by MBO investors, including management, is approximately the same as the excess return or premium earned by outside shareholders to take the company private—the two groups come close to splitting the gains.[12] At first pass this allocation suggests that there is no need for careful scrutiny of the fairness of the division of gain from the transaction. What could be unfair about an equal sharing of the gains from MBOs between shareholders on the one hand and management and the investing group on the other? The problem, however, is that there is a second, substantially larger, body of empirical evidence suggesting that an equal division of the gain from MBOs may be dramatically unfair to shareholders.

Surveys of the division of gain between acquiring and target company shareholders in third-party transactions present a single consistent pattern: target shareholders earn a substantial multiple of the return earned by acquiring company shareholders.[13] The puzzle thus presented by the two patterns of data is that in third party offers "companies that are the targets of takeovers receive the bulk of the value created,"[14] whereas in MBOs the acquirer, which now includes target management, shares equally in the value created. While the data do not demonstrate that the acquirer gets a larger cut in an MBO than in the third-party transaction *because* management is on its side, neither do they demonstrate that the law's traditional concern over fair division in conflict of interest situations is unwarranted.

Over the years, corporate law's approach to policing the fairness of the division of gain from transactions between management and the company has changed dramatically. Drawing on trust law doctrine by analogy, corporate law originally simply prohibited transactions between a corporation and its management.[15] This prohibition evolved over time, however, in response to the fact that, properly policed, such transactions could benefit shareholders. Accordingly, prohibition gave way to an overriding emphasis on the substantive fairness of the transaction. Where a transaction presented a conflict of interest between management and the company, a court would "subject [it] to rigid and careful scrutiny, and would invalidate the contract if it was found to be unfair to the corporation."[16] This remains a fair statement of the duty of loyalty, and is reflected in Part V of the project which covers interested transactions generally.

2. THE AMERICAN LAW INSTITUTE'S APPROACH
   TO MBOs

So matters stood when the Reporters of the Corporate Governance Project considered the governance standards that should apply to an MBO. A traditional and straightforward approach would have been to apply Part V's familiar duty of loyalty standards that are otherwise applicable to any interested transaction. On complaint, a court would be charged with assuring that the terms of the MBO, presumably with special attention to the price to be paid, were fair. The Reporters saw two problems with this approach.

The first was real skepticism that courts would be particularly good at determining the obvious touchstone against which to measure the fairness of an MBO's price: what the company would fetch if offered to third parties. Here it is important to recall the Delaware Supreme Court's performance in Smith v. Van Gorkom.[17] In that case the nation's most experienced court in corporate governance matters concluded that a board of directors could not rely largely on the fact of a substantial (some 60%) premium over market price in approving an arm's-length merger. Rather, the board was charged with determining the "intrinsic value"[18] of the company.

The second problem was that using litigation to police the division of gains from an MBO through application of the duty of loyalty would be very costly in terms of expense, delay and uncertainty. The goal of a corporate governance system is to assure that the discretion appropriately accorded management to use its expertise on behalf of shareholders[19] is neither abused by management nor so constrained in an effort to avoid managerial abuse that it is effectively eliminated. In seeking to achieve this balance between discretion and constraint, the Reporters were at pains to avoid too "legalcentric" a view of the available approaches. The variety of techniques that can serve to assure the proper balance of managerial discretion simply is not limited to traditional resort to judicial review. Other techniques, less expensive and less intrusive, can also be part of the corporate structure.[20]

The role of markets as a constraint on managerial discretion is of particular importance to the Reporters' approach to MBOs. Familiar elements of the governance structure of public corporation reflect the importance of the markets in which a company operates as a source of managerial discipline. Most important, the broad discretion given management by the business judgment rule is best understood not as a statement that management's conduct of the business is unreviewable. Rather, it is a statement that management's operating performance largely is shielded from judicial review. Because markets make both management's future and the shareholders' returns dependent on the company's commercial success, there is reduced need for liability rules to assure the compatibility of management and shareholder incentives concerning the company's efficient operation. In contrast, where markets do not align the incentives of management and the interests of shareholders, as when a transaction presents a conflict of interest, a liability rule may be necessary. Thus, standard applications of the duty of loyalty contemplate a traditional litigation-driven judicial review of the fairness of transactions in which management is interested.

In important respects, MBOs straddle the line dividing circumstances when management's actions are most efficiently reviewed by a court as opposed to the market. On the one hand, MBOs are a prototypical interested transaction in which management and shareholders are on opposite sides of the transaction. To be sure, the transaction does seem to create value,[21] and in that sense management and shareholders share the common goal of increasing the size of the pie. However, the transaction also serves to divide the pie, and management and shareholders have conflicting interests in how the gains from the transaction are shared. This analysis counsels in favor of judicial review, much as current law has evolved with respect to other interested transactions, with courts determining the fairness of the price paid.

On the other hand, determining the fairness of the price to be paid in an MBO is significantly more difficult than reviewing the fairness of the types of transactions for which the duty of loyalty has traditionally dictated judicial review. Quite simply, with respect to an MBO the task is to value the entire company on a going-concern basis where recourse to a thick market of comparable transactions likely will not be available.

In this setting, using the market to police the fairness of the division of the gains resulting from an MBO is particularly attractive. If there is a competitive acquisition market, then management in successful MBOs will garner only that portion of the gains from the transaction that is peculiar to their special skills. The portion of the gains that can be achieved as effectively by third-party bidders will go to shareholders because of competition among bidders. Thus, a market approach to policing the division of gain from an MBO is more likely than judicial review to result in a fair—that is, comparable to an arm's-length—division of the gain. Moreover, it has the potential to reduce substantially the enormous legal and investment banking costs associated with the litigation orgies that now routinely accompany MBO proposals.

Implementing a market approach to policing the fairness of MBOs, however, presents some problems. Most important, a management group has significant information and timing advantages over other potential bidders. With respect to information, management simply knows more about the company than a potential third-party bidder with access to publicly available information only. Presumably management discloses this information (or signals the information's content without actual disclosure by its very willingness to pursue the transaction) to the investment group with whom management is allied.

With respect to timing, management can do its investigation and secure its financing on its own schedule, announcing the MBO and triggering the various regulatory time limits only when it is ready to proceed. In contrast, a potential third-party bidder can begin its investigation only when the MBO is made public. In the meantime, the clock ticks away potential competitors' ability to field a viable competitive bid.

Section 5.15 of the Corporate Governance Project reflects the Reporters' preference for policing the division of gain from MBOs by a market oriented, as opposed to a litigation oriented, approach. Recognizing management's informational and timing advantages, however, §5.15 does not unconditionally subordinate litigation-driven judicial review. Rather, §5.15 assigns priority to market review only when management's informational and timing advantages have been neutralized. Thus, §5.15 *requires* litigation-driven judicial review of an MBO *unless* disclosure of the transaction is made and "responsible persons who express an interest are provided relevant information concerning the corporation and given a reasonable opportunity to submit a competing proposal." If these conditions are met, market review is treated as adequate and judicial review of the transaction is on a waste standard, essentially identical to the noninterventionalist standard applicable to arm's-length transactions under the business judgment rule.

The full text of §5.15, and the associated explanatory commentary, which contains both a detailed discussion of the section's operation and a justification for its approach, are set forth in Appendix 10-1. Rather than repeat that discussion here, I want to conclude the substantive consideration of §5.15 by evaluating two predictable objections, both to the conditions that must be satisfied before a market review of the fairness of an MBO's terms will displace judicial review and to the value of a market approach to the problem of policing gain sharing at all.

The attraction of a market review, and the informational and timing conditions §5.15 imposes on its applicability, are premised on the assumption that competition in the acquisition market is desirable because it assures target shareholders a larger share of the joint gains from a transaction. The objections to a market approach build on the observation that increasing the shareholders' portion of the gain decreases the gain received by the two other parties to the transaction: management and the investor group. Because these groups are typically the initiators of an MBO, reducing the returns to either, the argument runs, will result in reducing the number of transactions that are undertaken. Unless the increase in the portion of the shareholder gain that results from encouraging market review of the fairness of the transaction through competitive bidding offsets the decrease in the overall number of transactions that result from decreasing the initiators' return, shareholders end up net losers.[22] Because the incentives of the two categories of initiators of MBOs—management and investors— differ, it is helpful to consider each separately. In both cases, however, market review in the end proves beneficial.

The Impact of Encouraging Competitive Bidding on Management's Incentives

The analysis here builds on my earlier discussion of the quandary management faces when evaluating a positive net present value project that will result in increasing the company's diversifiable risk and, hence, the risk of management's nondiversifiable human capital investment in the company. An MBO eliminates management's reluctance to undertake the project by increasing management's potential gain from the project (through an increase in ownership) to offset the increased risk the project imposes on management. If encouraging competitive bidding prevents management from being compensated for bearing extra risk, then management will cause the company to forgo positive net present value projects, to the detriment of shareholders.

Put this way, the issue posed is one of compensation technique. Assume management justifiably must be paid to bear the additional risk that results, for example, from a dramatic increase in the company's leverage through a restructuring. The question then is how best to provide this additional compensation. The problem with providing it through an MBO is that the level of compensation actually received by management is difficult to monitor; there is thus an agency cost advantage to direct compensation.

Additionally, without better information concerning competitive conditions in the MBO market (and in the market for managers generally), we simply do not know whether a decrease in the return to management will result in a decrease in managerial activity. The conflict between shareholders and managers over division of gain in an MBO may be over the division of surplus.

In the end, the argument depends on the comparative efficacy of different compensation techniques. But precisely because setting the terms of an MBO and, as a result, management's compensation puts management in an inherent conflict of interest the outcome of which is difficult to monitor, the burden of proof is appropriately on those who argue that MBOs dominate other compensation techniques as a way of overcoming managerial resistance to risky net present value projects.

The Impact of Competitive Bidding on the Incentives of MBO Investors

Here the argument is that by reducing the returns to MBO investors, competitive bidding causes a decrease in investment in search for companies that could benefit from the change in policies typically implemented through MBOs. The ultimate outcome then is to decrease the number of beneficial MBOs. Although both the argument and the appropriate response are similar to those made with respect to the wisdom of encouraging competitive bidding in response to third-party offers generally,[23] an additional point is appropriate in the MBO context. If management's incentive problem can be solved by alternative compensation techniques,[24] third-party searches may be of dramatically reduced importance in the MBO process. By definition, management already has the information necessary to identify and implement any policy change that could be implemented through an MBO. Recall that an MBO brings no new resources to the target company; in this regard, there is no substantive advantage to (or, in the end, difference between) an MBO and an internal restructuring. Thus, the role of third parties in MBOs, whether in terms of search or implementation, is significantly smaller than in arm's-length acquisitions.

3. STATUS OF THE AMERICAN LAW INSTITUTE PROPOSAL

The Reporters' proposed §5.15 is still at a quite preliminary stage in the ALI approval process. At a meeting of the Council of the Institute in early 1988, §5.15 was approved as a "Discussion Draft." This means no more than that the Council believes the proposal warrants distribution to interested parties outside the ALI so that their comments can be considered. Such commentary may persuade the Council to proceed with §5.15 as currently formulated or, instead, to instruct the Reporters to reconsider their proposal. Should the Council determine to proceed with §5.15, the next step is Council approval as a "Tentative Draft," following which it would be submitted for consideration by the full membership of the ALI.

APPENDIX 10-1

AMERICAN LAW INSTITUTE, PRINCIPLES OF CORPORATE GOVERNANCE: ANALYSIS AND RECOMMENDATIONS

(COUNCIL DRAFT NO. 10, JANUARY 26, 1988)

§5.15 Transactions in control in which a director or senior executive or his associate is interested.*

(a)   If a transaction in control [§1.32] results in the transfer of control [§1.05] of the corporation to another person [§1.23] in which directors or senior executives of the corporations or their associates [§1.02] are interested [§1.18(a)(2)], then, if the transaction is challenged by a shareholder, such directors, senior executives, or associates fulfill their duty of fair dealing, by satisfying the burden of proving that the transaction was fair to the shareholders of the corporation, unless the conditions of subsection (b) are satisfied.

(b)   If in connection with a transaction specified in Subsection (a):

(1)   adequate advance public disclosure of the transaction is made;

(2)   responsible persons who express an interest are provided relevant information concerning the corporation and given a reasonable opportunity to submit a competing proposal;

(3)   the transaction is authorized by disinterested directors following compliance with the procedures set forth in Subsections (1) and (2); and

(4)   the transaction is authorized or ratified by disinterested shareholders [§1.11], following disclosure concerning the conflict of interest [§1.09(b)] and the transaction [§1.09(a)],

then a party challenging the transaction has the burden of proving that it constituted a waste of corporate assets [§1.34].

(c)   The fact that holders of equity securities are entitled to an appraisal remedy with the characteristics provided for in [Part VII] with respect to a transaction specified in subsection (a) should not make an appraisal proceeding the exclusive remedy of a shareholder who proposes to challenge the transaction.

---

*Bracketed references are to definitions contained in Part I of the Project and not reproduced here.

Comment:

a. Comparison with Existing Law.

1. Section 5.15(a).

State corporation statutes do not specifically address transactions where a director or senior executive, or an associate of a director or senior executive, is a participant in the transaction, except to the extent that the safe harbor statutes discussed in the comment to §5.02 are applicable. Section 5.15(c) expressly negates the exclusiveness of an appraisal proceeding as a remedy to challenge the transaction. Unless the special procedures of §5.15(b) are satisfied, the director, senior executive, or associate will have the burden of proving the fairness of the transaction.

2. Section 5.15(b).

If satisfied, the approval procedures set forth in §5.15(b) provide a safe harbor within which a management buyout can be challenged only on the grounds of waste, a result corresponding to that applicable in the case of transactions between a director or senior executive and the corporation under §5.02 which have been approved by disinterested shareholders. These procedures are designed to allow the market to operate as the primary check on the fairness of a management buyout. Even within the safe harbor, however, §5.15(c) expressly negates the exclusiveness of the appraisal remedy.

Existing law concerning management buyouts is conflicting. On the one hand, such transactions have not been treated as interested transactions that would explicitly trigger a full-scale fairness review. On the other hand, it is increasingly the case that even disinterested directors' approval of such transactions is not being accorded the full protection of the business judgment rule. A careful reading of *Revlon, Inc.* v. *MacAndrews & Forbes Holdings, Inc.*, 506 A.2d 173 (Delaware Supreme Court 1986), and *Hanson Trust PLC* v. *ML SCM Acquisition, Inc.*, 781 F.2d 264 (2nd Circuit 1986), indicates that those courts did not believe that director approval of the management buyout transactions there involved warranted substantial judicial deference. The resulting uncertainty concerning the appropriate level of judicial review forces courts and, as a result, directors to put increasing reliance on the role of third-party advisers such as investment bankers. Section 5.15(b) is consistent with those decisions in both questioning the likelihood of arm's-length consideration by directors of transaction in which directors, senior executives, or their associates participate, and in tempering the application of the full-scale fairness review. It differs, however, in its preference for market forces, rather than judicial review, as the primary means by which directors' decisions concerning management buyouts are policed.

b. Implementation.

Section 5.15 may be implemented by judicial decision, except where an amendment to an existing statute governing review of interested transactions would be required.

c. Operation of Section 5.15.
    1. Overview.

Section 5.15 treats a setting in which management's discretion to facilitate a negotiated transaction that they favor is appropriately constrained: when directors, senior executives, or their associates are participants in the transaction. Commonly referred to as a management buyout (or as a leveraged buyout, to reflect that most of the consideration used to complete the transaction is usually borrowed), this form of transaction typically involves the acquisition of a publicly-held corporation by a newly formed entity in which the public corporation's management has a significant albeit usually minority stake, with the remainder of the equity held by institutional investors or investment banking firms. (The effect of the transaction is usually to substantially increase the level of management's ownership interest. In a sample of 28 management buyouts occurring between 1979 and 1984, management's equity interest rose from a pre-transaction average of 24.3% in the acquiring entity. Lowenstein, "Management Buyouts," 85 Col. L. Rev. 730-737 (1985) (Table 1).) The consideration used in management buyout transactions is typically cash or nonconvertible debt, in order to eliminate public shareholders from future participation in the enterprise. As in freezeout transactions, management is inevitably on both sides of the transaction, representing both itself and public shareholders in setting the terms by which it will participate in purchasing the corporate enterprise.

The problem presented is to identify governance rules that provide reasonable assurance that the division of the gain resulting from a management buyout transaction approximates that which would be forthcoming in an arm's-length transaction. In approaching the same problem with respect to freezeout transactions including a controlling shareholder, §7.51 places primary reliance on a combination of an independent bargaining structure and the presence of an adequate appraisal remedy. If these protections are present in a particular freezeout transaction, then additional judicial review of the fairness of the transaction—essentially the fairness of the allocation of the gains from the transaction between public shareholders and the corporation as reflected in price—is unnecessary. No recourse to the market for corporate control for price protection is possible in connection with a freezeout transaction because the presence of a controlling shareholder eliminates the possibility of a competitive bid. In the context of a management buyout, however, the market for corporate control is potentially available to police the fairness of the non-arm's-length division of the gain from a management buyout transaction. If the price to be paid for the corporation is too low, the possibility exists that it will evoke a competing bid, thereby creating an incentive for management to fairly price the transaction in the first place.

Under current circumstances, there is substantial reason to doubt that bids competing with the management-sponsored bid will be forthcoming with sufficient frequency. Although there have been important instances in which announcement of the terms of a proposed management buyout has given rise to a competing bid, a party that might contemplate bidding against a management-sponsored group suffers under substantial information and timing disadvantages. Most important, the management-sponsored group, and its financing sources, have access to substantial, often non-public, information concerning the corporation at essentially no cost. Additionally, even if the potential competing bidder has the means to develop independent sources of information, the opportunity for the management-sponsored group to choose the moment when it makes its offer, and to act first, puts any potential competitor at a disadvantage.

Section 5.15 sets out governance rules that will allow the market for corporate control to operate as a realistic protection against non-arm's-length division of gains from a transaction in control of the corporation to which its directors, senior executives, or their associates are parties. Section 5.15(b) provides a safe harbor for transactions that are subjected to an adequate market test of the fairness of their terms. Because a transaction that satisfies the requirements of Section 5.15(b) will have been tested by the market, judicial review is limited to a waste standard. Where the requirements of Section 5.15(b) are not satisfied, there is no adequate market review of the fairness of the transaction. In that event, Section 5.15(a) provides for judicial review of the fairness of the transaction, as is the case under Part IV for other transaction in which directors or senior executives have a personal interest.

Section 5.15(a) does not cover a transaction in which directors, senior executives, or their associates simply sell a business to the corporation or buy a division or subsidiary from the corporation where senior management remains with the selling corporation. Such a transaction is not a transaction in control, as defined in §1.32, and the transaction will therefore be subject to review under other provisions of Part V.

Section 5.15(a) also does not cover a transaction in which senior executives are furnished employment contracts, stock options, or other normal management remuneration incentives to continue employment with a successor corporation, unless the executives also acquire such a significant investment interest in the successor corporation that they would be viewed as "interested" within the meaning of §1.18(a)(2), because their investment interest would reasonably be expected to affect their judgment with respect to the transaction in a manner adverse to the shareholders.

Section 5.15(a) applies where the senior executives primarily responsible for management of the business are interested in the transaction, either directly or through associates. Thus, the fact that an officer who is not within that limited group of senior executives is interested in the transaction would not normally render §5.15(a) applicable.

Section 5.15(c) explicitly negates the exclusiveness of the appraisal remedy for transactions described in Section 5.15(a). In the case of a buyout by directors or senior executives when there is not a majority shareholder, the considerations that may justify permitting a freezeout under §7.51 when there is a majority shareholder are not present. The most significant efficiency gain from a freezeout—facilitation of transactions between members of an affiliated group—is by definition absent. Moreover, shareholder expectations are likely to differ markedly from those existing when there is a majority shareholder, because shareholders anticipate that senior executives and directors normally will act on the shareholders' behalf in a combination—an expectation that is less appropriate with respect to a majority shareholder. This difference in expectations mirrors the historic distinction in corporate law between the obligations of directors and officers, who must always look first to the interest of shareholders, and the obligations of a majority shareholder, which is allowed to favor itself in certain circumstances. Finally, the analogy to short-form mergers does not apply.

Accordingly, unlike §7.50 and §7.51, §5.15 does not limit shareholders to an appraisal remedy even if an appropriate appraisal procedure is available.

2. Section 5.15(a)

Section 5.15(a) states the general rule that directors, senior executives, or their associates who are interested in a transaction in control have the burden of proving that the transaction was fair to the shareholders of the corporation. In this respect, the treatment of management buyouts parallels Part V's treatment of other interested transactions. The director, senior executive, or associate may show that the price paid for the shares was within a "range of reasonableness" within which conflict-of-interest transactions may be sustained. The commentary to §5.11(a)(2)(A) is relevant in determining fairness for this purpose. While a court may give weight to the presence of an independent negotiating structure to represent the corporation's interest (i.e., an independent negotiating committee of outside directors with the power to reject the transaction) in assessing the fairness of the transaction, such a negotiating structure would not be given weight unless the corporation also followed the procedures in §5.15(b) to allow the market to police the fairness of the transaction. In this connection, under [Part VI] directors or senior executives would not be permitted to grant a lockup option to the corporation in which they or their associates have an interest. See *Hanson Trust PLC* v. *ML SCM Acquisition, Inc.*, 781 F.2d 264, 283 (2d Cir. 1986) (concurring opinion).

3. Section 5.15(b).

Section 5.15(b) reflects two basic premises. The first is that a market review of the fairness of the terms of a management buyout is preferable to judicial review. Thus, when the requirements of §5.15(b) are satisfied, judicial review is limited to a waste standard in contrast to the fairness review contemplated by §5.15(a). The second is that before the market for corporate control can serve as a meaningful check on the pricing of management buyout transactions, and thus serve as a substitute for a judicial fairness review, the disadvantages under which potential competitive bidders currently operate must be significantly reduced. To this end

§5.15(b) establishes three transactional requirements that must be met before market review can be substituted for judicial review. First, there must be adequate public disclosure of the proposed transaction. Second, responsible parties who express an interest in making a competitive proposal must be given the opportunity to review relevant information concerning the corporation. Finally, parties who undertake to review information concerning the corporation must be afforded a reasonable opportunity to acquaint themselves with the information and to offer a competitive proposal.

Section 5.15(b) is thus intended to facilitate alternative proposals for an acquisition of the corporation as a means to police the fairness of a proposed management buyout. Consistent with an explicit theme of the treatment of transactions in control in Part VI, this approach reflects a general preference for shareholder self-help techniques, whether through voting procedures or through the marketplace, rather than judicial review, as a means of ensuring that shareholders are adequately protected in connection with a transaction in control. The availability of such a process, protected by [Part VI] from lockups of the character that have restricted competition with proposed management buyouts in the past (see *Revlon, Inc.* v. *MacAndrews and Forbes Holdings, Inc.*, 506 A.2d 173 (Del. Sup. Ct. 1986) and *Hanson Trust PLC* v. *ML SCM Acquisition, Inc.*, 781 F.2d 264 (2d Cir. 1986), makes judicial review of the fairness of the transaction unnecessary.

Section 5.15(b) specifies three requirements that must be met before the market for corporate control will be deemed to operate with sufficient rigor that judicial review of the fairness of transactions in control in which a corporation's directors, senior executives, or their associates are participants, is not necessary. The three requirements are designed to alleviate the major informational and timing disadvantages third parties otherwise suffer in attempting to compete with a proposed transaction in control sponsored by corporate insiders. The requirement of adequate advance public disclosure of the transaction involving management operates to alert the market to the opportunity to make a competitive proposal and to the terms against which bidding will take place. Thus, the quality of disclosure required under §5.15(b) is to be judged from the perspective of the needs of a potential competitor sophisticated enough to contemplate a corporate acquisition. In this respect, disclosure under §5.15(b) is measured by a different standard than under §7.51.

The requirement that responsible parties considering making a competitive bid be given access to relevant information contemplates provision of information of the same character as that provided to any investment banker representing any party to the transaction. Provision of such information poses the risk to the corporation that is the subject of the buyout offer that proprietary information disclosed will be misused to the corporation's detriment. Accordingly, the corporation should be entitled to condition the opportunity to review such information on the execution of an agreement to keep confidential the information disclosed and to refrain from using it for any other purpose than to determine whether to propose a transaction in control. Furthermore, the corporation would not be obligated to furnish such information to a person of questionable financial resources or as to whom there is a reasonable basis for concluding that a confidentiality agreement would not be respected, as, for example, when the information is requested by a competitor. The final requirement, that those given access to information be afforded a reasonable period of time to evaluate the information and to make a competing proposal, is intended to alleviate the timing advantage the management group possesses by virtue of its selection of when to announce its offer. What is a reasonable time for this purpose will depend on the size and complexity of the corporation and the transaction proposed by management. Where, for example, the transaction proposed by the management group contemplates high interest rate subordinated debt financing, determination of a reasonable period of time for competitors would take into account the time necessary to evaluate the availability of similar financing.

Where a bidder begins to actively compete with directors, senior executives, or their associates for the business, §5.15(b)(2) does not require that the directors or senior executives or their associates disclose to the competing bidder the price they are ultimately prepared to pay for the business. To come within §5.15(b)(2) they must publicly disclose the nature and amount of consideration they are initially prepared to offer for the business. Thereafter, however, they are under no obligation to advise competing bidders as to the extent to which they may be prepared to improve their initial offer. See also the Comment to §1.09.

It is a predicate of §5.15(b) that the directors, senior executives, and associates will disclose to responsible competing bidders all material information that they know concerning the corporation that would have an effect on the value of the corporation. If such disclosure is not made, the safe harbor of §5.15(b)(a) is unavailable, even if no greater disclosure is made to the corporation's investment bankers.

Section 5.15 will apply whenever directors, senior executives, or their associates are interested in a proposed acquisition of their corporation that constitutes a transaction in control [§1.32], whether the transaction was initiated by the directors, senior executives, or associates, or they submitted a competing offer in response to an unsolicited tender offer initiated by a third party. In the latter case, §5.15(b) does not require that the directors, senior executives, or associates give additional advance notice of the transaction, but they must furnish to the tender offeror who initiated the bidding process the same information they make available to the corporation's investment bankers.

Because the purpose of §5.15(b) is to substitute market review of the fairness of the terms of a transaction for judicial review, it would not be available in circumstances when meaningful market review would not be possible even if the procedures of §5.15(b)(1)-(3) were met. Thus, the §5.15(b) safe harbor would not be available in connection with a close corporation or in other circumstances when a realistic market review was not feasible.

When the procedures of §5.15(b)(1)-(3) have been satisfied so that the market has been permitted to police the fairness of the purchase price, a shareholder who challenges such a transaction must meet the burden of proving waste of corporate assets if the transaction was approved by disinterested directors and authorized or ratified by disinterested shareholders [§1.11], following disclosure of the conflict of interest [§9.09(a)] and the transaction [§1.09(b)].

Where disinterested directors approve the transaction, their decision will be subject to review as a business judgment decision under §4.01(c). In such event, the participation by interested directors in the decision (unless required to authorize the transaction) will have no effect either on the application of the business judgment rule to the actions taken by the disinterested directors, on the validity of the action taken, or on the exposure of the corporation to injunctive or rescissory relief.

4. Section 5.15(c).

Section 5.15(c) makes clear that even though the procedures specified in §5.15(b) are followed, the transaction will be subject to judicial review as to whether a waste of corporate assets occurred, and a complaining shareholder will not be limited to an appraisal remedy. This result is consistent with the provision for judicial review of transactions subject to §5.02 in which directors, senior executives, or associates are interested, that have been approved by disinterested shareholders. Section 5.15 is not designed to provide a lesser degree of judicial scrutiny to an interested transaction than would otherwise be provided under §5.02. Rather, §5.15 is intended to ensure that where a complex transaction in control is undertaken in which directors, senior executives or associates are interested, in order to have safe harbor benefits of the more limited judicial review provided for in §5.15(b), the procedures specified therein must be followed to ensure that the transaction was fair to the corporation.

Illustrations:

1. The board of directors of X Corporation announces that it has approved a transaction in control pursuant to which a purchasing group, in which certain X Corporation directors and senior executives (who currently own 5% of X Corporation's common stock) would own 23%, would make a tender offer for 53% of X Corporation's voting common stock at a price 40% above the average closing price of X Corporation common stock over the month preceding approval of the transaction. Following the tender offer, the purchasing group would cause X Corporation to be merged into a new corporation formed for that purpose. In exchange for their shares in the merger, X Corporation shareholders would receive

high interest rate subordinated debentures. Although the announcement of the transaction disclosed that X Corporation's investment bankers had valued the debentures to be issued in the second stage transaction at a specified price, the terms of the debentures' subordination were not disclosed. Unless the subordination provisions are so unusual as to be essential to an analysis of the transaction by a sophisticated investor, disclosure of such provisions would not be required by §5.15(b).

2. The facts being otherwise as stated in Illustration 1, the disclosure of information necessary to satisfy §5.15(b)(1) involves confidential proprietary information concerning X Corporation whose public disclosure or competitive use would result in significant injury to X Corporation. A, an individual acting as an agent for an undisclosed principal, requests the opportunity to review such information. X Corporation refuses to provide the information until A's principal delivers to X Corporation his agreement that the information disclosed will be kept confidential, and not be used for any other purpose than in connection with evaluation of whether to make a competitive bid. X Corporation does not fail to satisfy §5.15(b)(1) by conditioning review of the information called for by §5.15(b)(1) on delivery of such an agreement.

3. The facts being otherwise as stated in Illustration 1, the purchasing group required approximately 30 days to secure a commitment for the financing necessary to complete the tender offer that was the first step in the contemplated transaction in control. In determining a reasonable opportunity to submit a competing proposal under §5.15(b)(2), it should be presumed that potential competitors need equivalent time to investigate the availability of financing for a competitive bid.

4. The facts being otherwise as stated in Illustration 1, no director or senior executive of X Corporation, or their associates, is formally a member of the purchasing group. Certain directors and senior executives, however, have entered into employment agreements with the purchasing corporation, conditioned on the success of the tender offer, which allow the officers or directors to increase significantly their investment in the surviving company in the contemplated merger on terms that reflect a price substantially below that paid by the purchasing group. For purposes of analysis under §5.15, those directors and senior executives who have executed such agreements are part of the purchasing group.

NOTES

1. The complete name of the project is *Principles of Corporate Governance: Analysis and Recommendations*. As currently contemplated, it ultimately will consist of seven parts: Part I (Definitions); Part II (The Objective and Conduct of the Corporation); Part III (Structure of the Corporation); Part IV (Duty of Care and Business Judgment Rule); Part V (Duty of Loyalty); Part VI (Transactions in Control); and Part VII (Remedies).
2. The origins and early history of the Corporate Governance Project is succinctly treated in Eisenberg, 1984, An introduction to the American Law Institute's Corporate Governance Project, *George Washington Law Review, 52,* 495.
3. Although developed as part of Part IV, the Reporters' proposal concerning MBOs was placed in Part V to reflect that part's primary focus on transactions in which management has a personal stake. The relative lack of controversy concerning §5.15 may result less from a consensus about the appropriateness of its substance than from the attention given to the other areas originally treated in Part VI, including defensive tactics, greenmail, lock-ups, and a corporation's selection of alternative governance rules concerning transactions in control by adopting charter amendments.
4. See R. Gilson, 1986, *The Law and Finance of Corporate Acquisitions*, Chapter 11.
5. See Ibid., at Chapter 10.
6. See, e.g., Lowenstein, 1985, Management buyouts, *Columbia Law Review, 85,* 730; K. Schipper & A. Smith, July 1986, Corporate income tax effects of management buyouts, University of Chicago Graduate School of Business mimeo; S. Kaplan, November 1987, Management buyouts: evidence on taxes as a source of value, Harvard Business School mimeo.
7. R. Gilson, M. Scholes & M. Wolfson, 1988, Taxation and the dynamics of corporate control: The uncertain case for tax motivated acquisitions, in *Knights, raiders and targets: The impact of the hostile takeover,* p. 271. J. Coffee, L. Lowenstein & S. Rose-Ackerman, eds.
8. Gilson, 1987, Evaluating dual class common stock: The relevance of substitutes, *Virginia Law Review, 73,* 807, 826, Note 52. In contrast, Kaplan, Note 6 above, argues that the increased interest deductions that follow an MBO do uniquely result from the transaction's buyout structure. Kaplan's point is an empirical observation, based on the claim that companies the subject of MBOs did not appear to have unused debt capacity prior to the transaction. This observation, in turn, is based on the fact that the MBO companies did not have lower leverage than a control group of similar companies in their industry. But these data also are consistent with an industry-wide pattern of unused debt capacity, only corrected when a firm is the subject of an MBO (or of a hostile offer— apparently companies that were the subject of a successful third-party acquisition

were excluded from the control group). On this analysis, the puzzle then is what prompts the change for the MBO firms. Gilson, above, and Shleifer & Vishney, 1988, Management buyouts as a response to market pressure in *Mergers & Acquisitions*, 87, argue that the selection of the technique for achieving the tax benefit (Gilson), or the decision to seek it at all (Schleifer and Vishney), results from an agency conflict between managers and shareholders.

9. Jensen, 1986, Agency costs of free cash flow, corporate finance, and takeovers, *American Economics Review, 76,* 323.

10. See, e.g., Jensen, 1988, Takeovers: Their causes and consequences, *Journal of Economic Perspectives, 2* (21), 29-31.

11. See Gilson, above, Note 8, at 826, Note 52. Shleifer and Vishney, above, Note 8, argue that a threat of a hostile takeover may be necessary before management is willing to accept higher leverage for any reason.

12. See Chapter 4.

13. See, e.g., Jarrell, Brickley, & Netter, 1988, The market for corporate control: The empirical evidence since 1980, *Journal of Economic Perspective, 2,* 49; Jensen & Ruback, 1983, The market for corporate control: The scientific evidence, *Journal of Financial Economics, 11,* 5; R. Gilson, above, Note 4, at 433-445.

14. Jarrell, Brickley, & Netter, above, Note 13, 53.

15. See generally, March, 1966, Are directors trustees? *Business Law, 22,* 35.

16. Ibid., 43.

17. 488 A.2d 858 (Delaware Supreme Court, 1985).

18. 488 A.2d, 881. Consider, for example, the court's explanation of its difficulty with relying on market price as a measure of value:

   A substantial premium may provide one reason to recommend a merger, but in the absence of other sound valuation information, the fact of a premium alone does not provide an adequate basis upon which to assess the fairness of an offering price. Here the judgment reached as to the adequacy of the premium was based on a comparison between the historically depressed Trans Union market price and the amount of the Pritzker offer. Using market price as a basis for concluding that the premium adequately reflected the true value of the company was a clearly faulty, indeed fallacious, premise, as the defendants' own evidence demonstrates. (Ibid., pp. 875-876.)

   The court does not address the issue of whether the fact that the market price had been historically depressed suggests something about the company's intrinsic value. For a critical discussion of the Van Gorkom court's approach to valuation, see R. Gilson, above, Note 4, p. 814; Fischel, 1985, The business judgment rule and the Trans Union case, *The Business Lawyer, 40,* 1437.

19. Every corporate statute specifies that the business of the corporation will be managed by or under the direction of the board of directors. See, e.g., Delaware General Corporate Law §141(a).

20. See The American Law Institute, (January 26, 1988), *Principles of corporate governance: Analysis and recommendations*, (Council Draft No. 10) 6, introductory note.
21. See, e.g., Kaplan, November 1987, Management buyouts: Efficiency gains or value transfers? Harvard Business School mimeo.
22. In the context of MBOs, this argument is thoughtfully presented by Yakov Amihud, in Chapter 1.
23. See, e.g., Easterbrook & Fischel, 1981, The proper role of a target's management in responding to a tender offer, *Harvard Law Review, 94,* 1161; Gilson, 1982, A structural approach to corporations: The case against defensive tactics in tender offers, *Harvard Law Review, 95,* 1028; Bebchuk, 1982, The case for facilitating competing tender offers: A reply and an extension, *Stanford Law Review, 25,* 23; Easterbrook & Fischel, 1982, Auctions and sunk costs in tender offers, *Stanford Law Review, 25,* 1; Gilson, 1982, Seeking competitive bids versus pure passivity in tender offer defense, *Stanford Law Review, 25,* 51; Schwartz, 1986, Search theory and the tender offer auction, *Journal of Legal Economics and Organizations, 2,* 229. To summarize my own position in the debate, I believe the answer is indeterminant. Auctions encourage search activity by those participants who earn their returns by tendering their shares to the eventual winner. Auctions discourage search activity by those who actually want to implement the acquisition or sell their information to such a party. The net impact of auctions depends on empirical observations on the investments in search by different categories of market participants. To my knowledge, the empirical investigation remains to be undertaken.
24. See Note 22 above.

ABOUT THE AUTHOR

Ronald J. Gilson is Professor of Law and currently a Visiting Scholar at the Hoover Institution, both at Stanford University. He is also a Reporter of the American Law Institute Corporate Governance Project, with special responsibility for standards governing transactions in control, and is a member of the California Senate Commission on Corporate Governance, Shareholder Rights and Securities Transactions. Professor Gilson is the author of *The Law and Finance of Corporate Acquisitions* (Foundation Press, 1986, with 1987 and 1988 Supplements), and has published numerous articles in leading law journals on aspects of the operation of the market for corporate control.

CHAPTER 11

MANAGEMENT BUYOUTS AND LEVERAGED BUYOUTS: ARE THE CRITICS RIGHT?

Joseph A. Grundfest *

1. INTRODUCTION

MBOs and LBOs have been subject to extensive criticism.[1] They have been reviled as unfair to stockholders, threatening to employees, and inhospitable to long-term corporate planning. The companies involved in these transactions are allegedly dangerous to themselves and others because their high debt-to-equity ratios leave them economically vulnerable, particularly if interest rates increase or if the economy suffers a recession.

The bankruptcy of Revco Drugstores only 18 months after its MBO has added fuel to these fears. Further concern has been generated by the rapid growth of multibillion-dollar LBO funds. Here, the apprehension is that, in order to "do deals" necessary to commit billions of dollars in available capital, fund managers will be pressured into paying premium prices that lead to unsustainable leverage, thereby further threatening the competitive fabric of an increasingly large number of MBO and LBO companies.[2]

These concerns are expressed by many respected observers of the economic scene and, as Congressman Markey makes clear in Chapter 9,

*The views expressed herein are those of Commissioner Grundfest and do not necessarily represent those of the Commission, other Commissioners, or Commission staff.

they are shared by influential policymakers in Washington.[3] These concerns are, I believe, quite understandable. The academic and financial communities have an obligation to respond with credible evidence that either supports or rejects the factual premises upon which these concerns are based.

My review of the evidence leads me to conclusions that are, however, quite different from those expressed by many critics of MBO and LBO transactions. Experience to date demonstrates that some of these transactions succeeded while others failed. Among the successes are reinvigorated companies that have regained a sharp competitive edge as a result of an MBO.[4] Among the failures are companies that may well have encountered difficulties as a result of the financial pressures imposed by leveraged transactions.[5]

Public policy cannot be guided solely by successes nor solely by failures. Rational public policy must be guided by the best available evidence regarding the aggregate consequences of these transactions measured on average and over time. Anecdotal evidence, no matter how compelling when considered in isolation, can easily mislead. Viewed from this perspective, and taking full account of the undeniable risks involved in many of these transactions, the preponderance of the evidence strongly suggests that MBOs and LBOs are beneficial for the companies involved and for the economy as a whole. The successes far outnumber the failures, and many of the costs associated with these transactions have been substantially exaggerated.

In order to appreciate the benefits that result from these transactions, it is useful to draw an analogy between buyouts and the operation of the venture capital sector. Venture capital is an undeniably risky business. It is a trivial matter to identify startup companies that have quickly gone bankrupt, costing their backers many millions of dollars—and occasionally making even the most technologically and financially sophisticated investors look foolish. If the venture capital industry were judged solely by its risks and failures, that entire sector of the economy would be a candidate to be shut down.

Fortunately, the public policy process has not proved so short-sighted or risk averse. Policymakers are able to appreciate the tremendous successes spawned by the venture capital industry. They appreciate the extraordinary value that can be called forth when entrepreneurs have a substantial equity stake in the businesses they run and when those businesses are overseen by a relatively small group of knowledgeable, active investors who have a direct and significant financial stake in the success or failure of the enterprise. The value added by the entrepreneurial energy associated with venture capital operations is so well recognized that many foreign countries have specifically sought to replicate the United States' venture capital success by providing inducements to entrepreneurs and investors willing to take venture capital-type risks.[6]

Buyouts are closely related to venture capital enterprises. Instead of starting a firm from scratch, a buyout recreates venture capital-type incentives within existing firms by providing management with strong, equity-based incentives combined with aggressive oversight from investors who have substantial capital at stake. The economic benefits that result from reinvigorating large, established corporations that may have grown a bit lazy or sluggish are every bit as real as the benefits that result from the formation of new firms. Thus, just as society applauds the risk-taking inherent in venture capital operations, it makes sense, I think, to view buyouts in an equivalent light as risky but beneficial opportunities for industrial rebirth at firms that may not be living up to their full potential.

While there is extensive debate over the sources of gain that result from buyouts, the most significant gains result, I believe, from the reduction in agency costs that occurs when management is given an opportunity to share a substantial equity stake in the firm it operates.[7] Buyouts thus reintegrate management interests with equity incentives and resolve the classic Berle-Means problem that arises when ownership is separated from control.[8] Managements are thereby motivated to adopt the kinds of efficiency-enhancing measures that are rarely if ever implemented in publicly traded firms with diffuse ownership.[9]

As the co-head of corporate finance at McKinsey & Company explains, MBO and LBO transactions "are so immensely successful because they are better managed."[10] Indeed, there is no shortage of war stories describing how a firm taken private in an MBO or spun off in an LBO increased productivity as a direct result of management improvements that were unthinkable or infeasible under prior ownership structures.[11] There is also no shortage of testimonials from business executives who participated in buyout transactions and say "[i]t's amazing what a little motivation does for the bottom line."[12]

Even economists skeptical of the benefits associated with hostile takeovers concede that MBOs result in

> a nontrivial amount of value creation. The enterprises emerging from MBOs are invariably structured to give managers greater incentives to cut costs and to budget capital more responsibly. Increased management ownership,

concentrated ownership in the hands of knowledgeable profit-motivated investment bankers, and reduced free cash flow all contribute to the value created in MBOs. Finally, managers who know their firms best get to keep them, and all of the upheaval costs associated with hostile takeovers are avoided... From the point of view of promoting efficiency they appear to be a good thing.[13]

Journalists sometimes make the same point in a more colorful fashion:

> When management or new owners take over a company in an LBO, they suddenly stop managing so they can get to the country club by 3 p.m. Instead, they start to notice what the difference in internal rate of return is if they sell a low-yielding parcel in Palm Springs tomorrow instead of earning 1% on its present value. When management of LBOs goes into action, it suddenly starts to notice arbitrages between liquidation value and yield value. Out goes the three wood. In comes the HP-12.[14]

Accordingly, the best available evidence urges a "steady as she goes" course for policymakers and provides little support for those who would further regulate or restrict MBO or LBO transactions.

The literature analyzing MBOs and LBOs is substantial and, in the context of this article, it is impossible to summarize the full policy implications of this large and growing body of work. Instead, this chapter focuses on five specific points that help put the policy debate in better focus by relating identified policy concerns to relevant economic evidence.

First, I describe the current regulatory environment as applied to takeover transactions in general and MBO transactions in particular. MBOs and LBOs are already among the most intensely regulated transactions in our economic system. Calls for further regulation should be tempered by a careful appreciation of the extensive regulation already in place.

Second, I address the argument that shareholders are not treated fairly in takeover transactions. Contrary to the position espoused by some critics, the data indicate that average premiums paid in MBO and LBO transactions are comparable with the premiums paid in takeovers involving arm's length negotiations with independent third parties. Shareholders bought out in MBO and LBO transactions thus appear to be earning competitive takeover premiums.

Third, I consider the argument that takeovers are predominantly tax-motivated transactions that constitute a raid on the public fisc. Here, the evidence suggests that tax incentives are not properly characterized as dominant forces behind MBO and LBO transactions. Careful tax planning is certainly a crucial component of MBO and LBO transactions, and there is evidence that the size of premiums paid is related to tax factors. There is, however, no evidence that MBOs and LBOs are tax-motivated or reduce aggregate federal tax revenues. Moreover, tax factors account for only a fraction of the gains available in MBO or LBO transactions, and those tax effects can generally be replicated through transactions that do not involve MBOs or LBOs.

Fourth, in the wake of the recent Revco bankruptcy, this chapter considers policy concerns raised by the spectre of MBO and LBO failures. The available evidence, and the specific experience of the Revco transaction, suggests that many concerns associated with MBO and LBO failures are exaggerated from a macroeconomic perspective. Bankrupt MBOs or LBOs are not fire-bombed. Their productive capacity does not disappear from the economy. While bankruptcy certainly imposes real costs, firms in reorganization continue to operate as debtors in possession as their capital structures are renegotiated.

Fifth, and finally, this chapter discusses the implications of the vast pool of capital now committed to financing MBO and LBO transactions. As a practical matter, the growth of this capital pool makes it probable that the average risk adjusted rates of return earned by MBO and LBO investors will decline, just as rates of return to venture capital fund investors declined after rapid growth in that sector. Fund managers do not, however, have effective carte blanche to bid as high as they like: they are responsible to sophisticated and aggressive investors who strongly oppose overpricing and must persuade lenders that transactions are reasonably priced. Moreover, there is no evidence that MBO-LBO firms have consistently overpaid to date, and MBO-LBO firms are often outbid in takeover battles. Thus, natural market forces appear to be the most effective disciplinary measure to guard against overpayment or excessive investment of capital in MBO or LBO ventures.[15]

2. MBOs AND LBOs ARE HIGHLY REGULATED TRANSACTIONS

Critics of MBOs and LBOs occasionally proceed from the assumption that these transactions are relatively unregulated phenomena. Little could be farther from the truth. MBOs and LBOs rank among the most intensely regulated transactions in our entire marketplace.

At the federal level, the Williams Act imposes substantial disclosure requirements on all participants in MBO and LBO transactions.[16] The purpose of these requirements is to assure that investors are fully informed when deciding whether to accept or reject an MBO or LBO offer.[17] The disclosure requirements imposed on MBOs are even more stringent than those imposed on third-party takeover transactions. In particular, participants in MBOs are required to disclose additional appraisal and valuation information in order to assure that management is not exploiting an informational advantage.[18] The staff of the Securities and Exchange Commission has, over the past few years, expanded the scope of these disclosure requirements so that a board considering an MBO proposal must now disclose the valuation information provided by investment bankers who have provided advice regarding the transaction.[19]

At the state level, courts have become substantially more aggressive in scrutinizing the conduct of all takeover transactions. MBO transactions have, however, been singled out for particularly close attention because of the potential for self-dealing that disadvantages public stockholders. As a result, a board's decision to accept an MBO proposal is almost certain to be construed as a signal that the company is for sale. At that point, the corporation's directors become subject to a duty to conduct an auction designed to assure that stockholders obtain the highest price for their shares.[20] The board is generally advised to form a separate committee of independent directors to handle negotiations with management and other bidders.[21] That committee often retains its own independent counsel and investment bankers.[22] The auction is typically subject to extensive judicial supervision with courts setting standards for the disclosure of information to competing bidders,[23] the reasonableness of any "hello" or "good-bye" fees to be paid to bidders,[24] the validity of lockup agreements,[25] the exercise of "poison-pills" rights,[26] and the timing of any decisions that may be subject to shareholder vote.[27]

A management group therefore cannot, as a practical matter, buy out its own company without giving competing bidders an opportunity to at least top management's own bid. As this chapter is written, an MBO that is in its earliest stages of development demonstrates the open auction environment that has evolved in conjunction with those transactions. The management of Insilco Corporation, in conjunction with First Boston Corporation, recently proposed a $29-per-share MBO.[28] Documents filed with the SEC indicate that other bidders may have been willing to pay $30 a share or more. Insilco's board asserts it acted reasonably in accepting management's $29 proposal because of the contingent nature of the other potential bids and First Boston's insistence on a rapid response to its offer. Nonetheless, counsel for the committee of Insilco's outside directors concedes that First Boston's bid was only an opening bid and explains that "if somebody wants to bid more than $29, they still can. The best test of the process is what happens now."[29]   In other words, an auction with a reservation price of $29 has begun.

No doubt, stockholders and competing bidders may challenge the board's initial decision to accept management's $29 bid, as well as expense reimbursement and termination fee arrangements with First Boston.[30] However, management and First Boston are not assured of success because if a higher bidder comes along the board may well find it impossible to accept management's offer.

3. ARE SHAREHOLDERS BEING TREATED FAIRLY?

A frequent concern in MBO transactions is that the managers purchasing the company are acquiring it at an unfairly low price.[31] In support of this theory, critics often point to transactions in which management earns substantial returns in short periods of time on relatively modest initial capital investments.[32]

These individual instances, however, prove little if anything about the equity of premiums paid in MBO transactions. Shareholders are clearly taken advantage of if management acquires the company at a price below that which would be paid by an independent third party purchaser in an arm's-length transaction. The available evidence, however, indicates that the premiums paid in MBO transactions are comparable with the premiums paid in third-party merger transactions.[33] These results should not be surprising: if the board of a company considering an MBO proposal has an obligation to conduct a fair auction that yields stockholders the highest possible price, then management will be unable to complete an MBO unless it is willing to pay at least as much as competing third-party interests.

Managers might also be suspect if they purchased corporations on the basis of projections that consistently understate the future performance of the enterprise. Such evidence would suggest that managers might be "bad-mouthing" their companies in order to drive down the price they have to pay in an MBO. Here, the evidence is surprising and suggests managers are, on average, overly optimistic about their corporations' future performance.[34]

Thus, if anyone is potentially disadvantaged by management's projections it is the lenders and financiers who may be providing capital on the basis of an unrealistically rosy scenario—assuming, of course, that these investors aren't savvy enough to discount such overly optimistic projections.

The data also suggest that, on average, the gains that result from an MBO transaction tend to be divided evenly between the selling stockholders and the MBO group.[35] No rational bidder will ever offer a price so high that he eliminates all opportunity for future profit from the MBO transaction. The observation that the gains from the transaction appear to be split evenly between buyer and seller further supports the conclusion that, on average, the process does not unfairly disadvantage selling stockholders.

Any examination of data that focuses solely on averages overlooks outliers at both extremes. Thus, just as there are situations in which MBO purchasers have, in hindsight, profited quite handsomely, there are also situations in which selling stockholders are the ones who made out like bandits, because they collected substantial premiums while the buyers were stuck with failed transactions. Public policy must, however, be guided by central tendencies, and the data here fail to support the claim that stockholders consistently wind up on the short end of the stick.

Before leaving this topic, however, it should be noted that the concern over the adequacy of premiums stands in sharp conflict with the criticism that MBOs are dangerous because the high prices paid induce excessive leverage. Either shareholders are being paid too little or they are being paid too much. Both propositions cannot simultaneously hold true. Critics of MBO and LBO transactions should therefore be careful to choose between these allegations and should, at a minimum, strive for internal consistency in their attacks on MBO and LBO transactions.

4. ARE MBOs AND LBOs MERELY TAX-INDUCED TRANSACTIONS?

Another frequent criticism of MBOs and LBOs is that they are primarily motivated by tax considerations and that they amount to little more than a shift of wealth from the federal treasury to financial market participants brazen enough to leverage themselves to the hilt at the public's expense. Here again, the data fail to support the common wisdom. In reality, the relationship between federal tax revenues and MBO-LBO activity is sufficiently complex that policymakers should keep an open mind regarding the possibility that these transactions may actually increase the net present value of federal tax revenues.

Although MBO and LBO firms tend to reduce their corporate tax liabilities for a period of years,[36] it does not necessarily follow that the federal treasury loses revenue as a consequence of these transactions. In order to calculate the marginal tax revenue effect of MBO and LBO transactions, the net present value of taxes paid as a result of the MBO and LBO must be compared with the net present value of taxes that would have been paid in the absence of a takeover transaction. To the best of my knowledge, no one has attempted this calculation. It is, however, important to note that there are plausible MBO-LBO scenarios that may well be correlated with increased tax receipts or with little or no aggregate tax revenue effect.

MBO-LBO transactions result in substantial premiums for stockholders and typically cause a recognition of gain that would not occur but for the buyout. Frequently, in order to pay down debt rapidly, firms subject to MBOs or LBOs engage in asset sales or spinoffs that generate additional taxable gains. If the restructured corporation is later sold for a profit, that profit again will be subject to tax. If the MBO-LBO transaction transforms a money-losing corporation into a profitable enterprise, the transaction creates a stream of potentially taxable revenues that otherwise would not have existed. The lenders and bondholders involved in the transaction also receive interest payments that, while deductible to the corporation, may be taxable to some recipients.[37] Accordingly, a narrow focus on the revenue loss to the Treasury that results when deductible interest is substituted for nondeductible dividends cannot possibly lead to a balanced conclusion about the aggregate effect of these transactions on federal tax revenues. That question remains open, and the only safe conclusion is that it is incorrect to assume that MBOs and LBOs cause tax receipts to fall because they substitute debt for equity.

Another significant and often overlooked point is that tax benefits correlated with MBO and LBO transactions generally have many substitutes that do not involve MBOs and LBOs.[38] In particular, corporations can increase their leverage without engaging in an MBO or LBO and obtain tax benefits identical to those that result from the leverage associated with MBO-LBO transactions.[39] Because a corporation need not engage in an MBO or LBO in order to take advantage of the interest paid deduction, it is not logically correct to conclude that the corporate tax savings associated with MBO-LBO transactions are a cause of or incentive for those transactions.

Put another way, the presence of tax benefits "is a necessary condition for tax factors to influence merger activity, but not a sufficient one."[40]

Studies that have examined the relationship between taxes and MBO-LBO activity conclude that the intracorporate tax benefits that result from MBO-LBO activity are positively correlated with the size of the premium paid to stockholders.[41] They also find that the value of these tax benefits appears largely to be paid out to stockholders and is not captured by the firm's new owners.[42] This result should not be surprising because, absent special circumstances, many bidders will be equally capable of structuring transactions that minimize tax burdens. The competitive bidding process thereby forces a substantial portion of these tax savings to be passed on to stockholders through the takeover premium.

The available evidence thus suggests that "income tax savings do not appear to be the driving force behind leveraged buyouts. Tax savings are important, and entrepreneurs are not blind to that benefit, but the evidence suggests leveraged buyouts would occur with no tax savings at all."[43] These transactions could continue because "expected improvement in efficiency and profitability are important reasons for leveraged buyouts. These are real gains, they are not tax generated."[44]

5. THE REVCO BANKRUPTCY: AN OMEN OF THINGS TO COME?

Although the majority of MBOs and LBOs conducted to date have been successful, only the most incorrigible optimist would claim that these transactions are without risk. Indeed, as a supporter of MBO-LBO activity, I think it important that failures not be swept under the rug and that policy assessments be continually adjusted in light of most recent experience. It is particularly valuable to study MBO-LBO failures because they (1) help point out pitfalls that should be avoided in future transactions and (2) demonstrate that many critics of MBO-LBO activity exaggerate the adverse macroeconomic consequences that result from MBO-LBO failures.

The largest MBO failure to date occurred on July 28, 1988, when Revco D.S., Inc., a retail chain of 2,000 drug stores, filed for bankruptcy-law protection. Revco's bankruptcy came just a year and a half after a $1.3 billion buyout and stands, in many respects, as a shining example of what can go wrong in an LBO transaction.[45]

Following a tumultuous period, during which Revco experienced internal management strife and made an expensive and ill-fated acquisition, Revco's management decided that an MBO held the solution to many of its problems. At the time of the transaction "many people believed it shouldn't be done in the first place,"[46] and hindsight proves them correct. Projections underlying the buyout assumed that sales would grow by 13% and that profits would surge by 42% in the year ended May 31, 1988. Instead, sales rose by only about 6.5% while the company ran up fiscal 1987 and 1988 losses in excess of $100 million.[47]

Revco's problems appear to have been caused by bad management and intense competition. In the wake of the buyout, Revco departed from its previously successful strategy of concentrating on pharmaceutical sales and began stocking a broader set of product lines. Revco failed, however, to carry sufficient inventory to support its broader product base. Thus, while increased advertising drew more customers, the customers often found that the shelves were bare. In addition, "the company ran a huge promotion to clean out inventory but neglected to replenish shelves for the all-important Christmas season."[48] Vigorous price competition added to Revco's problems by reducing its margins and sharply limiting its ability to generate necessary cash flow.[49]

On April 15, 1988, Revco missed a $46 million interest payment, and there followed an intense period of negotiation among stockholders, bondholders, and investment bankers over a restructuring plan that would reduce Revco's debt payments and realign the interests of Revco's stockholders and bondholders.[50] Revco's stockholders and bondholders were, however, unable to reach a voluntary agreement. Revco thereupon filed for bankruptcy protection and the restructuring that Revco's creditors could not design for themselves will now be designed for them through the bankruptcy courts.

Viewed with the luxury of hindsight, one of Revco's management errors was that it adopted a strategy that required additional cash flow to support inventory and advertising at the same time that cash flow was necessary to finance the firm's debt obligations. Thus, to many analysts, "the company appears to have been brought down not by problems like high interest rates or disappointing growth in consumer spending, but by its own managerial failings."[51] Strategies that add substantial new cash flow demands on enterprises that have pressing obligations to pay down debt are strategies asking for trouble. Such strategies either should not be attempted at all in an MBO-LBO context, or the transaction should be structured in a manner that gives management some breathing room by lightening up on interest payment obligations in the buyout's early years. MBOs may be excellent management motivators, but they cannot draw blood from a stone.

Significantly, the bankruptcy filing does not mean that Revco goes out of business. Most of Revco's 2,000 stores remain profitable,[52] and "Revco doesn't have any plans to sell off drugstores, lay off employees, or to abandon print or television advertising as a result of the filing."[53] Instead, the major loss will be felt by investors who financed the transaction. Revco's most actively traded bonds were selling for 50 cents on the dollar shortly before the bankruptcy filing.[54] Analysts expect the reorganization to take about three years and project that Revco's most active bonds are now worth about 41 cents on the dollar; other issues are worth as little as 16 cents.[55] Large investors have, however, acquired substantial positions in Revco's debt securities in anticipation that they will rise to 80 cents on the dollar within two years as the firm moves out of bankruptcy.[56]

From a macroeconomic perspective it is difficult to identify any major dislocations that result from the failure of the Revco transaction. The drug store industry is highly competitive and there is no evidence or reason to believe that Revco's failure has adversely affected prices paid by consumers or the availability of product. All else equal, the aggregate sales of the industry are also unaffected, so whatever sales are lost by Revco will be made up by increased sales from Revco's many competitors. Moreover, if employees were laid off at Revco, the increased demand at Revco's competitors would have created additional employment opportunities at those firms. Further, even if hiring by Revco's competitors did not offset Revco job losses on a one-for-one basis, the fact that the industry's aggregate sales did not decline materially suggests that productivity, measured by sales per employee, would have increased. Productivity gains are generally considered economic benefits.

Revco's failure thus seems to have generated few, if any, externalities that have meaningful macroeconomic consequences, and the persons most injured by the failure may well be the sophisticated investors who knowingly assumed the risks involved in the transaction. No doubt the transaction costs associated with bankruptcy proceedings will be substantial and resources could have been saved had Revco not failed, but again, these losses will be borne by the participants in the transaction and appear to generate no substantial externalities. Protection of these sophisticated investors does not, however, seem to be the central concern of MBO-LBO critics—nor should it be.

Critics of MBO-LBO activity may thus be overstating the adverse consequences that result upon failure of these transactions.[57] In bankruptcy, firms are reorganized and continue to operate as productive entities while their obligations are renegotiated. Bankrupt firms are not shut down or fire-bombed. Thus, while not all MBO-LBO failures may be as benign as Revco's, the fears generated by the spectre of bankruptcy may not be as real as critics often claim.[58] More to the point, the investors in each MBO-LBO transaction have a powerful incentive to adopt an appropriate debt-equity ratio given the costs of bankruptcy, and there is no reason to believe that the government can do any better than the market in determining these optimal debt-equity ratios.[59]

6. WHAT ARE THE CONSEQUENCES OF INCREASED CAPITAL AVAILABLE FOR LBO AND MBO FINANCING?

The amount of capital available for MBO and LBO transactions has grown significantly in recent years. According to data tracked by Wilshire Associates, 42 buyout funds raised at least $20 billion in 1987 and at least 40 funds are trying to raise $8 billion in 1988.[60] The 10 largest buyout firms have at least $15 billion in committed capital, and the largest of these firms, Kohlberg, Kravis, Roberts, can deploy $5.6 billion.[61] Estimates of the total amount of capital available for MBO and LBO financing range as high as $60 billion, taking into account assets available to corporations willing to invest directly in such ventures.[62] When multiplied by the leverage ratios often used in MBO-LBO transactions, it is clear that MBO-LBO firms have the ability to finance a large number of substantial acquisitions.

The concern is that fund managers, in order to collect fees and "do deals," will be pressured to invest these substantial sums and will therefore bid up prices beyond reasonable levels. It is feared that the pressure to invest and the leverage associated with these high prices will cause target firms to assume unsustainable debt obligations and stimulate a wave of failures that will be damaging to the firms involved and to the economy as a whole.[63]

The problem with this scenario is that it vastly oversimplifies the incentive structure facing MBO-LBO fund managers. MBO-LBO fund managers have as their clients some of the largest and most sophisticated investors in the country. While these investors may be limited partners, they will not be shy in disciplining fund managers who appear to be overpaying or taking risks that are out of line with potential returns. After all, it is not in any investor's interest to put up the money for an overpriced deal.

Fund managers who develop reputations as "suckers" by consistently overpaying in transactions will also find it more difficult to attract investors for future funds. While growth in funds available for MBO and LBO financing has been substantial, it has not been indiscriminate. Investors in these funds are quick to reject proposals that fail to meet stringent criteria, and many new funds have had difficulty raising capital.[64] Managers with reputations for paying prices that are too high will almost certainly find themselves at a real disadvantage in this market.

A further incentive against overpayment is generated by the market itself. Overpriced deals are tougher to finance because outside creditors have strong incentives not to place themselves at risk. Lender oversight can thus temper excessive spending enthusiasm by MBO-LBO fund managers. Overpriced deals are also likely to require that the fund increase its equity contribution, which in turn lowers the amount of capital available to invest in other transactions. These disciplining effects are real, and there have been cases where the prices offered in successful MBO transactions were lowered because of difficulties in obtaining financing.[65]

Recent experience also suggests that, while MBO-LBO firms occasionally pay prices that are criticized as "too high,"[66] MBO-LBO funds are often outbid by industrial or foreign acquirers. While no studies have yet examined the issue closely, my quick review of prices paid in recent takeover transactions suggests that MBO-LBO purchasers are not developing a reputation as consistent over-bidders in takeover contests.

One probable consequence of the sharp increase in funds available for MBO-LBO transactions is a reduction in future rates of return to MBO-LBO investors. In fact, many investors are "quick to concede that...phenomenal results will be hard to sustain"[67] and expect returns to moderate for a wide variety of reasons. In particular, sizable MBO-LBO transactions are relatively new phenomena. The first LBO of a major New York Stock Exchange firm, Houdaille, took place in 1979; the first $1-billion buyout, Wometco, occurred in 1984; and the first major buyout accomplished through a tender offer, Malone & Hyde, also occurred in 1984.[68] Early entrants in the field were able to earn the substantial economic rents that are typically part of the economic rewards of innovation. Early entrants also faced less competition in identifying and pricing transactions because the number of firms active as buyout principals was relatively small. However, as the innovations inherent in MBO-LBO transactions diffuse through the marketplace and as the number of MBO-LBO firms increases, the ability to earn supercompetitive rates of return is likely to decline and will probably approach levels more commensurate with risk-adjusted rates of return. These returns may, nonetheless, be quite handsome because the risks to equity investors in highly leveraged transactions can be substantial and because there may be a limited pool of management teams able quickly to restructure a specific firm as part of a buyout transaction.

This process again has an analogue in the venture capital industry. Early venture capital funds earned astronomical returns that attracted many new funds and investors. Rates of return subsequently declined. The same evolution is likely to occur among MBO-LBO funds.

The concern about systematic overpayment resulting from an embarrassment of riches thus appears to be far more conjectural than real, based on currently available data. While managers certainly have strong incentives to "do deals," their investors and outside lenders have strong incentives to make certain they do not overpay in the process. No doubt, given the size and volume of transactions currently observed in the marketplace there will be situations in which overpayment concerns will be raised, but it is doubtful that such problems will become endemic.[69]

NOTES

1. See, e.g., L. Lowenstein, 1985, Management buyouts, *Columbia Law Review, 85,* 730; Lipton 1987, Corporate governance in the age of finance corporatism, *University of Pennsylvania Law Review, 136,* 1; Morrisey, 1988, Law, ethics and the leveraged buyout, *University of Detroit Law Review, 65,* 403. The term "leveraged buyout" refers generally to an acquisition in which the purchase price is financed predominantly with debt to be repaid by cash flow generated by the acquired firm. If management of the acquired company participates significantly in the buyout by holding equity in the new leveraged firm, the transaction is referred to as a management buyout. Management buyouts are thus a subset of leveraged buyouts.

2. See, e.g., A.C. Wallace, August 6, 1988, All dressed up and no place to go? *New York Times*, col. 2, p. F1; J. Lewis, July 1988, Everybody into the pool, *Institutional Investor*, 141.

3. Markey, Chapter 9. See also *Leveraged buyouts and the pot of gold: Trends, public policy and case studies*, a report prepared by the Economics Div. Cong. Res. Serv. for the House Subcommittee on Energy and Commerce, Comm. Print No. 100-R, 100th Congress, 2nd Session (December 1987).

4. See, e.g., When power investors call the shots, June 20, 1988, *Business Week*, 126 (discussing Borg-Warner, Igloo Holdings, Cortec Industries, spinoffs of ITT Corp., Seven-Up, Dr. Pepper, Beatrice, and Cain Chemical).

5. Ibid. (discussing Revco, Republic Health, and Dart Drug).

6. See, e.g., John W. Wilson, 1986, *The New Venturers*, pp. 219-230; Melcher, August 29, 1988, A continental spending spree for venture capitalists, *Business Week*, 41.

7. See generally Jensen, 1986, Agency and costs of free cash flow, corporate finance and takeovers, *American Economic Review*, 76, 323.

8. See generally A. Berle & G. Means 1932, *The modern corporation and private property*.

9. Critics of MBO-LBO transactions occasionally contend that such management improvements should be forthcoming without MBO-LBO transactions and that shareholders are shortchanged because they must be bought out before these improvements take place. The available evidence, however, suggests that the strategies involved in MBO-LBO transactions "increase the risk associated with the managers undiversified human capital" and that managers will not consent to such levels of risk without being offered the opportunity at least to participate in the larger rewards associated with MBO-LBO transactions (Gilson, Chapter 10).

10. When power investors call the shots, above, Note 4.

11. See, e.g., Magnet, March 2, 1987, Restructuring really works, *Fortune*, p. 38; Russell, February 16, 1987, Rebuilding to survive, *Time*, p. 44; When power investors call the shots, above, Note 4.

12. Magnet, above Note 11, p. 43, quoting B. Halsey, Chief Executive of James River Corporation.

13. A. Schleifer & R. Vishny, 1988, Management buyouts as a response to market pressure, *Mergers and Acquisitions*, University of Chicago Press, pp. 101-102. Professors Schleifer and Vishny also raise questions about the fairness of these transactions to various participants. These concerns are addressed below.

14. Stein, January 12, 1987, Shooting fish in a barrel: Why management always makes a bundle in an LBO, *Barron's*, p. 6, 20.

15. This bill of particulars by no means exhausts the allegations levied against MBO and LBO transactions. It does, however, describe a large part of the financial concern associated with these transactions. By focusing on these

financial issues I do not mean to suggest that concerns over job loss and other social implications of MBO-LBO transactions are irrelevant. These concerns also deserve close scrutiny, but they do not sway me from the conclusion that, on balance, the economy is stronger because of MBO-LBO transactions. In particular, corporate restructuring can certainly generate substantial dislocations in communities with undiversified industrial bases, and these job-loss concerns must be factored into the policy debate. See, e.g., Grundfest, March 11, 1988, Job loss and takeovers, address to the University of Toledo College of Law, Third Annual Colloquium on Corporate Law and Social Policy.
16. Pub. L. No. 90-439, 82 Stat. 454 (1968) (codified at 15 U.S.C. §§ 78m(d)-(e), n(d)-(f)).
17. Even in situations in which management owns a majority stake and the success of the going-private transaction is assured, the Williams Act's disclosure requirements are valuable because they help investors decide whether to challenge the terms of the transaction and whether to elect appraisal remedies available under state law. See, e.g., Meyers Parking System, Inc., Rule 13e-3 Transaction Statement (No. 88-47), Amendment No. 2, at 9 (filed July 19, 1988).
18. See Schedule 13E-3, 17 C.F.R. 240.13e-100, Item 8 (Fairness of the Transaction), Item 9 (Reports, Opinions, Appraisals and Certain Negotiations), and Item 17 (Material to be Filed as Exhibits).
19. Ibid. See also, A.M. Borden, May 11, 1988, A fresh look at going-private disclosure, 21 Rev. Sec. & Commod. Reg. 73, 77-78.
20. See, e.g., Revlon, Inc. v. MacAndrews & Forbes Holdings, Inc., 506 A.2d 173, 182 (Del. 1986) (Board's authorization to management to negotiate a merger or buyout with a third party was "a recognition that the company was for sale." At that point, "the directors' role changed from defenders of the corporate bastion to auctioneers charged with getting the best price for the stockholders at the sale of the company").
21. Simpson, 1988, The emerging role of the special committee—ensuring business judgment rule protections in the context of management leveraged buyouts and other corporate transactions involving conflicts of interest, *Business Law, 43,* 665, 678.
22. Ibid. The hazard of a board's failure to maintain adequate independence from management is well illustrated by the recent battle for control of MacMillan, Inc. See Robert M. Bass Group, Inc. v. Evans, [Current] Sec. L. Rep. ¶93,924 (Del. Ch. July 14, 1988). In part because MacMillan's management did not form a special committee with truly independent advisors to evaluate competing proposals for control from the Bass Group and from management (see ibid., p. 90, 192), the directors were denied the benefits of the business judgment rule when the Bass Group challenged the decisions to adopt the management proposed restructuring and to reject the Bass offer.

23. See e.g., Edelman v. Fruehauf Corp., 798 F.2d 882, 890-91 (6th Cir. 1986).
24. See e.g., ibid., pp. 885, 887; Revlon, Inc. v. MacAndrews & Forbes Holding, Inc., 506 A.2d at 184.
25. See e.g., Edelman v. Fruehauf Corp., 798 F2d, pp. 885, 887; Revlon, Inc. v. MacAndrews & Forbes Holdings, Inc., 506 A.2d, pp. 184-5; Hanson Trust PLC v. ML SCM Acquisition, Inc., 781 F.2d 264, 267 (2d Cir. 1986).
26. See e.g., CRTF Corp v. Federated Department Stores, Inc., [Current] Fed. Sec L. Rep. (CCH) ¶93,711 (S.D.N.Y. 1988).
27. AC Acquisitions v. Anderson Clayton & Co., 519 A.2d 103,114 (Del. Ch. 1986).
28. B. Burrough, August 11, 1988, Insilco discloses board declined to talk with others suggesting higher bids, *The Wall Street Journal,* p. 5, col. 1.
29. Ibid.
30. Shareholder lawsuits challenging the transaction have already been filed; see Shareholders file seven suits to try to block acquisition, August 19, 1988, *The Wall Street Journal,* p. 14, col. 3.
31. See e.g., Hector, January 19, 1987, Are shareholders cheated by LBO's? *Fortune,* p. 98; Lowenstein, above, Note 1; Lipton, above, Note 1; Stein, above, Note 14.
32. Ibid.
33. See e.g., Amihud, Chapter 1; Kaplan, Chapter 4; M. Marais, K. Schipper, A. Smith, 1988, *Sources of shareholder gains in leveraged buyouts,* (Chicago: University of Chicago Press). These studies generally rely on older data that may fail to reflect higher premiums paid in recent transactions. Third-party mergers may nonetheless constitute the most comparable set of transactions because they, along with MBO-LBOs, generally involve transactions that initially have management support.
34. Kaplan, above, Note 33. "MBOs tend to underperform their projections."
35. Kaplan, above, Note 33, points out that the excess return earned by the buyout investors is approximately the same as the premium earned by outside shareholders when the company is taken private. Thus, the two groups come close to splitting the gains.
36. Kaplan, above, Note 33; Bull, Chapter 3; M. Marais, K. Schipper, A. Smith, above, Note 33.
37. Of course, to the extent that these instruments are held by tax-exempt institutions, the Treasury receives no revenues as a result of these payments.
38. For a more detailed analysis, see R. Gilson, M. Scholes, & M. Wolfson, 1988, Taxation and the dynamics of corporate control: The uncertain case for tax motivated acquisition, in J. Coffee, L. Lowenstein, & S. Rose-Ackerman, eds., *Takeovers and contests for corporate control;* M. Scholes & M. Wolfson, *The effects of changes in tax laws on corporate reorganization activity,* Stanford Business School working paper; Amihud, above Note 33.

39. For further examples of transactions that are tax substitutes for MBOs and LBOs, see materials cited in Note 38, above, and by Gilson, Chapter 10.

40. A. Auerbach & D. Reishus, 1988, The effects of taxation on the merger decision, *Corporate takeovers: Causes and consequences*, National Bureau of Economic Research.

41. Kaplan, above, Note 33; M. Marais, K. Schipper, A. Smith, above, Note 33 "Tax savings estimates explain a substantial portion of the cross-sectional variation in buyout premia"; K. Lehn & A. Poulsen, February 1987, *Sources of value in corporate going private transactions*, (St. Louis: Washington University).

42. Kaplan, above, Note 33.

43. Bull, above, Note 36.

44. Ibid.

45. See Stircharchuk, June 14, 1988, Revco's leveraged buyout comes apart, *The Wall Street Journal*, p. 6, col. 1; Stircharchuk, July 29, 1988, Revco taken private with junk bonds, files for protection under chapter 11, *The Wall Street Journal*, p. 2; Kaletsky, July 29, 1988, Revco files for chapter 11 in largest buyout failure, *Financial Times*, p. 17, col. 3; Holusha, July 29, 1988, Revco drugstore chain in bankruptcy filing, *The New York Times*, p. D1.

46. Stircharchuk, above, Note 45.

47. Stircharchuk, above, Note 45.

48. Holusha, above, Note 45.

49. Ibid.; Stircharchuk, above, Note 45.

50. "Revco's LBO ends with a whimper," August 15, 1988, *Business Week*, p. 22; Stircharchuk, above, Note 45.

51. Kaletsky, above, Note 45.

52. Holusha, above, Note 45.

53. Stircharchuk, above, Note 45.

54. Ibid.

55. Ibid.

56. Stircharchuk, August 1, 1988, Strong stand by Revco's bondholders helped push firm's bankruptcy filing, *The Wall Street Journal*, p. 20.

57. Similar overstated criticisms are often leveled at transactions that cause firms to reduce capital expenditures. For example, in the wake of a takeover, an oil firm may reduce its exploration expenditures. Does that mean consumers will have less petroleum in the future? Not necessarily. If the forgone projects have the potential to earn a competitive rate of return, then the projects will likely be developed by competing firms. Only if the projects don't present the prospect of earning a competitive return in anyone's hands are they likely to remain idle—in which case the question is why were those projects being pursued in the first place? For a discussion of the circumstances in which reduction of capital expenditures can be economically rational and socially beneficial,

see,e.g., Jensen, 1986, Agency costs of free cash flow, corporate finance and takeovers, *American Economic Review, 76*, 323; Jensen, 1988, The free cash flow theory of takeovers: A financial perspective on mergers and acquisitions and the economy, in L. Browne, E. Rosengren, eds., *The merger boom*, Federal Reserve Bank of Boston, p. 102.

58. A distinction should be drawn between bankruptcies that result as a consequence of changes in market fundamentals (e.g., a sharp decline in steel prices makes it uneconomic to produce at a particular firm) and bankruptcies that result as a consequence of a viable firm's inability to meet its financing commitments. In the former case, real macroeconomic losses will be associated with, though not necessarily caused by, the failure. In the latter case, there is little reason to tamper with the firm's viable operations. Instead, the primary consequence of the reorganization is a realignment of creditor interests.

59. For a discussion of the relationship between bankruptcy costs and optimal debt-equity ratios, see T. Copeland & J. Weston, 1988, *Financial theory and corporate policies*, 3rd ed., pp. 498-500.

60. Wallace, above, Note 2.

61. Ibid.

62. Lewis, above, Note 2.

63. See e.g., above, Note 2; Bartlett, June 20, 1988, Power investors, *Business Week*, p. 116.

64. See e.g., Lewis, above, Note 2, at 142.

65. Barmash, December 20, 1985, Macy bid cut $2, to $68 a share, buyout group has problems with financing, *The New York Times*, p. D1, col. 6; see also Bleakley, December 20, 1984, Brakes on leveraged buyouts, bankers take harder stand, *The New York Times*, p. D1, col.

66. Loomis, July 4, 1988, Buyout kings,'' Fortune, pp. 53, 55 (criticism of price paid in Duracell buyout).

67. Bartlett, above, Note 63.

68. Loomis, above, Note 66.

69. There is a sense in which it can be argued that the winner of any auction—whether for a Monet or a company—has overpaid because the very fact of his victory indicates that he was the most optimistic market participant. This "winner's curse" argument has spawned an interesting literature and suggests that "the rational bidder in a common-value sealed bid auction [as occurred in the sale of Duracell] avoids becoming a victim of the winner's curse by presuming that his own estimate of the item's value is higher than any other bidder's [and] then setting his bid equal to what he estimates to be the second highest perceived valuation given that all the other bidders are making the same presumptions" (R. McAfee & P. McMillan, 1987, Auctions and bidding, *Journal of Economic Literature, 25*, 699, 721).

ABOUT THE AUTHOR

Joseph A. Grundfest is a Commissioner of the Securities and Exchange Commission. Mr. Grundfest is both an attorney and economist. Immediately prior to his appointment, Mr. Grundfest served as counsel and senior economist for legal and regulatory matters at the Council of Economic Advisers in the Executive Office of the President. Prior to his current government service he practiced law with Wilmer, Cutler & Pickering and was an economist with The Rand Corporation and the Brooking Institution. Mr. Grundfest is a graduate of Yale University (BA 1973) and the joint law and economics program at Stanford University (JD-PhD (ABD) 1978), and has also completed the MSc program in Mathematical Economics and Econometrics at the London School of Economics (1972). Mr. Grundfest is author or co-author of numerous research reports and publications dealing with a range of topics, including contests for corporate control, insider trading, international securities regulation, regulation of markets subject to kickback schemes, the economics and regulation of broadcasting, and the role of citizen participation in administrative proceedings.

CHAPTER 12

LBOs AND THE REEMERGENCE OF INSTITUTIONAL MONITORING OF MANAGERS

Michael C. Jensen

The controversy surrounding the so-called LBO issue is a mystery to me because the facts reveal no evidence of a problem. Congressman Markey has said that he wasn't considering a bill to restrict, regulate, or oversee MBOs, and I encourage him to continue down that path. I recommend that Mr. Markey consider adopting for his legislative program one of the principles on which I run my life: *If you never miss an airplane, you're getting to the airport too early.* I urge his sub-committee not to arrive at the airport the day before the flight's departure, which, in spite of what he says, is what may happen with MBOs. Congressional legislators rarely schedule hearing with the idea that they will do nothing. We should wait to see more than a few LBOs in trouble before we start thinking about further restricting a system that has worked well.

Before I comment on some of the ideas presented in this book, let me try to give a broader perspective from my recent research on the LBO market, the takeover market, and the control market in general.

There has been a massive change in the role of institutional investors and financial institutions in the corporate sector over the last 50 years. Institutions have been driven out of the role of active investors. By "active investor" I don't mean one who indulges in portfolio churning. I mean one who actually monitors management, sits on boards, sometimes is involved in dismissing management, often is intimately involved in the strategic direction of the company, and on occasion even manages. That description is worth thinking about. It fits Carl Icahn and Irwin Jacobs and Kohlberg, Kravis, Roberts (KKR) well. Before the mid-1930s, investment banks and commercial banks played a much more important role on boards of directors, in monitoring management, and on occasion even in engineering changes in management.

What happened over the past 50 years to change the bankers' roles? Some general causes are obvious. The concept of "insider" was defined by the 1934 SEC Act. In addition, the 16-b Short Swing Profit Rules require an institution satisfying any insider conditions to give the company 100% of the profits earned on investments held less than six months. An institution is an insider if it owns more than 10% of the shares, serves on the board of directors, or holds a position as officer. These insider rules increase the cost of being an active investor and contribute to the forces driving institutions out of this role. In addition, the 1940 Investment Company Act put restrictions on the maximum holding of a company. Money managers do not serve on boards today, and seldom think of getting involved in the strategy of their portfolio companies. Banks risk legal liability if they are too closely involved in a company to which they have loaned funds.

The result of these forces and others over the past 50 years has been to leave managers increasingly unmonitored. As financial institution monitors left the scene, managers commonly came to believe the company belonged to them and that stockholders were merely one of many "stakeholders" the firm had to serve. The banning of financial institutions, which now own more than 40% of corporate equity, from fulfilling their critically important monitoring role has resulted in major inefficiencies. The evidence indicates managers have been able to destroy up to 50% of the value of the organizations they lead before facing serious threat of disturbance. This destruction of value generates large profit opportunities that are causing the creation of innovative new financial institutions to help capture the lost value. Takeovers and LBOs are some of the products of these institutions. By my estimate, over the 10 years from 1975 to 1986 alone, these activities have created more than $400 billion in value for investors (Jensen, 1988).

Along with the takeover specialists came other new financial institutions such as the family funds (the Bass Brothers, Pritzkers, and Bronfmans) and others such as Warren Buffet who figured out ways to bear the cost associated with insider status. They purchase entire companies and play an active role in them. These new institutions have discovered a different way from that of J.P. Morgan to resolve the monitoring problem. The modern trend toward merchant banking in which Wall Street firms are taking equity interest in their own deals is another manifestation of this phenomenon. KKR is much more than an expediter of LBO transactions. It plays an important role in management after the transaction. In fact, LBO specialists generally are the boards of directors in the companies they help take private. They choose the managers of the firm and influence the corporate strategy in important ways.

Buyout specialists are very different from the usual outside or public directors supposedly representing shareholders. Buyout specialists who own or represent in the buyout funds an average of 60% of the firm's equity (see Kaplan, 1988) have great incentive to take the job seriously, in contrast to public directors with little or no equity interest. This development of new financial institutions is a response to problems caused by the lack of effective monitoring of corporate managers. It is important that Congressman Markey and his subcommittee carefully assess the damage done by various federal laws and regulations that have driven financial institutions out of the boardrooms. When the holders of over 40% of the equity in this country are dissatisfied with management, they have no option other than to sell their shares. Do not be misled by managers' complaints about the churning of financial institutions' portfolios: they much prefer that to a system in which those institutions actually try to correct a management problem. The last thing most CEOs want is to have institutions sitting on their corporate board that own substantial amounts of their stock. That would bring about close monitoring of managerial activities by people who more closely bear the wealth consequences of managerial mistakes and who are not beholden to the CEO for their positions .

I have a great deal of respect for the people involved in the ALI proposal, but I'm concerned about the proposed provision regarding MBOs. I am concerned about vague words and concepts in the language such as "adequate advance public disclosure of the transaction." Virtually every word here is vague and will, I suspect, generate litigation. Consider several others: "responsible persons who express an interest" and "will provide relevant information concerning the corporation, given a reasonable opportunity to submit a competing proposal."

The MBO environment is already intensively regulated. Moreover, there is no evidence that shareholders are being harmed. Regulation has substantially damaged the takeover market and thereby harmed the very shareholders that proponents of these actions have said they want to protect.

And now we are on the verge of damaging the MBO market where we have voluntary transactions between shareholders and managers that seem to benefit everyone. Kaplan's work shows that MBOs generate a 100% increase in total value and that about 50% of the gain goes to public shareholders, with 50% going to managers and buyout specialists. New laws regulating MBOs will increase their costs and prevent some otherwise desirable transactions from occurring. As a result, Congress will have further locked us into inefficient use of corporate assets.

One of the major sources of pressure for buyouts comes from the inadequacies of executive compensation. I have been studying this system for several years with Kevin Murphy at the University of Rochester. We have found a system with many problems (Jensen and Murphy, 1988), and MBOs are an effective way to correct many of them. The gains generated by MBOs are particularly interesting; these are situations where the same assets are being managed by the same managers. Kaplan has documented clearcut increases in operating earnings and cash flows of MBOs. Thus the gains are not the result of financial legerdemain, and the evidence indicates that they are not coming out of the hides of either labor or bondholders. Tax savings can be an important benefit in some transactions, but they cannot explain all the gains.

The 100% increase in value is apparently generated in large part by changing the compensation and organizational structure. After an MBO, managers own about 30% of the equity, debt is significantly increased, and the board of directors is composed of people with substantial equity ownership. This suggests that the problems leading to the reduced value prior to the buyout are due to the wrong structure and not to incompetent managers. Let's not damage a system that allows managers and shareholders to generate large gains through transactions that correct the structure of their companies.

It has been asserted that managers do not make proper disclosure before an MBO offer: Kaplan's evidence (Chapter 4) indicates that managers do publish pro forma statements which forecast how they are going to do. But contrary to the assertions, managers are not publishing underestimates of their future earnings performance in order to con shareholders into selling at a low price. Kaplan's evidence indicates the MBO firms, while performing significantly better after than before the buyout, do not meet their forecasts. Thus, contrary to the assertions, there is a great deal of information available to shareholders, and to the extent the information is biased it goes in the wrong direction for the critics. The pro forma statements tend to systematically overestimate future performance and, therefore, value. (We suspect the positive bias has to do with it making it easier to sell the debt.) Moreover, DeAngelo's (1986) evidence indicates that information in the accounting reports prior to the buyout is not biased. It is also interesting to note that she finds considerable bias in the accounting reports issued around proxy fights, where managers are manipulating the numbers to mislead shareholders (DeAngelo, 1988).

LBOs represent the invention of a superior organizational form. Unfortunately, politicians, bureaucrats, and people in general are often suspicious of new inventions, even when they are productive. As the takeover market itself becomes more restricted, LBOs become a primary vehicle for change and increased efficiency. Thus, it is important to examine the evidence before rushing to change a system that is generating large benefits. We ought to be sure—much surer than we've been in the past—that any proposed changes are more likely to improve the current system than to damage it. I plead with Congress and the ALI to move slowly until we are certain there is a problem to be resolved.

REFERENCES

DeAngelo, L. E. (1986). Accounting numbers as market valuation substitutes: A study of management buyouts of public stockholders. *Accounting Review, 61*, 400-420.

DeAngelo, L. E. (1988). Managerial competition, information costs, and corporate governance: The use of accounting measures in proxy contests. *Journal of Accounting and Economics, 10*, 3-36.

Jensen, M. C. (1988, winter). Takeovers: Their causes and consequences. *Journal of Economic Perspectives, 2*, (1) 21-48.

Jensen, M. C. & Murphy, K. J. (1988, May). Performance pay and top management incentives. (Working paper 88-059, Harvard Business School, Cambridge, MA).

Kaplan, S. N. (1988, May). Sources of value in management buyouts. (Unpublished doctoral thesis, Harvard Business School, Cambridge, MA).

ABOUT THE AUTHOR

Michael C. Jensen is Professor of Business Administration at the Harvard Business School. He held joint appointments at Harvard and Rochester since 1985. He was LaClare Professor of Finance and Business Administration at the William E. Simon Graduate School of Business Administration, University of Rochester from 1984 through 1988, Associate Professor from 1971 to 1979, and Assistant Professor from 1967 to 1971. He founded the Managerial Economics Research Center, at the University of Rochester in 1977 and served as its Director until 1988. Professor Jensen earned his Ph.D. in Economics, Finance, and Accounting and his M.B.A. in Finance from the University of Chicago and received the A.B. degree from Macalester College.

Professor Jensen is the author of more than 50 published papers, comments, and articles on a wide range of economic-, finance-, and business-related topics in scholarly journals, books, and the popular and business press. He is editor of *The Modern Theory of Corporate Finance* (with Clifford W. Smith, Jr., McGraw-Hill, 1984) and *Studies in the Theory of Capital Markets* (Praeger Publishers, 1972). In 1973 he founded the *Journal of Financial Economics,* a leading journal in financial economics, and is now Managing Editor of that journal.